MW01040848

DEMAGOGUE

DEMAGOGUE

THE FIGHT TO SAVE
DEMOCRACY FROM ITS
WORST ENEMIES

Michael Signer

ST. MARTIN'S PRESS ⚲ NEW YORK

St. Martin's Press are registered trademarks in the United States,
the United Kingdom, Europe and other countries.

ISBN-13: 978–0–230–60624–1
ISBN-10: 0–230–60624–5

Library of Congress Cataloging-in-Publication Data is available from the
Library of Congress.

A catalogue record of the book is available from the British Library.

Design by Newgen Imaging Systems (P) Ltd., Chennai, India.

First edition: February 2009

P1

For my family

Sicinius Velutus:

> What is the city but the people?

Citizens:

> True, the city is the people.

—William Shakespeare,
Coriolanus

CONTENTS

ACKNOWLEDGMENTS

First of all, I thank my family—my mother, Marjorie Brahms Signer; my father, Robert Signer; and my sisters, Rebecca, Mira, and Rachel—for their support through the eight years it has taken to bring this project from dissertation proposal to book. I would especially like to thank my mother and father for their close and helpful reading and editing of the manuscript. My grandfather Herbert and grandmother Esther, now passed, deserve gratitude for the dedication to progress and to ideas they shared so generously with their children and grandchildren. They also had unusual connections to some of the characters in this story. My grandfather was a student at the City College of New York during the same time period as Irving Kristol, and he took remarkable (and very different) intellectual lessons from that tumultuous time and place. My grandmother was an executive secretary at the New School while Hannah Arendt was there, and often spoke to me about the "great woman" she had the privilege to work with—but in her empathy and concern about the world, my grandmother was just as great.

Many friends and colleagues throughout the years have provided assistance, inspiration, and support. At Princeton, George Kateb was a formative and eloquent teacher, advisor, and mentor; years later, he provided extremely helpful commentary on this manuscript. Stan Katz originally alerted me to the idea of constitutionalism. While in graduate school at Berkeley, Mike Rogin, Shannon Stimson, Paul Thomas, and George Lakoff were supportive members of my dissertation committee. Mike—who tragically passed away just before 9/11—was an especially gracious and challenging mentor, and Shannon has continued to be a friend and supporter of this project over the years. I also had the privilege of a one-on-one reading seminar with Hanna Pitkin. While I was in law school at the University of Virginia, A. E. Dick Howard provided warm and constant mentorship, and his focus on constitutionalism has been especially inspiring. Vince Blasi and Mike Klarman were also a pleasure to work with on their studies of free speech and civil rights, respectively.

Friends and colleagues who deserve special thanks for their helpful readings of the manuscript and related materials include Matt Dallek, Peter Beinart, Derek Chollet, Rachel Kleinfeld, Andrei Cherny, Brian Katulis, Anne-Marie Slaughter, Barry Blechman, Mike Gubser, Frank Lovett, James Ceaser, Matt Duss, Vanessa Mobley, Michael Lind, Dave Oliver, Rick Gilmore, Jonathan Morrow, and David Greenberg. I also would like to thank my original colleagues from Democracy Arsenal, including Suzanne Nossel, Heather Hurlburt, Lorelei Kelly, and Mort Halperin, for their energetic and engaging discussions of foreign affairs in that forum. While I was a contributor at Democracy Arsenal, it was always a privilege to develop some of these ideas by sparring with and linking to other writers on foreign policy, including Kevin Drum, Matt Yglesias, Ezra Klein, Ivo Daalder, Laura Rozen, Ilan Goldenberg, and David Shorr.

Other friends, family, and colleagues who provided invaluable support at various stages of this project include Paul Nace and Sally Jackson, Deborah Signer and Mark Balaschak, Sheila Drummer, Sean Roche, Abbie Kinnebrew, Jonathan Morgenstein, Walker Richmond, Andy Kaufman, Matt Seidman, Dan Hunt, Carrie Nixon, Dmitri Mehlhorn, Dallas Dickinson, Frank DiStefano, Mark Brzezinski, Jon Cohen, Sam Loewenberg, Christine Salmon, Simon Stow, Alex Rossmiller, Jordan Tama, Thad Kousser, Matt Spence, Ganesh Sitaraman, Stephen Bailey, Lisa Ellman, Siddarth Mohandas, Shadi Hamid, John Sides, John Dervin, Aaron Myers, Adam Lord, Anne Ledyard, Christine Whelan, Trevor Corson, Rafe Sagalyn, Ryan Chiachiere, Massie Ritsch, Jon Cohen, Reuben Brigety, Dan Restrepo, Caroline Wadhams, Peter Swire, Gayle Smith, Stephanie Miller, Winnie Chen, Peter Juhl, John W. Wright, and Russ Linden.

The Center for American Progress was very supportive during the writing of this book, especially John Podesta, Rudy deLeon, P. J. Crowley, and Peter Ogden. Third Way was extremely gracious, including Matt Bennett (whose father David is one of the original scholarly authorities on demagogues) and Jon Cowan.

The founders and staff of *Democracy: A Journal of Ideas,* including Ken Baer, Andrei Cherny, and Clay Risen, deserve special thanks for publishing my article "A City on a Hill," which I allude to in the Conclusion of this book. The community of the Truman National Security Project, including the co-founders Rachel Kleinfeld and Matt Spence as well as dozens of colleagues and friends in the organization, deserve thanks for their support and their accomplishment in creating a space for progressives committed to our national security. I also am grateful to my former law firm, Wilmer Cutler Pickering Hale & Dorr, including partners such as Jamie Gorelick, Todd Stern, Ed Tobin, and Jen O'Connor, for providing a comfortable and supportive work environment while I taught and worked on this book and related projects.

It was a privilege to work with those on the John Edwards presidential campaign to include democracy in the campaign's foreign policy proposals, including Senator Edwards, Elizabeth Edwards, Admiral Dave Oliver, General Speedy Martin, General Les Lyles, General Mike Hough, General Paul Kern, Admiral Bill McDaniel, General Allen Youngman, Gordon Adams, Bruce Jentleson, James Kvaal, Miles Lackey, Heather McGhee, and Alex Navarro-McKay.

In assisting the Obama campaign, it was a privilege for me to work with and be inspired by the Senator's advisors and staff, including Susan Rice, Greg Craig, Denis McDonough, and Wendy Morigi.

Many of the lessons and ideas of this book stem from experiences in my home state of Virginia. I thank Gerard Toal and the staff of Virginia Tech for inviting me to teach about democracy and political theory in the Master's Program for Government and International Affairs and my terrific students for their interrogation and their insights. When I worked in the Office of Governor Mark Warner, first as a law student and then as Deputy Counselor to the Governor, I learned many practical lessons about democratic politics and government from leaders including Governor Warner, Bob Blue, and Bob Crouch. In the electoral reform effort in Virginia, colleagues including Carrie Nixon, Ivy Main, and Carol Doran Klein were a joy to work with and learn from.

The original research for this book was completed with the assistance of a National Science Foundation Graduate Research Fellowship. The Friedrich Ebert Stiftüng graciously hosted me at the panel in 2008 in

Berlin that I describe in this book. The Political Science Department at the University of California at Berkeley provided a warm and supportive environment for the initial research and dissertation on this topic as well as a very gracious fellowship for completing my doctoral studies there.

Finally, I am grateful to Jake Klisivitch, my editor at Palgrave, for his faith in this project; Alan Bradshaw at Palgrave, for superb editing assistance; my two research assistants, David Korn and Evan Munsing, for their good natures and hard work; and my agent, Larry Weissman, without whom this project about the strange and compelling struggle between democracy and the demagogue almost certainly would never have seen the light of day.

INTRODUCTION

FREEDOM AT THE BRINK

SADDAM HUSSEIN WAS EXECUTED ON DECEMBER 30, 2006. A CROWD of chanting Iraqis, most of them Shi'a, watched as he was led, hand-cuffed, up the stairs of a wooden gallows. A hood was placed over his head, a trapdoor was released, and he suddenly dropped, his neck breaking. A cell phone video immediately circulated around the world on YouTube, showing grainy footage of the execution and the edgy, restless audience.

Aside from the stark fact of witnessing someone die by hanging—something that does not happen in most developed nations—the most memorable element of the famous cell phone video was the crowd's chant of "Moqtada! Moqtada! Moqtada!" For even the staunchest opponents of the Iraq War, Saddam's death marked the end of an old era and the beginning of a new one. But with the call of Moqtada al-Sadr's name, Iraq's bloody past instead echoed in the execution room. Iraq, it seemed, was not escaping from tyranny. Perhaps it was just trading one tyranny for another. And the great irony was that Moqtada al-Sadr was supposed to be in jail.

More than two years earlier, Paul Bremer, President George W. Bush's viceroy in Iraq, had announced that Moqtada al-Sadr would be arrested for his alleged involvement in the murder of Abdul Majid al-Khoei, a leading cleric. Sadr's militia had recently begun attacking coalition forces and had taken control of many provincial capitals in southern Iraq. President Bush now ordered the military to capture or kill him: "We can't allow one man to change the course of the coun-try," he said in a video teleconference. "He must be wiped out."

Sadr never was arrested. Within a week, the White House reversed course and ordered coalition forces to walk away from the mission, reasoning that negative media coverage of the failure to capture Sadr could endanger the transfer of sovereignty planned for July 1, 2004. That, in turn, could impact Bush's reelection that November.[1] As American policymakers hastened Iraq's political transition to suit their domestic political schedule, Sadr continued his meteoric rise, unimpeded by police, arrest warrants, or prison. He single-handedly led his personal Mahdi militia's rebellion against coalition and government forces while creating a broad social movement of hundreds of thousands of Shiites devoted solely to him. These forces launched waves of attacks against the central Iraqi government, against American targets and coalition forces, and against other militias. In 2007, retired Lieutenant General Ricardo Sanchez, who commanded coalition forces in Iraq in 2003 and 2004, observed that "by turning up the level of violence at will," Sadr was "able to control the coalition war-fighting environment, disrupt Iraq's political progress and affect American public opinion." Sanchez predicted an ominous future in the years ahead: "Today, as Iraq moves toward provincial elections, [Sadr] is in a position to alter world events."[2]

We won't know the result of the Iraq invasion and subsequent installation of democracy for years. As of this writing, a fragile cease-fire between the Sadr and government forces, introduced in 2007, is still in force, and there are signs that Sadr could ultimately decide to join forces with the central government. But we already know the cost of Sadr's movement. There is no question that American leaders' misapprehension of the endemic threat a demagogue like Sadr would pose to the democracy we had created in Iraq dramatically increased the expense of the Iraqi operation—measured in time, treasure, and blood.

The issue of democracy's struggle with demagogues today is much broader than Moqtada al-Sadr and Iraq. These political leaders were players in a drama much larger than themselves: the struggle of democracy to survive. The political scientist Samuel Huntington has famously demarcated the story of democracy into three "waves," each followed by a "reverse wave." The first wave, from 1828 to 1926, included the series of European revolutions in 1848, the ensuing economic modernization, and the political freedoms that followed early in the twentieth century. The first reverse wave began in 1922, with Mussolini's takeover of Italy's fragile democracy, and continued through World War II, sweeping up many European and Latin American countries. The second "short wave" extended from 1943 to 1962, as the Allied Powers installed democracies in the conquered Axis countries, and democracy increased in Latin America, Asia, and Africa. A second reverse wave crashed down from 1958 to 1975, when authoritarian regimes took root across the world. The third wave began in Portugal in 1974 and crested with the fall of the Soviet Union, the various recent "color revolutions" in Eastern Europe, and, again, the rise of democracies in Asia, Africa, and Latin America today. In recent years, many countries, including Poland, Mexico, and South Africa, have seen freedom expand.[3] The question is whether we stand today on the brink of a third reverse wave. Beginning in the first decade of the new millennium, a new cast of cagey, aggressive mass leaders confronted the United States while threatening to install or expand autocratic governments in their home countries. In September 2006, for instance, Hugo Chávez, the president of Venezuela, stood behind the podium of the United Nations General Assembly in Manhattan and drew a deep breath of air through his nose. "The devil came here yesterday," he declared to the audience. "And it still smells of sulfur today."[4] Chávez was referring to President George W. Bush, who had appeared at the same podium the previous day. Four months later, Chávez pushed a bill through Venezuela's General Assembly that gave him the right to rule by decree, creating in essence a fresh new tyranny in the Western Hemisphere. Chávez's belligerence was alarming partly because he seemed so comfortable with violence, having risen to power in a bloody coup.

Also in 2006, in the summer, Hassan Nasrallah, the furiously charismatic leader of Hezbollah in southern Lebanon, launched an unprovoked war against Israel. Lebanon was still enjoying a freshet of freedom after the sudden "Cedar Revolution" revolt against Syria's occupation the prior year. A new democracy had been installed; liberty's flag rose. Or did it? Israeli forces responded to Nasrallah's aggression by essentially destroying the infrastructure of southern Lebanon, unintentionally helping to entrench Hezbollah as the leader of an aggrieved populace and as a challenger of the Lebanese state. After the war with Israel, Nasrallah bided his time, building up forces and becoming one of the most popular figures among Muslims in the Middle East. One Lebanese woman contacted Nasrallah's political party and begged for the *abaya* he wore during his televised addresses. Her request was granted, and she traveled the country wearing the simple brown cloak. Across the country, the *abaya* was treated "with a reverence usually afforded to an ancient holy relic."[5] In 2008, Nasrallah's forces attacked the Lebanese government in the capital, seizing property before an uneasy truce.

In other countries around the globe, democracies slipped and strongmen rose. In Russia, President (and then Prime Minister) Vladimir

Putin consolidated his power and established a quasi-authoritarian state, as political opponents and journalists were poisoned or shot; in 2008, under Putin's shadowy direction, Russia invaded the sovereign nation of Georgia. Meanwhile, enormous majorities of Russians cheered the new autocrat. In Iran, President Mahmoud Ahmadinejad, the former mayor of Tehran who fashioned himself as a "little street-sweeper," attacked the state of Israel's right to exist and subtly threatened to create a nuclear arsenal, while strengthening the authoritarian rule of the country's governing clerical elite. In Zimbabwe, President Robert Mugabe for months refused to allow a democratically elected opposition leader, Morgan Tsvangirai, to take office, employing violence to turn back his supporters. In Bolivia, President Evo Morales led violent riots in the streets before winning election as that country's first indigenous president. Riots erupted over corruption and disputed election results in Nigeria, which previously had been Africa's shining example of democracy. In Gaza, where the Bush administration had pushed Israel to allow democratic elections as part of Bush's "Freedom Agenda," the terrorist group Hamas gained power, lifting up minor demagogues such as Khaled Mashal, the group's political leader. In Central Asia, from Uzbekistan to Belarus, authoritarian leaders rose and freedom retreated.[6]

In most of these cases, the leaders threatening to convert democracy into tyranny were demagogues: political figures who fashioned themselves as leaders of the masses and who would go to almost any extreme to hold and expand their power. And in most cases, they were capitalizing on a powerful sentiment that surged through the world during the Bush presidency, gathering nations and groups together against America and Americans, often with a militaristic bent. During the 2008 presidential campaign, these obnoxious figures stormed across the world stage, fulminating against many of the ideas we hold most dear, from a peaceful nuclear order to the humanitarian advantages of liberal democracy.

Democracy's tipping point has become dizzyingly clear in recent times. With the free election of Barack Obama as president of the most powerful country in the world, the example of American democracy shone, once again, around the globe. But at the same time, democracy teetered. Autocratic China continued its meteoric rise while suffocating the freedom of speech, newly tsarist Russia bullied its neighbors and clamped down on dissidents, and the world's citizens shared a widespread skepticism about an American "democracy agenda" that seemed to ignore anti-democratic regimes such as those in Saudi Arabia, Egypt, and Belarus and that, for several long, tragic years, incompetently fused democracy with regime change in Iraq.

At this potent historical moment for humanity's two millennia-long experiment with political freedom, the question is whether the world's twenty-first century demagogues represent isolated shocks or tremors signaling a broader quake. Democracy, after all, does not necessarily face disaster at the hand of demagogues; there are glimmers of hope. In a constitutional referendum, the Venezuelan people denied Hugo Chávez an infinite presidency. The Iranian people voted for an opposition party—against the will of Ahmadinejad. Iraq seemed to be edging toward political compromise, with the predations of al-Sadr potentially a thing of the past. Nasrallah's ambitions seemed to be constrained by an international agreement that would contain Hezbollah in Lebanon. The new demagogues can perhaps be driven into retreat.

The philosopher George Santayana said that those who do not remember history are condemned to repeat it. Democracy is clearly in our future. The questions are: How can we avoid making mistakes like those we made in Iraq and Gaza in the future? How can we promote democracy while including the people and convincing them to side with the state rather than a demagogue? How can we maintain democracy as a goal for American power?

In such a pregnant, uncertain time, answering these questions requires a deep understanding of democracy's eternal struggle with the demagogue. Scholars today are generating, reading, and digesting nuanced ideas about democracy's advanced problems, such as how to use foreign aid to expand civil society in other countries,[7] how American constitutionalism has historically influenced democracies abroad,[8] and how to strengthen democracy through an emphasis on international free markets.[9] Such worthwhile work has a rich lineage that includes Presidents James Monroe, Woodrow Wilson, F.D.R., and George W. Bush—all distinctly different leaders, but partners in the cause of promoting liberal democracy throughout the world.

This book is about a related but very different challenge. It is not about how to make good democracies better, or mediocre democracies decent. In contrast to such relatively sophisticated challenges, this book concentrates on a more basic problem: how to make sure democracy lives rather than dies. The re-emergence of demagogues amid a generally perceived crisis in democracy means we all need to take a deep look at this system that we think we know so well. In reality, the system will present both promise and peril if we don't grasp its true inner workings. This book is about the interrelationships between democracy, demagogues, constitutionalism, and foreign policy. It employs both political theory and American history to argue that preserving democracy is not primarily about economics and the relative wealth of a country; it is not about institutions such as checks and balances or running successful elections. Instead, democracy rises or falls with the *people*. It will survive if the people possess what we will refer to as a "constitutional conscience"; it will die if a demagogue attacks it with the support of people uncommitted to the basic values of democratic self-governance.

To tell this story and make this argument, this book recounts the stories of a number of demagogues from history, from Cleon of Athens to Adolf Hitler. While many people see these demagogues as self-contained demented or outright evil figures, they are instead a phenomenon endemic to democracy itself. Whenever we see a demagogue, therefore, we should see not just another villain but instead another challenge in humanity's ongoing struggle for a lasting state of liberty. It's especially essential to understand demagogues because they expose the most central danger to democracy: How much ownership are ordinary people willing to take of their countries, and what happens when they fail? Are they willing to deny the demagogue the power he seeks? And, from America's perspective, are we willing to do what it takes to help protect democracy from the demagogues around the world?

To reshape a new foreign policy of democracy we cannot focus only on history, politics, and current policy; we have to understand ideas as well. In the following pages, we will follow the stories of seven great political thinkers who personally grappled with the fight to save democracy: the Greek philosophers Plato and Aristotle; the American Founding Father Thomas Jefferson; the French sociologist Alexis de Tocqueville; the German émigré and professor-father of the neoconservatives, Leo

Strauss; another German émigré and professor, Hannah Arendt; and the poet Walt Whitman.

Taken together, these thinkers and their ideas are essential to understanding where we have been and where we can go with democracy. Each grappled with the problem of the demagogue and came up with a different answer—in some cases, these answers have made the problem worse. On the one hand, we find that Aristotle, Jefferson, de Tocqueville, and Whitman all answered the problem of the demagogue by calling for a strengthened political role for ordinary people, coupled with greater civic education and a stronger sense of responsibility and obligation. On the other hand, Plato and then Strauss repeated the devastating error of imagining that the demagogue could somehow be stopped through an elite, authoritarian, metaphysical order. The heroine of this book is Arendt, a writer and political theorist who fled Nazi Germany, embraced her new homeland of America, and went on to provide profound insights into democracy that help explain the greatness of America's constitutional accomplishment and help solve the riddle of how foreign policy can genuinely promote democracy.

Some may argue that it's naïve to charge the people with responsibility for democracy's success and that changing economics or institutions are more important goals. Such critics fail to appreciate the role that ideas play not just in describing what has been, but what can be—inspiring people to pursue democracy. While plenty of good books explain through complex equations or historical studies how democracy can succeed, comparatively few books attempt to demonstrate how ideas and individuals can help democracy win the fight with its worst enemy. One of the great benefits of political theory is that it is normative as well as empirical; in other words, it can prescribe as well as describe. The Greek word *theoria* meant "to see," and political theory, at its best, can help explain how the world ought to be and how we ought to behave within it. A world where superpowers pursue constitutionalism, and where people adopt anti-authoritarian values within their hearts and their governments, is a world that will defy demagogues. But that world will need political theory as guidance. This book is an attempt in that direction.

In defiance of recent events, we can tell a much more hopeful story about the future of democracy. In this narrative, people learn that their gullibility and passions can generate demagogues and make democracy self-destruct. They realize that the constitution, which lends order and enables progress, must out-rank any demagogue. And they develop a "constitutional conscience" that shuts down what the ancients first deemed the "cycle of regimes"—during which democracy begets tyranny through demagogues—by placing the greater good above any demagogue. This culture of beliefs and attitudes is intrinsically anti-authoritarian. The constitutionalism we have developed in America, which can be used to shape a new foreign policy of democracy promotion, works in two directions. The first drives outward, "chastening authority," in the words of one scholar,[10] and forcing those who seek power to accept limits as a precondition of that quest. The second turns inward, leading individuals to value their human potential as free citizens and to take responsibility for their role in the future of their democracy.

As we will see, American history shows that the American people, for the most part and increasingly over time, have internalized a set of constitutional values that essentially short-circuit national demagogues. It has not been economics, or checks and balances, or political institutions that have been primarily responsible for keeping us safe. While all these factors have been necessary to ensure constitutional success and the victory over demagogues, the sufficient element is simple but profound— the people themselves have refused to accede to a national demagogue's seductions. It is the American people, in other words, who prevent demagogues from rising on the national stage. In the 1830s the visiting French sociologist Alexis de Tocqueville first observed Americans' "*mores,*" the social values that give our Constitution strength. A century later, the famous Yale political scientist Robert Dahl observed, "To assume that this country has remained democratic because of its Constitution seems to me an obvious reversal of the relation; it is much more plausible to suppose that the Constitution has remained because our society is essentially democratic."[11]

Understanding how to stop the demagogue is especially pressing today. Despite Americans' success with democracy at home, the early difficulties of democracy in Iraq had serious costs not only in lives and suffering but also in the damage to America's standing in the world and our sense of our own potential. Other countries are losing faith in America's ability to do good through democracy, and the American people themselves today are flirting with isolationism, turning away from the engagement that marked America's greatest foreign policy successes during the previous century.

George W. Bush's 2005 State of the Union address placed democracy promotion as the central pillar of America's mission in the world. But shortly after his speech, 53 percent of Americans said it "should not be in the role of the United States to promote the establishment of democratic governments in other countries."[12] Americans today routinely perceive a zero-sum relationship between democracy and security. A survey completed by the think tank Third Way in February 2007 asked people whether the main purpose of American foreign policy should be "protecting the security of the United States and our allies," "promoting freedom and democracy," or "advancing our economic interest." Sixty-six percent chose protecting security, and less than one-quarter—21 percent—chose promoting freedom and democracy.[13] Amid all of this, Americans were "wary of sweeping visions that portray the movement toward democracy as inexorable and desired by all people."[14] On the basis of these trends, it should come as no surprise that today democracy does not seem very much like the future. In fact, the future looks less bright. One 2005 poll found that 64 percent disagreed that "eventually, nearly all countries will become democracies."[15]

The fact is that many Americans no longer hold democracy as a universal ambition. At the same time, a number of prominent recent books have questioned America's standing in a post-Bush world, from Fareed Zakaria's *The Post-American World*[16] to Parag Khanna's *The Second World*.[17] Such works envision a world where America has dramatically lost its influence, and where we must accede to the loss of both practical and moral authority as a result of the Bush years.

———————————

We must challenge this new phenomenon of "democracy fatigue." Too much is at stake. Democracy is a driving factor in humanity's efforts to escape the tragedies of our shared past. The story of demagogues opens the door to a broader underlying story about the possibility of progress for humanity. Demagogues, like the proverbial canary in a coal mine, alert us to a deeper paradox that has plagued human society since classical times: that as democracy expands, it increases the potential for its own destruction. In other words, demagogues are a symptom rather than a cause. When they emerge, it is because the people, rather than using their freedom, their wits, and their self-restraint to select leaders who would ensure liberty for the ages, willingly hand over their power to a leader who enslaves them. Democracy self-destructs, and the most hopeful and optimistic of dreams—a system based on pure freedom, and on possibility itself—becomes the most monstrous of nightmares.

In this sense, the demagogue is linked to a fundamental question about human history. Will the "cycle of regimes" forever entangle humanity—not only holding our progress static but also dragging us down to failure? Or can we shrug off democracy's paradox and transcend our own vulnerabilities? The goal of worldwide freedom has been a broadly shared horizon at least since Immanuel Kant first published his masterful essay *A Project for Perpetual Peace* in 1796.[18] We need to reclaim democracy as a primary goal of our foreign policy, but with a new heart—constitutionalism. As we will see, the people hold the ultimate answer to democracy's paradox. If the people dedicate themselves to the rule of law, they will defy the demagogue. If, on the other hand, the people are more interested in the roller-coaster of the demagogue's ambitions than their own small part in maintaining the rule of law in their own nation, democracy can disintegrate into authoritarianism, corruption, and murder.

Basing a foreign policy of freedom on constitutionalism rather than structural democracy will involve a new set of ideas, language, and instruments. We are going to need to think about, communicate, and work directly with *peoples,* rather than just leaders and institutions. We will need to learn to view a successful liberal order in a country as a product of culture and values. And we will have to accept that there are certain countries—such as the Gaza Strip, where the terrorist group Hamas won elections in 2006—where creating the conditions for constitutionalism are more important than short-term "democratic" outcomes that ultimately end up, perversely, damaging freedom in the world.

In the final analysis, democracy's demagogue problem matters for America's national security interest. We are today still generally considered the most powerful nation in the world. Most Americans agree we should do what we can to remain in that position. The question—with a new president, a new century, and a new horizon—is what we use this power *for*. To regain our stature and become a source of admiration and leadership for the world—the "city on a hill" that John Winthrop first invoked aboard the ship *Arbella* in the seventeenth century—we need to fully comprehend both the majesty and complexity of our accomplishment. Sharing the success of the American democratic experiment demands restraint and self-discipline instead of braggadocio and belligerence. In our promotion of democracy, from the rhetoric of our leaders to the substance of our governmental programs to the actual efforts undertaken by multilateral organizations such as the United Nations and NATO, we need to stop grasping for a metaphysical democracy that magically solves its own problems and instead begin cultivating constitutionalism.

In the end, we need to think of the United States in the world not as a conqueror on a divine mission, but as a leader of crowds spread through hundreds of nations. We can draw strength from the peoples of the world, just as an elected leader rises through the citizens who support her. By connecting more directly and powerfully with the citizenries of the world, whether in the Middle East, Asia, Africa, or Latin America, we can begin to undermine demagogues and enforce constitutionalism. And we will, in the process, share perhaps our greatest gift: what we have learned over the centuries about the hard practice of freedom. A foreign policy of constitutionalism will bring our success at home to bear on our greatest challenges abroad, while lending a muscular hand to democracy in its perpetual struggle with the demagogue.

PART I

THE CYCLE OF REGIMES

Revolutions in democracies are generally caused by the intemperance of demagogues.[1]

—Aristotle, *The Politics*

———————————◆———————————

THE FOUNDING FATHERS' NIGHTMARE

THE *FEDERALIST PAPERS* LITERALLY OPENED AND CLOSED WITH demagogues. In the first article of this series of eighteenth-century op-eds, written to urge the voters of New York to ratify Congress's recently passed Constitution,[2] Alexander Hamilton wrote that "of those men who have overturned the liberty of republics, the greatest number have begun their career by paying an obsequious court to the people, *commencing demagogues and ending tyrants.*"[3] In Number 86, Hamilton concluded the *Papers* by warning against the *"military despotism of a victorious demagogue."*[4]

These words might just as well have been written in Greek or Latin—which is not to say they were complex but that they literally drew from Athens and Rome. The Framers of the Constitution were all classically educated and literate, if not fluent, in the classical languages. In 1785, two years before the Constitutional Convention, for instance, James Madison wrote his friend Thomas Jefferson, who, as Minister to France, had access to the world's greatest bookstores, to send back "Treatises on the ancient or modern Federal Republics, on the law of nations, and the History, natural and political, of the new world." He specifically requested works "such of the Greek and Roman authors . . . where they will be got very cheap, as are worth having, and are not on the common list of school classics."[5] His budget issues aside, Madison received and read hundreds of books that Jefferson sent over the next five years.[6]

Madison and the other Framers read Plato, Aristotle, Aristophanes, and Cicero, among others. These were dark books with sordid plots and ominous endings. Ancient stories of democracy's self-destruction at the hand of demagogues shaped the Founding Fathers' own thoughts. They wanted raw democracy about as much as they wanted another revolution. Elbridge Gerry, for instance, a fiery representative from Massachusetts (and later vice president under President James Madison), thought that allowing ordinary Americans to vote for the president was madness. "A popular election in this case is radically vicious," Gerry lectured his fellow Founding Fathers during the Constitutional Convention. "The ignorance of the people would put it in the power of some one set of men dispersed through the Union & acting in Concert to delude them into any appointment."[7] Two months later, he declared that democracy was simply "the worst . . . of all political evils."[8]

What was Gerry so worried about? The demagogue. At the time, the nation was still recovering from a revolt of debtor-farmers in western Massachusetts led by a man named Daniel Shays. While Shays' Rebellion in 1786 cost only a handful of lives, it struck terror deep into the hearts of the Founders about whether the ancient cycle of regimes would replay in the modern new nation. Rather than placing trust with the people, Founders like Gerry abandoned hope instead. As the delegates sweltered indoors in the Philadelphia heat, Gerry proclaimed, "The people are uninformed, and would be misled by a few designing men."[9]

To understand the concerns that drove the formulation of the American Constitution and that linger in our thoughts even today (though we might not realize it), we need to understand the intimate connection between the most hopeful of political ideas and the most dreaded political villain.

———————————◆———————————

DEFINING THE DEMAGOGUE

A FEW DEFINITIONS WILL FIRST BE HELPFUL. LET'S BEGIN WITH democracy. At its simplest level, democracy is a political system that grants power based on what large groups of people want. Democracy is unlike an oligarchy, which makes decisions based on what a small group of rich people wants to do, or a monarchy, where only a single person matters. Democracy instead lets the people make decisions. So in a democracy, whoever controls the people, or the authorized representative of the people, has great power. That power can lead to a wide range of actions, from justice to massacres.

There is spirited discussion among experts about how to define democracy, which has only become more complicated over the centuries since its invention. Today we see electoral democracies, liberal democracies, illiberal democracies, quasi-democracies, and incomplete democracies, among others.[10] Electoral democracies are defined simply by the fact that they have elections. However, the basic existence of elections does not tell you much about a country's overall politics, just as a judicial system does not mean a country actually has justice if all it can assemble are sham trials. Saddam Hussein, for instance, was routinely "elected" with more than 90 percent of the vote in Iraq. Liberal democracy is what we familiarly think of in America as "democracy"—its elements include political accountability for everyone with power (meaning the military or royalty do not have a monopoly or some reserved jurisdiction beyond the control of the people), checks among the various branches and institutions of government, freedom of speech, a free flow of information, and judicial review.[11] "Illiberal democracy" is a term made famous by the political scientist and journalist Fareed Zakaria. It describes the backsliding that can occur in formal democracies that substantively are governed by autocracy and, in many cases, demagogues.[12]

The debate about defining democracy is important both to understand how to improve freedom and to dissect the various causes of failed democracies. This book focuses not on democratic institutions or systems, per se, but rather on the relationship of people to individual mass leaders. This connection can channel tremendous power to a demagogue; it's also a means by which the people can recover control of their country. Most fundamentally, however, the connection between leader and people can create tremendous volatility. Democracy suffers from an intrinsic paradox—left to its own devices, freedom, humanity's ultimate ambition, can disintegrate into its opposite: tyranny. It is as if humanity is somehow bent on suicide or even matricide, where the demagogue attacks the very system that gave him birth. The pattern emerged in the first democracy in ancient Athens, as well as in the

Roman Republic. In the last century, it reappeared most vividly in the destruction of the democratic Weimar Germany under the dictatorship of Adolf Hitler. And it has replayed in recent years in Iraq.

At the center of this dynamic is the demagogue. The ancient Greeks first invented the word "demagogue" to describe a new class of mob leaders who quickly evolved to fill a power vacuum left by the demise of a reigning class of elite statesmen. The word meant "leader" (*agogos)* of the "people" (*demos)*. Then, as now, demagogues can always emerge in a political system that grants power, even if initially a small amount, to those who connect with the people. In empires, by contrast, demagogues are unimaginable, because power depends exclusively on a grant from the emperor or his counselors. In strongly party-based or elite systems, a connection with the people generally will not lead to political power. But a democracy—and any other system with an element of democracy—intrinsically creates an opening for a demagogue.

Aristotle likened the demagogue to a gadfly, an insect that you cannot shake free, that has a bitter sting. In this metaphor, democracy is a beast bedeviled by the maddening pest, who goads and pesters and stings until the animal bolts—stampeding away, trampling everything underneath, perhaps rushing off a cliff. But a better metaphor is perhaps a retrovirus, in which the body's defense mechanisms literally begin rewriting the body's DNA until the body turns on itself. Biologists speak reverently of these viruses as gorgeous things—intricate works of nature that, taken alone, inspire comparisons to abstract art or fine lacework. But when left to run their own path, they turn on their host and destroy it, using the host's own raw material as their weapon of death.

The word demagogue has always fascinated people; in 1649 the poet John Milton called it a "goblin word."[13] The word immediately invokes political villains from a hall of horrors, ranging from epic sociopaths such as Hitler and Mussolini, to a modern "ethnic cleanser" like Slobodan Milosevic, to a rabble-rousing bigot like George Wallace. But the word is actually far more precise. In ancient Greek, *demos*, or the "people," was a specific socioeconomic classification describing a range of lower- to middle-class citizens, generally unsophisticated, who could easily congeal into an angry mob. Their leader, mirroring this group of commoners, exhibited a volatile, even violent character. In short, the demagogue, championed by the people themselves, challenged order.

Today, defining and even recognizing demagogues is made more difficult by the casual, ill-informed usage of the term. There are only a handful of books in English on demagogues, and nothing that deals with them systematically at the conceptual level.[14] The word is often used carelessly in daily language to describe any political leader we think of as manipulative, pernicious, or bigoted. This sloppy usage means that we miss the precise lessons a demagogue can teach about the health of democracy itself.

The best systematic account of demagogues was actually given almost two hundred years ago, in an essay written in 1838 by James Fenimore Cooper called, simply, "On Demagogues." Cooper wrote, "A demagogue, in the strict signification of the word, is a 'leader of the rabble.' . . . The peculiar office of a demagogue is to advance his own interests, by affecting a deep devotion to the interests of the people."[15] As Cooper recognized, true demagogues meet four rules: (1) They fashion themselves as a man or woman of the common people, as opposed to the elites; (2) their politics depends on a powerful, visceral connection with the people that dramatically transcends ordinary political popularity; (3) they manipulate this connection, and the raging popularity it affords, for their own benefit and ambition; and (4) they threaten or outright break established rules of conduct, institutions, and even the law. They can break these rules, institutions, and laws internally, by threatening tyranny in their own countries, or externally by attacking other nations or groups or by testing the international rule of law. Either way, they are intrinsically violent.

As these rules suggest, demagogues do not need to reach the extremes of a Hitler to undermine democracy. The political scientist James Ceaser has usefully distinguished between "hard" and "soft" demagogues. "Hard" demagogues actively stir the passions through antagonism and division. "Soft" demagogues, on the other hand, employ flattery, currying favor through impossible promises.[16] In both cases, demagogues connect with large groups of ordinary people. And in either instance, they often earn the reputation of a villain, which they usually deserve. But the hostility in Cooper's words above can obscure how a demagogue actually works. Cooper, like many others, thought that demagogues lie, that they merely "affect" devotion. But this isn't always the case. A demagogue can be sincerely committed to his own causes—as long as they facilitate his own relentless ambition and forge a powerful connection with the common people.

This popularity enables the demagogue to carve out a space that he alone dominates, to undermine legitimate constitutional authority, and, in the most extreme instance, when democracy succumbs to tyranny, to create his own state within the state. This is why the fourth and last rule is the most important, distinguishing demagogues from populists. Populists play by the rules, but demagogues most often bully the rule of law. The point was emphasized by Aristotle, who wrote that the most dangerous form of democracy is the one in which "not the law, but the multitude, have the supreme power, and supersede the law by their decrees. . . . This is the state of affairs," he concluded, "brought on by demagogues."[17] The rule of law is the *sine qua non* of a successful democracy; conversely, demagogues break rules of order and, often, order itself.

This point helps explain why the most dangerous kind of demagogue is the one in power. But the rule also helps explain a paradox: demagogues occasionally can have a positive, progressive effect, if the system of law they subvert is intrinsically corrupt. We might refer to the two different kinds as "destructive" and "beneficial" demagogues. Boris Yeltsin, the populist president of Russia after the fall of the Soviet Union, for instance, was a demagogue with extreme ambition and a powerful connection with the masses. The crumbling Soviet system that he helped subvert was repressive—so this beneficial demagogue was, in the end, a general force for good. The same could be said of the Polish labor leader Lech Walesa, a bearish leader who stirred the masses against a corrupt and brutal system.

A couple of qualifiers are necessary before completing the definition of a demagogue. First, there are inherent subjective hazards to the definitional enterprise. As with any attempt to define political leaders, beauty (or ugliness) will often lie in the eye of the beholder. Many will disagree about whether a demagogue is destructive or beneficial, for instance, because they have personal biases toward the system the demagogue threatens. Second, we shouldn't spend too much energy disputing whether someone "is" or "is not" a demagogue. To borrow the terminology of social scientists, demagogue is a "continuous" rather than a "binary" variable. In other words, the category is a sliding scale. A leader can have different scores on the four rules, meaning he can be more or less of a demagogue and can range from a minor to a major threat to democracy. But it's certainly true that the most extreme demagogues pose the greatest challenges to democracy and to history itself.

By any measure, demagogues rank among history's most fascinating figures. In the last century in America alone, we can count Huey Long, Father Coughlin, Theodore Bilbo, George Wallace, and Joseph McCarthy as demagogues who met the four rules: they fashioned themselves as leaders of the common people, triggered enormous emotional reactions, used these reactions for political benefit, and tested or broke established rules of political conduct. On the fourth element, they each operated differently. Huey Long consolidated power so effectively in Louisiana that he established one-man rule; Coughlin created a massive, millions-strong movement of angry poor and later turned to anti-Semitism; Wallace actively militated against the federal government and against African Americans; and McCarthy blatantly exploited fears of Communists to violate the civil rights of thousands of Americans.

Internationally, the list of demagogues includes Hugo Chávez in Venezuela, Hassan Nasrallah in Lebanon, Moqtada al-Sadr in Iraq, Mahmoud Ahmadinejad in Iran, Slobodan Milosevic in Serbia, Vladimir Zhirinovsky in Russia, Jörg Haider in Austria, Fidel Castro in Cuba, Charles Taylor in Liberia, Juan Perón in Argentina, Benito Mussolini in Italy, and, of course, Adolf Hitler. Going back in time, we include Georges Danton during the French Revolution, the radical priest Savonarola in Renaissance Florence, and the golden-haired Athenian warrior, Alcibiades. These demagogues all broke boundaries. Their magnetism lay in their recklessness—in the disregard they manifested for the way things were done. This was the secret to their success, and also to their madness and their danger.

Some try but do not succeed. In recent American history, figures like Jimmy Hoffa, Louis Farrakhan, and Pat Buchanan tried to become demagogues, though their political success was limited and they were never really able to test the rules. Hoffa never met the third

rule of achieving political success; Farrakhan did not meet either the
third or fourth rules; Buchanan failed the second, third, and fourth
rules. But they all introduced the same unnerving kind of political
dynamic we see even in just the attempt to demagogue.

Demagogues are a fearsome adversary as old as democracy itself. But
they can be stopped. In the ancient world, where democracy was
invented, demagogues emerged almost as quickly as freedom itself.
After a period of intense struggle, the Athenians discovered a solution
to the demagogues. To remember how to defy the demagogue, we
need to travel back in time and visit the birthplace not only of democracy, but of its own worst enemy.

DEMOCRACY'S OWN WORST ENEMY

The tale is that he who has tasted the entrails of a single human
victim minced up with the entrails of other victims is destined to
become a wolf. . . . And the protector of the people is like him;
having a mob entirely at his disposal, he is not restrained from
shedding the blood of kinsmen; by the favorite method of false
accusation he brings them into court and murders them, making
the life of man to disappear, and with unholy tongue and lips
tasting the blood of his fellow citizen; some he kills and others he
banishes, at the same time hinting at the abolition of debts and
partition of lands: and after this, what will be his destiny? Must
he not either perish at the hands of his enemies, or from being a
man become a wolf—that is, a tyrant?[18]

—Plato, *The Republic*

THE CYCLE BEGINS SIMPLY, WITH A DEMAGOGUE, AMBITION, AND
charisma. Connecting with the people's hopes and dreams, fears, and
hatreds, he begins to grow more powerful by the day. For whatever

reason, the people choose to abandon their self-respect and commitment to the rule of law and reward the demagogue not with wariness and rebellion but with devotion. Soon enough, the people give him the government itself. The democracy rapidly becomes a tyranny. But the tyrant quickly becomes corrupt, tyrannical, implacable. His enemies begin to die; the ship of state starts to founder. Unsettled by the convulsions, a group of noblemen decide to take matters into their own hands. They rise up and overthrow the demagogue-*cum*-tyrant. The nobles hold power for a while, but jealously begin squabbling among themselves. The people, disquieted, watch their new leaders carefully. After a time, the people themselves conspire and overthrow the noblemen. And then the cycle begins again when the next ruthless, charismatic personality with political ambitions emerges.

So goes the ancient "cycle of regimes," a powerful historical logic that, unless countered by a mighty collective effort of thought and purpose, will trap humans over and over again, whether in Weimar, Germany, in Mussolini's Italy, or in Iraq today. The Greek historian Polybius powerfully explained this cycle, with a traumatic personal story that informed his perception of the tragic cycle's human costs.

Two centuries after the peak of Athens' fame, the Greek intellectual was captured by Roman conquerors in 168 B.C. and transported to Rome, where he was imprisoned for seventeen years.[19] This punishing stay concentrated Polybius's mind on the rise and fall of regimes. A harsh, empirical style dominated his famous histories, but the pressure created gems of insight. He described for his adoptive countrymen a "cycle of constitutional revolutions" seen in the dozens of competing Greek city-states hundreds of years earlier. He argued that there were three kinds of rule, each of which disintegrates into a base form. Kingship becomes tyranny, aristocracy oligarchy, and pure democracy, he said, collapses into a "government of violence and the strong hand."[20] A demagogue rises from the ashes of a destroyed democracy , sacrificing freedom for order. And the cycle then produces a despot. After a "reign of mere violence" comes worse: "Tumultuous assemblies, massacres, banishments."[21]

Polybius wove into his discourse on the cycle of regimes a terribly pessimistic account of human nature itself, echoed many centuries later by the English philosopher Thomas Hobbes' invocation of a state of nature that was "poor, nasty, brutish, and short." The "lawless ferocity" of democracy, Polybius wrote, comes because it is "inevitably transformed."[22] Polybius likened the cycle disintegrating democracy to rust acting as a "natural dissolvent" of metal and to a grub devouring timber. In all three cases, the enemy destroys the host "without any external injury."[23] The destruction takes place through internal, organic decay; it isn't apparent until it's too late.

Notions of vast, almost galactic patterns that inevitably sweep up mere mortals have dominated much of history. The medieval philosophers were fascinated by the idea of a "great chain of being."[24] This chain linked together all living things, from insects to wild animals to human beings to the gods, in a celestial pattern that gave a sense of order, reassurance, and well-being to medieval people contemplating an otherwise chaotic universe. Similarly, Polybius's cycle of regimes saw human beings as pawns in a drama much larger than themselves. The cycle revolved around a single figure: the demagogue. Polybius was fixated on this leader who was "sufficiently ambitious and daring" to capture the people's fancy in a democracy—in him, they have "once more found a master and a despot."[25] According to Polybius, the same figure who would haunt the Founding Fathers millennia later always leads the revolution that transforms democracy into tyranny. In his cycle, the demagogue turns human history like a great, merciless wheel, crushing people and their dreams in its gears.

The hand-to-hand combat between democracy and the demagogue dominated centuries of history, unleashing violence that forever shadowed our ideas about human freedom. After decades of struggling to control demagogues, Athenians ultimately realized that the problem of the demagogue rested not in some foreign enemy and not in the spirits and demigods they usually blamed for most human mishaps. Responsibility lay instead in a very different location: their own hearts and minds.

CLEON OF ATHENS

ONE OF THE MOST BRUTAL DEMAGOGUES THE WORLD HAS KNOWN NOT only brought Athens' democracy to its knees, but also toppled a revered statesman, took over the Athenian government, came within a hair of executing a powerful playwright who dared challenge him, attempted the mass murder of the inhabitants of a vanquished island, launched reckless military expeditions, and brought Athens into a war that ultimately would defeat its democracy for a time. Cleon was a political tsunami. As the waves receded and Athenians surveyed the wreckage, they resolved to build warning systems and barricades that would prevent another disaster in the future. He triggered a wave of self-criticism and self-restraint among Athenians that ultimately helped democracy survive; their example echoes today as a powerful but forgotten answer to democracy's demagogue problem.

Cleon is not well-remembered by history, but many readers may dimly recognize his name. In international relations classes across the country, thousands of undergraduates every year read a famous passage from Thucydides' *The Peloponnesian War*. The passage, called the "Mytilenean Debate," teaches students about *realpolitik* in international politics, illuminating the theory that pure morality should play no role in foreign policy. This theory holds that political decisions should be guided by a harsh calculation of self-interest, no matter the human cost or the sacrifice of our ideals. The passage is assigned so frequently because it illustrates the argument in the harshest, most memorable terms possible. Fittingly, the character who makes the most ruthless argument is the demagogue.

The debate occurred before several hundred Athenian citizens at the Assembly on the Pnyx, the hilltop meeting place where Athenian democracy would live and die. The meeting was convened to consider a single question: how to deal with a rebellion in the city of Mytilene, which Athens had conquered. The Athenians had particularly venomous feelings about the Mytileneans. The city, a former ally, had recently switched allegiance to Sparta, an unpardonable offense to Athens' famous self-regard. After Athens conquered them, the Mytileneans revolted, with Sparta's assistance. According to Thucydides, the Athenians, "in an angry mood," decided to execute not only the military perpetrators of the revolt, but also the entire male population of the city. A boat had already been dispatched to Mytilene carrying the order to the Athenian commanders. The day after the decision, however, a wave of remorse and indecision swept over Athens. The hilltop crowd reconsidered; its decision would literally have to outrun fate.

As the ship sailed to Mytilene, Cleon stood before the restless crowd and made the case, with terse brutality, for letting the order to kill all the men stand. Athenians, Cleon said, needed to stick to their original decision. To do otherwise would signify weakness. "[Y]ou fail to see that when you allow them to persuade you to make a mistaken decision and when you give way to your own feelings of compassion," he berated the crowd, "you are being guilty of a kind of weakness which is dangerous to you and which will not make them love you any more." Taking a breath, pausing, and slamming his hand into his thigh for emphasis, the general continued. He said the Mytileneans deserved harsher than ordinary punishment because their revolt was "calculated aggression," rather than simple warlike passion. As a relatively wealthy city, Mytilene had grown arrogant, and Athens should have suppressed it earlier. The example set by Athens' leniency in this case, Cleon told the crowd, would set off a domino chain of revolts in other cities.

And then Cleon turned the argument against his audience. The Athenian empathy for the Mytileneans revealed why people like him were needed to make difficult decisions like this. High-class intellectuals, he told them, were less capable of governing in political matters where "lack of learning combined with sound common sense is more helpful than the kind of cleverness that gets out of hand." The people themselves were to blame: "To feel pity, to be carried away by the pleasure of hearing a clever argument, to listen to the claims of decency are three things that are entirely against the interests of an imperial power. Do not be guilty of them." He concluded with a damning charge: "You are simply victims of your own pleasure in listening, and are more like an audience sitting at the feet of a professional lecturer than a parliament discussing matters of state."

And he then gave an astonishing description of his own purpose. "I am trying to stop you behaving like this."[26] That charge was almost tragic, with Cleon revealing to the crowd his own inevitability. Even if Athens wised up, he would still be in control. There was no escaping the demagogue. Like the worst kind of bully, he was unable to refrain not only from taking advantage of weakness, but also from taunting his enemy about it.

We know very little about the man who made this horrifying argument with such methodical brutality, who goaded Athens' elite and claimed that only a demagogue like him, who would eschew "cleverness" in order to assert "the interests of an imperial power," was qualified to make foreign policy. We do know a few things about him, however. Cleon came from a relatively well-off family—his father ran a leather-tanning business. But he was still only a soldier, not a priest or a tradesman (Athens' higher classes), and was therefore excluded from high society. His enemies mocked him as a drunkard, and they claimed that they could smell the heavy odor of the oils and herbs used in his family's tanning business when he passed them on the street. By his manner, his dress, and his peers, Cleon was seen as vulgar and lower class by the elites of Athens. He certainly cultivated this condescension for its political dividends, but it also generated in him a politics of constant resentment and anger.

Cleon was a professional soldier, and most of his values, experiences, and friends would have derived from Athens' military culture as well. He appears to have been a brave if reckless fighter. He never hesitated to put himself at peril in military missions—he was not, in other words, a coward. But his politics also had a combative, violent tone, common to the warrior ideal in Athenian society. We also can infer from writings about him that Cleon was tremendously ambitious, ruthless, intelligent, vulgar, physically powerful, charismatic, and bold. Even Thucydides—a pessimistic, cranky historian, a brilliant writer of a bloody tragedy, and hardly one to praise idealists—painted Cleon in particularly harsh hues in his writings. One scholar says that Thucydides writes of Cleon "with more personal animus than he allows himself anywhere else."[27] For Thucydides, Cleon's premeditated inhumanity crossed the line.

Cleon paired his violent sensibility with raw, native intelligence to drive public policy decisions unimaginable by anyone with even a modicum of sympathy in their politics. As another scholar writes, Cleon had a "clear head which was clever at simplifying things, a trenchant logic which readily made its way by incontrovertible deductions, and which imposed its conclusions by systematic severity."[28] Logic, for Cleon, was a weapon, and the people themselves were only a means to an end.

———

All demagogues begin with a distinctly ruthless, inexorable ambition. A wary political society must take for granted that there will always be tremendously aggressive democratic entrepreneurs who will pursue every opening and cross every boundary in a quest for personal power and political success. This ambition can have tragic human costs. The trail of any successful demagogue is littered with the bodies of victims—sometimes figuratively, but often enough literally.

Cleon's first victim in his rise to power could not possibly have been more majestic: Pericles, a statesman and Athens' ruling general, who was at once father and grandfather to the city. Legend had it that Pericles' mother dreamed about a lion the week before he was born. The lion's traditionally elevated qualities of courage and moral stature manifested themselves both in Pericles' intellect and his bearing.[29] Plutarch wrote that Pericles had a "dignity of spirit and a nobility of utterance which was entirely free from the vulgar and unscrupulous buffooneries of mob-oratory, but also a composure of countenance that never dissolved into laughter, a serenity in his movements and in the graceful arrangement of his dress which nothing could disturb while he was speaking."[30] Pericles' power seemed to concentrate the extraordinary accomplishment of Athenian democracy in the single point of himself. As Plutarch wrote, "So, in what was nominally a democracy, power was really in the hands of the first citizen."[31] During Pericles' reign, Athens—a city-state at once strong, free, and the envy of the world—was itself a complex hybrid, a meld of freedom and hero-worship.

Unsurprisingly, Pericles also had enemies. Some said that he had a "rather disdainful and arrogant manner of address" and that "his pride had in it a good deal of superciliousness and contempt for others."[32] He was aloof in his public manners, too. He "took care not to make himself too familiar a figure, even to the people, and he only addressed them at long intervals."[33] As Thucydides described him:

[P]ericles, because of his position, his intelligence, and his known integrity, could respect the liberty of the people and at the same time hold them in check. It was he who led them, rather than they who led him, and, since he never sought power from any wrong motive, he was so highly respected that he was able to speak angrily to them and to contradict them.[34]

The Athenians had a custom of burying the bones of those who had died in battle during the previous year in the most beautiful spot in Athens. At a mass funeral for all of the war's dead, Pericles presented a funeral oration that echoed throughout the Greek world in which he praised Athens' democratic accomplishment in glowing terms. "Our constitution is called a democracy because power is in the hands not of a minority but of the whole people," he told his flock. "We give our obedience to those whom we put in positions of authority, and we obey the laws themselves, especially those which are for the protection of the oppressed, and *those unwritten laws which it is an acknowledged shame to break*."[35] Pericles was attempting to recall Athenians to their own democratic values—to the underlying beliefs that made them both free and strong.

Despite the obvious power of such words and ideals, Pericles' elite status had a perverse consequence: it created a natural opening for political opponents to fashion themselves as mirrors for the masses. Over time, his elevated standing became not a means to draw the people to him, but a wedge for others to drive them away.

Three years before Cleon's brutal prosecution of the case against the Mytileneans, he engineered Pericles' collapse. Cleon's great political insight was that the masses were growing restless under the tight grip of elites like Pericles. He recognized that the people were ready to place other matters—among them the hatred of Sparta, their panic at a faltering economy, and the sheer thrill of Cleon's vulgar style—above Pericles' cool statesmanship.

A series of disasters befell Athens during the last two years of Pericles' rule, unsettling the people's hearts and minds. First, a band of Spartans had plundered an Athenian neighborhood.[36] Pericles thought the ragged foreigners were too exhausted to pose a serious threat, so instead of going to war with Sparta, he announced to the Athenians his plan to send one hundred ships to loot the Peloponnesian coast.[37] But as the ships were about to sail, the moon went into eclipse, and the skies turned black. The people began to panic. Hundreds began streaming up the rocky stairs to the Pnyx, where they began chanting against Pericles' mission. Pericles rushed to the Pnyx and somehow managed to calm the mob, and the ships finally were able to leave port.[38] The heavens, however, were not on Pericles' side. The next week, an epidemic struck, and hundreds of people began dying, in agonizing fevers and sweats.[39]

Cleon glimpsed his opportunity and seized it. Prior to Cleon, very few politically ambitious Athenians spoke before the Athenian Assemblies for the purposes of influencing opinion and achieving political power. Under Pericles' reign, Athenian politicians did not rabble-rouse because they were simply not allowed to do so. But Cleon discovered and asserted an untraveled path to power—oratory. During a meeting of the Assembly, he staged an attack on Pericles for the "misuse of public funds"—corruption. Such inquiries were common in Athens' extremely litigious society, and Pericles had escaped them before. But this time he was entangled in the people's anger. Led by Cleon, the Assembly fined Pericles the great sum of fifty talents. Worse than this, they voted to revoke his generalship.[40] Athens now entered the wilderness of the demagogue.

Pericles recovered his generalship when the *demos,* fickle as always, voted him back into office several months later. But he never recovered his political status, and his tragedies continued inproportion to Cleon's rise. Pericles' two sons died in the plaguethe next year. Cleon, now an elected general, was making waragainst Sparta. More demagogues now emerged, less politically skilled than Cleon but even more bombastic. As Thucydideswrote, "[Pericles'] successors, who were more on a level with eachother and each of whom aimed at occupying the first place,adopted methods of demagogy which resulted in their losing control over the actual conduct of affairs."[41] They saw the politicalbenefit of militating against the hated enemy, regardless of thedamage that intervention and belligerence could do to Athens' national security interests. The cycle of regimes now began playing out geopolitically, as the demagogues took over military decisions and sapped Athens of the cool strategic sensibility that had led to decades of preeminence.

After Pericles, Cleon's next victim was a playwright—not just an artist, but a dominant political figure in the city. Athenians knew not to trifle with Aristophanes, who was rich, arrogant, and brilliant. Aristophanes fashioned himself as both an overseer and protector of Athens' democracy, and he despised Cleon. Over the years, the playwright fumed as Cleon increased his power. Lying awake at night, he would play out the scenario in his mind. The general—the *demagogue*—would pitch the state into a black hole of chaos. The democracy that had been so carefully built would spiral downward and disappear into the bottomless drain of the demagogue's monomania. The people who had been given power only a century before would give it away and Athens' magnificent experiment in freedom would be torn apart by the *demos* itself.

The tough playwright was hardly one for hand-wringing. Athens was now in the fourth year of the wasteful and ominous Peloponnesian War with Sparta, and Aristophanes held Cleon largely to blame. One day, after watching Cleon manipulate the people with his bombast, flattery, and bellicose rhetoric yet again, Aristophanes began formulating plans for a masterpiece—a great new play that he was sure would savage the demagogue and wake up the people. Several months later, his play (now lost) was produced in the Theatre of Dionysus, presenting Cleon as a comical robber idiot, a plunderer of the public weal. The *demos* roared with laughter at the caricature of their hero. The playwright watched, satisfied that he had cut Cleon down at the knees.

But it didn't work. Several months later, Aristophanes stood on the knotty grass of the Pnyx as Cleon assailed the playwright from the cold stone *bema*. Cleon thundered to the crowd: "With his play, he slandered our city in the presence of foreigners." This was a serious crime, but a bogus charge. Foreigners always attended the Festival of Dionysus, so it would be impossible to present a serious play *not* in the presence of foreigners. The jury voted the ridiculous charge down, but the feud only gathered momentum.

Aristophanes wouldn't back down. With the war now in its sixth year, he responded in a new play called *The Acharnians,* "Nor have

I forgotten how Cleon treated me because of my comedy last year; he dragged me before the Senate and there he uttered endless slanders against me; 'twas a tempest of abuse, a deluge of lies. Through what a slough of mud he dragged me! I nigh perished."[42] The play was beautifully written but, again, had little political effect, and Cleon's popularity continued to increase. Tossing and turning one night, the frustrated playwright suddenly sat up. This struggle, he realized, was larger than the general. It was larger than Athens. It was the struggle of the human race to achieve something larger than itself. How could you give the people so much freedom if they would just as quickly give it away? He pulled himself off his mattress, lit a candle, and began taking notes for a new play that would finally stir the people against their destroyer.

Two years later, with the war in its eighth year, 17,000 people shivered in the Theatre of Dionysus, pooled in the enormous shadow of the Acropolis. They shifted impatiently on the cold, stone benches. Beneath them, the playwright watched, scratching absentmindedly at a rough seam on the fat-suit the stagehands had pushed and pulled him into. The suit, stuffed with goose feathers, itched, but that was hardly the primary thing on Aristophanes' mind. The audience burst into applause, then hushed, while the playwright watched from the wings as three masked actors strolled onto the stage. A stagehand approached Aristophanes with his hands full of something red and dripping. He raised his hands to the playwright's face and almost tenderly smeared the grape skins on his cheeks, his forehead, his chin, even his eyelids. Aristophanes had no mirror, but he was sure the effect of mimicking Cleon's famously drunken visage was complete. He would bury this demon of democracy with blood on his face.

His cue came. Gathering the fat-suit around him, Aristophanes paused a moment—and then rushed on stage, startling even the other actors. The audience gasped; they had never before seen an actor on stage without a mask. The playwright then bellowed his lines, smacking his hands on his thighs for emphasis, mimicking Cleon: "By the twelve gods! Woe betide you, who have too long been conspiring against Demos." A second, greater gasp surged through those citizens seated in the rows closest to the stage, as they realized that the playwright himself was playing his nemesis.

Aristophanes acted his heart out on the stage. With *The Knights*, he thought he could finally make the citizens *understand*. In the script, he employed a powerful Greek verb—*tarattein*—no fewer than nine times. This was a word the Greeks used to signify one of four types of profound agitation: the disturbance of startled horses, the appearance of mentally or physically agitated persons, the stirring up of bodies of water, and the disruption of the unity of groups of people. Aristophanes used the third meaning several times in his play, likening Cleon to the ocean during a storm or a blustering squall.[43] But while some of the writing was precise, even surgical, the playwright's frustration occasionally got the better of him. At one point, the Chorus simply shouted that Cleon was "this public robber, this yawning gulf of plunder, this devouring Charybdis, this villain, this villain, this villain!"

Throughout his play, Aristophanes drew an aspirational picture of a *demos* that would use its native intelligence to finally challenge Cleon. The people of Athens actually appeared as a character named "Demos" (a typical device by Greek playwrights who often wanted to give the audience a metonymic representation of themselves). Aristophanes' Demos was a comic figure—a gullible, weak-willed, wealthy landowner. Part of the play's drama was Aristophanes' push to get Demos to stand up to Cleon. In one exchange, when the Chorus collectively threw up its hands and attacked Demos for listening to Cleon "with gaping mouth," Aristophanes had Demos retort, "'Tis rather you who have no brains, if you think me so foolish as all that; it is with a purpose that I play this idiot's role, for I love to drink the lifelong day, and so it pleases me to keep a thief for my minister. When he has thoroughly gorged himself, then I overthrow and crush him."[44]

The *demos* that Aristophanes imagined inspiring to act against Cleon was canny and self-aware, and much less stupid than their prior approval of Cleon implied. With evident hopefulness, Aristophanes described for the audience how he wanted them to turn on Cleon: "Look, see how I play with them, while all the time they think themselves such adepts at cheating me," his Demos said. "I have my eye on them when they thieve, but I do not appear to be seeing them; then I thrust a judgment down their throat as it were a feather, and force them to vomit up all they have robbed from me."[45]

Aristophanes clearly wanted his audience to understand that one element above all others was central to Cleon's appeal and to his demagoguery: war. The unkempt, ravenous Demos would match the expansion of his own waistline with his country's boundary; the increase in his pocketbook would parallel the growth in a war economy. Aristophanes charged about a current campaign: "[L]ittle you care for his reigning in Arcadia, 'tis to pillage and impose on the allies at will that you reckon; you wish the War to conceal your rogueries as in a mist, that Demos may see nothing of them, and harassed by cares, may only depend on yourself for his bread."[46] War coursed through Cleon's veins, so the city he led would naturally be warlike as well. In another passage, his Chorus (a stand-in for the playwright himself) described Cleon's reaction to Demos with a horrible rapacity: "[W]hen you find one simple and timid . . . you seize him by the middle, throttle him by the neck, while you twist his shoulder back; he falls and you devour him."[47]

The imagery strikes a modern-day reader as particularly ghoulish, even cannibalistic. This so-called friend of the people, this leader of masses, seduces the people before utterly destroying them. But Aristophanes' rhetoric—admittedly overheated—may have been proportional to the phenomenon he was witnessing. At the peak of Cleon's power, Athenians commonly said, he was so terrifying that a single glance from him could make a man vomit from fear.

The battles between Cleon and both Pericles and Aristophanes took place amid Athenians' tortured reflection about whether they had gone too far with democracy, which had been introduced only a century earlier. Although Athens had pretensions of being purely democratic—anyone who attended the Assembly on the Pnyx could speak, similar to a New England town meeting today—their system was actually highly constrained. Only a very small percentage of Athens' land-owning men could actually attend Assembly and vote; women, slaves, the poor, and foreigners were all locked out of the system. When Cleon erupted, he broke open the locks that had kept the poor from politics. The resulting flood swamped the city's power structure. And the new entrants in the political system did not share the values of the smaller number who had worshiped Pericles' dignified leadership. This new electorate was interested in higher jury pay, in war with Sparta, and in a strong man like Cleon. And so Cleon naturally rose with them.

The demagogue was therefore a symptom of a larger force roiling under the surface of society: the people's confidence in themselves. What would it take to trust the people with power? What values did they need to survive their own worst impulses?

Aristophanes' attempt to topple Cleon created great theater for his audiences and tremendous plays for the ages; we are lucky that his satires remain. But the elite playwright failed in his political objective. Despite Aristophanes, Cleon continued, unscathed, to attack his opponents, to hand out money to the *demos* with abandon, and to provoke military expeditions. He was even re-elected general by the people. In the end, the demagogue ultimately fell prey not to the people or his political enemies but, fittingly, to his own *hubris*. On a typically brash mission, Cleon was killed while attempting to recover the city of Amphipolis. His downfall came at the hands of Brasidas, a general of Cleon's hated Spartans.

◆

AN ENEMY OF THE PEOPLE

IN THE LAST YEARS OF THE FIFTH CENTURY B.C., ATHENS WAS A democracy, but an unruly, aggressive one plagued by demagogues. In 415 B.C., seven years after Cleon died, Athens launched a disastrous mission to Sicily that unnecessarily provoked Sparta and exposed Athens to attack both internally and externally. Four years later,

Athens was overthrown by an oligarchic coup of 400 noblemen. A counter-revolution followed shortly, restoring the democracy. But in 405 B.C., seventeen years after Cleon's death, Athens suffered a crushing naval defeat by Sparta in a new phase of the near-perpetual Peloponnesian War—in large part because Athens had overextended itself again through the military demands of jingoistic demagogues. Athens was soon under siege.

After a quick victory over its nemesis city, Sparta installed a puppet government of thirty Athenian noblemen. The "Thirty," as they were called, presented the most direct assault on Athens' democracy yet. After taking control, they undertook a series of brutal measures to consolidate the oligarchy and root out democracy. In the eight months they were in power, they created a group of 300 floggers, executed 1,500 people, and banished 5,000—in a city with only about 25,000 free citizens.[48]

These bloody events bring us to our first major character in the story of the fight to save democracy from the demagogue. A broad-shouldered young man watched the violence unfold around him with brooding melancholy. His given name was Aristocles, but his good-natured classmates had nicknamed their intense fellow student "Platon" (or "Plato") after the word for "broad," because of his wrestler's shoulders. His father had died when he was a boy, and his mother remarried a man who was a close friend of Pericles—as a teenager, Plato witnessed Cleon fell Pericles with the blunt weapon of democracy.[49] Plato was twelve years old when the Sicilian expedition was launched and twenty-two when the puppet government was installed. He watched bitterly as democrats were forced to drink hemlock—an herb that made the stomach clench and the body seize up, turn rigid and numb, and ultimately led to a massive coronary. Ironically, some of the leaders of the new regime recognized the young man as a natural leader and offered him a government appointment. He was flattered, and briefly tempted, but he ultimately refused, unwilling to join in such savagery.

The young man resolved to use his only real weapon—his mind—to solve the problem once and for all. The former wrestler spent his career bullying democracy to the ground with an intellectual aptitude so extraordinarily powerful that his ideas would come to dominate the Western mind for two thousand years—now going on three. His masterpiece, the *Republic,* is often remembered for Plato's allegory of the cave, for its description of an ideal state run by mysterious "Guardians," and for its condemnation of poets and actors. Yet, in many ways, the book can be read in a different way. In its simplest form, the world's most famous book of philosophy is also a book about demagogues.

The *Republic* is composed of ten sections, or "books," which together construct a hermetic, perfectly logical case for a fictional utopia—a small state where injustice is impossible, where people live in perfect economy and harmony, and, most importantly, that utterly eliminates the very possibility of political violence stirred up by demagogues. Plato's solution to the problems he watched in Athens was to create a state where a group of "Guardians" made every important political decision. Each young potential Guardian was culled from the general population at a young age and carefully cultivated—like a kind of human orchid—his entire adult life, until he was adjudicated competent to become one of the rulers of the city.

This certifiably nutty scheme has entranced generations of thinkers with a penchant for authoritarianism and a distrust of the messiness and unpredictability of mass decision making. Plato's end result does not hold much interest for a modern democracy; what is interesting, however, are two things: the extraordinary lengths that he believed were necessary to avoid the problems he saw in democracy, and the stories he told about democracy's own instability.

Plato had little direct experience in politics. His only real flirtation with political action ended as he watched his city collapse around him. In a letter he wrote when he was over seventy, he recalled an episode when friends and relatives who belonged to the Thirty asked him to help the regime, on the "assumption that theirs was a sort of work appropriate for someone like me." But Plato hesitated: "It is no wonder, since I was a young man, that my feeling was that they would govern the city by leading it from an unjust way of life to a just one, and I was intensely interested to see what would happen." His ominous feeling about the future under this new regime turned out to be true: "But after a short time, I saw that these men made the former constitution seem like a golden age by comparison."[50]

The tarnishing of the "golden" constitution occurred, in Plato's eyes, through Athens' abuse of the most important person in his life. Socrates was an unkempt, irreverent, but improbably lovable old man who made a profession of wandering Athens, sharing deep thoughts on subjects ranging from ethics to aesthetics to politics with the young men who were both his students and his lovers, and attacking corrupt public servants. Plato was his closest and most beloved student. In dozens of the "dialogues" he wrote in which characters discussed his philosophical ideas, Plato never in fact featured himself; most of his thoughts were communicated instead through the character of Socrates.

In his old age, Plato recounted with evident pain the regime's horrible treatment of Socrates. "Among other things, they sent my aged friend, Socrates, whom I wouldn't hesitate to call the most just man of his time, along with some others, to fetch one of their fellow citizens by force, so that he could be executed." Plato recorded Socrates' principled stand: "Their purpose was to involve Socrates in their activities, whether he wished it or not. He refused, however, and risked the most extreme penalties rather than take part in their unholy deeds."[51] Plato's squeamishness at his mentor's torment is striking. He would ultimately conclude that the cycle of regimes itself had undertaken the sickening attempt to press the aged philosopher, the "most just man of his time," into its machinery of violence.

This oligarchy, and the democracy that preceded and followed it, were all bound up, for Plato, in a horrific whole. Five years after the Thirty were deposed at the hands of the *demos*, Plato watched as Socrates was put to death. In extinguishing one life, however, the cruel act of the mob would take on a life of its own, reverberating throughout Plato's political philosophy, Western history, and (through an improbable set of twists and turns) our most recent experiments with democracy and our encounters, once again, with the demagogue.

The drama of Socrates' trial is one of history's most celebrated and infamous episodes. Plato's teacher was called to trial in 399 B.C. on two charges: corrupting the youth of Athens and worshiping false gods. Plato recounted the story of the trial in beautiful, tragic detail in his *Apology,* and he assayed Socrates' eventual death by hemlock in the *Crito.* In this haunting dialogue, Socrates' friend Crito attempts to persuade him to flee the cave where he is imprisoned, but Socrates—in a famous display of self-abnegation—says that because he was convicted under the laws of Athens, and because he loves Athens above all else, he cannot break the law.

In Athens, juries consisted of hundreds of citizens making decisions in a heavily emotional manner that could take dramatic twists and turns. The nature of juries was equivalent, in the critics of democracy's eyes, to the flaws of democracy itself. The jury that found Socrates guilty had more than 500 members. In it, Plato saw the mob. The vulnerability of crowds of common people to demagogic appeals would haunt much of what he would later write. Democracy, in other words, was not only a flawed and erratic system of governance to Plato. It was a murderer.

After Socrates' death, Plato set about a philosophical career with one political goal: to punish democracy. Like Polybius, Plato had a dark view of human nature that informed and reinforced his dark political philosophy. He believed that the urge for change was like a dark form of gravity in politics, and that all political systems, no matter how ambitious and hopeful, would eventually be suctioned back to the depths from whence they came. Plato thought decay was the governing logic of history. He wrote, "[E]verything that comes into being must decay," and likened political systems to seasons—coming, going, living, and dying: "All plants that grow in the earth, and also all animals that grow upon it, have periods of fruitfulness and barrenness of both soul and body as long as the revolutions complete the circumferences of their circles."[52] The cycle would particularly afflict democracy: "[D]oesn't the insatiable desire for freedom and the neglect of other things change this constitution and put it in need of a dictatorship?"[53]

In Book 8 of his *Republic,* the wrestler-philosopher squared off with the figure of the demagogue, depicting a horrifying vision of violence reminiscent of the paintings of Brueghel centuries later—men becoming wolves, sons striking fathers, and people succumbing to "civil wars in their souls," ripped apart by lust, disorder, and their own madness. Driving the madness was a familiar figure: the demagogue. A simple plot drove Plato's account of democracy. Plato began the *Republic* by describing democracy as an easily distracted child. Of the democrat, he wrote, "And so he lives on, yielding day by day to the desire at hand. Sometimes he drinks heavily while listening to the flute; at other times, he drinks only water and is on a diet; sometimes he goes in for physical training; at other times, he's idle and neglects everything. . . ." This was an almost touching description of a happy-go-lucky sort—aggravating, perhaps, but harmless. Plato even gave a positive dimension to the democrat, who embodies diversity and pluralism: "[H]e's a complex man, full of all sorts of characters, fine and multicolored, just like the democratic city," he wrote. In fact, "many men and women might envy his life, since it contains the most models of constitutions and ways of living."[54]

But this happy bumbler could quickly become a menace. "Democracy's insatiable desire for what it defines as the good," Plato explained, is "also what destroys it."[55] Democracy's appetite for everything at once sets a monstrous cycle in motion: "[D]oesn't the insatiable desire for freedom and the neglect of other things," Plato asked rhetorically, "change this constitution and put it in need of a dictatorship?"[56] Here the demagogue makes his entrance, filling the vacuum with discipline. Importantly, even here, Plato placed blame squarely on the people for their demise. The demagogue does not manipulate the people; instead, the "ruler who behaves like a subject"[57] slavishly follows the will of the people and fails to chart a course for the city beyond the narrows of popularity and passion. The demagogue runs democracy into the ground.

But it gets worse—this relationship between people and demagogue is "the fine and impetuous origin from which tyranny seems . . . to evolve."[58] The rule of decay holds; liberty falls apart. "Extreme freedom can't be expected to lead to anything but a change to extreme slavery, whether for a private individual or for a city." And "the most severe and cruel slavery" results from the "utmost freedom."[59] This occurs because the people are "always in the habit of setting up one man as their special champion, nurturing him and making him great."[60] Plato explained that this demagogue can quickly transform: "It is clear that, when a tyrant arises, this special leadership is the sole root from which he sprouts."[61]

Now the demagogue reaches his full demonic form, as democracy convulses before him. In response to the question, "What is the beginning of the transformation from leader of the people to tyrant?" Socrates answers, simply, "[A]nyone who tastes the one piece of human innards that's chopped up with those of other sacrificial victims must inevitably become a wolf." The demagogue, by the logic of his own connection with the hungry, disorderly people, is drawn ineluctably to violence, becomes addicted to blood, and cannibalizes the body politic itself. In a haunting passage, Plato described how the demagogue "dominates a docile mob and doesn't restrain himself from spilling blood." He spelled out a numbing sequence of terror: "He brings someone to trial on false charges and murders him (as tyrants often do), and, by thus blotting out a human life, his impious tongue and lips taste kindred citizen blood. He banishes some, kills others, and drops hints to the people about the cancellation of debts and the redistribution of land."[62]

The collapse of democracy into terror claims many victims, including, even more perversely, the tyrant himself. Plato explained that the demagogue himself suffers the moral consequence of murder: "And because of these things, isn't a man like that inevitably fated to be killed by his enemies or to be transformed from a man into a wolf by becoming a tyrant?"[63] The demagogue can never have peace, political success collapses in on itself, and even the victors cannot survive the cycle of regimes.

The savage, wolf-like demagogue who haunted Plato's imagination helped spawn a political philosophy based on control, crushing the passions stirred by the demagogue, and eliminating the possibility of a demagogue ever becoming a tyrant. Seared by the scene of Socrates' death at the hands of a mob, Plato endeavored never to let it happen again. Some, like the philosopher Karl Popper, have attacked Plato for subsequently launching a school of political thought that directly inspired totalitarianism and fascism.[64] Regardless of whether authoritarians cite him directly, Plato's *method*—to respond to the struggle between democracy and demagogue by locking the people away from real political power—has always attracted those in pursuit of the most immediate and forceful response to democracy's paradox.

Rather than disentangling democracy from the demagogue, Plato simply locked both in a cage and threw away the key. His goal, he said, was "to be fashioning the happy city, not picking out a few happy people and putting them in it, but making the whole city happy."[65] The only way to do this was to establish absolute control. As noted, Plato's city would genetically cultivate "Guardians" to run the city. These Guardians would procreate only with each other, raising children in common. The people would be told a "noble lie": "All of you in the city are brothers . . . but the god who made you mixed some gold into those who are adequately equipped to rule, because they are the most valuable." ("Gold" refers to the quality of one's soul, which Plato thought differentiated the elites from the rabble.) The stakes were high among the Guardians. Perfection had to be maintained at any cost. With a strange dispassion, Plato wrote, "If an offspring of theirs should be found to have a mixture of iron or bronze, they must not pity him in any way, but give him the rank appropriate to his nature and drive him out to join the craftsmen and farmers."[66]

From this elite class of home-grown Guardians, a singular figure would emerge—a shining "philosopher-king" with a monopoly on knowledge, virtue, and power. In a famous passage, Plato invoked an impossible world. "Until philosophers rule as kings in cities or those who are now called kings and leading men genuinely and adequately philosophize," he wrote, "that is, until political power and philosophy entirely coincide, while the many natures who at present pursue either one exclusively are forcibly prevented from doing so, cities will have no rest from evils. . . , nor . . . will the human race."[67] In his own person, in every judgment he would make, this mythical philosopher-king would forever rid the city of the disorder, madness, and murder that Plato saw in democracy that horrible day when his beloved mentor was executed by the mob.

A well-regarded classics professor once told me, in a discussion about Plato, "You know, I try not to assign Plato to first-year graduate students." "Why?" I asked. "He's too powerful," he said. "His equation of truth and beauty and justice overwhelms them. It is like a religion. They need more of a foundation before they can tackle him." It might seem bizarre that a professor would seek to keep students away from any important texts, let alone Plato. But these were the lengths to which this professor was driven by his judgment of Plato's impact on young scholars. After all, there *is* something intoxicating about the kind of thinking Plato promoted, and the professor's point was that, for young minds in search of a great idea with which to make their mark—typical of graduate students—the strong stuff of Plato sometimes needs to be taken slowly.

Plato inducts his adherents into a world governed by a spiritual trinity. In his realm, the knowledge of truth leads to the perception of perfect beauty, opening the path to justice—to political perfection, a state of the world where problems have dissolved in the acid broth of pure philosophy. The Platonic equation is Truth = Justice = Beauty. If you do not engage in this quest, or if you do not entertain the equation's possibility in the first place, you are locked out of a crystalline world. You become, in the eyes of Platonists, a subaltern philosophical seeker.

We can understand this a little better through the writing itself. There is a famous passage in Plato's dialogue *Phaedrus* in which the philosopher imagined the soul as a pair of winged horses led by a charioteer. One of the horses is "noble and of noble breed," meant to symbolize the philosophical temperament that Plato hoped to inspire among his followers; the other is "ignoble and of ignoble breed." It is the job of the noble horse to pull the chariot upward, into the universe, toward the upper realm where "abides the very being with which true knowledge is concerned; the colourless, formless, intangible essence, visible only to mind, the pilot of the soul."[68] In this celestial realm, the true nature of the universe—an underlying unity of truth, justice, and beauty—can finally be discovered. Why strive for the higher realm? "The reason why the souls exhibit this exceeding eagerness to behold the plain of truth," Plato explained, "is that pasturage is found there, which is suited to the highest part of the soul. . . ."[69] In other words, those with an elevated nature—or who think they have one—are destined for the higher realm.

In the story Plato told, the winged steed "long[s] after the upper world" where truth resides, plunging the chariot into chaos, as the ignoble steed fights back, leading to "confusion and perspiration and the extremity of effort."[70] The noble horse keeps soaring upward, toward the "plain of truth . . . suited to the highest part of the soul"; the ignoble steed, exhausted, fails, as "her wings fall from her and she drops to the ground."[71] Plato described the flight as so emotional and intense, it's more like love than philosophy. But even if you take leave of your senses during the search, you are ennobled by the quest— indemnified, if you will, from the judgments of history. He wrote, "For those who have once begun the heavenward pilgrimage may not go down again to darkness and the journey beneath the earth, but they live in light always. . . ."[72]

How high the noble steed soars determines the charioteer's own path to political power. The soul that has seen the most truth, Plato wrote, will "come to birth as a philosopher, or artist, or some musical and loving nature." The one who perceives truth in the "second degree" will be "some righteous king or warrior chief." The third degree begets a politician, economist, or trader. Only at the eighth degree of truth—the level, basically, of lies—can the "sophist or demagogue" be found. Demagogues are condemned to their status not because they are evil, but because they have not seen, they do not know, and their souls have not ascended to the highest levels.[73] Conversely, those who seek political power need only achieve—or believe they have achieved—truth.

◆

THE STUDENT REBELS

PLATO, THE FIRST MAJOR CHARACTER IN OUR STORY, ATTEMPTED TO resolve democracy's struggle with the demagogue by essentially ending the possibility of each ever coming into existence. He embarked upon a unique enterprise, fixating the minds of his students on the pursuit of an ideal city whose inhabitants would strive to achieve perfect knowledge. But Plato's solution was the far swing of the pendulum, which began to return to a center of common sense with the rebellion of a great student against his teacher. The first true answer to the demagogue can be found in the thoughts of Aristotle—the great pragmatic philosopher who hated the authoritarian metaphysics of Plato, and the second key figure in our story. Aristotle's confrontation with Plato would frame and shape humanity's attempts to grapple with democracy. Simply put, the question wasn't whether the demagogue ought to be defused, but how: As Plato proposed—from the top, through control and power, and by removing the people from power? Or from the bottom, by educating and entrusting the people with their own salvation? That distinction— between force and trust, between imposed structure and organic growth, and between metaphysics and simple experience—continues today.

Aristotle's father was the court physician to Philip, the King of Macedonia and father of Alexander the Great, so from birth the philosopher already belonged to a circle closely attached to royalty. A preternaturally gifted student, he was sent at the age of seventeen to study under Plato at his school of philosophy, the Academy. Aristotle remained there for twenty years, but developed a rebellious and ultimately completely contradictory philosophy to Plato's. When Plato died, twenty years after Aristotle's arrival, Aristotle was considered as a candidate to take over the school—but his philosophy differed too radically from his teacher's, and he was passed over. Aristotle, then in his late thirties, was hired by Philip of Macedon to tutor his son Alexander. After Alexander became emperor, Aristotle returned to Athens and set up his own school, the Lyceum, where Aristotle directed his students and teachers systematically to refute Plato's metaphysical school of philosophy.[74] There was a crisp logic to Aristotle's revolt against Plato's vision. Just as Aristotle placed faith in the people, he also had to have faith in himself to rebel so openly against the dominance of his former teacher.

Aristotle reacted violently to Plato's solution to the cycle of regimes. Scarred and horrified by what he saw in Athens' civil war, Plato had essentially escaped to an ivory tower, living out the rest of his years teaching students how to control democracy and imagining castles in the sky and a reign of Guardians. Aristotle, on the other hand, plunged into the hard world of *realpolitik*. He was the world's first true empirical political scientist, teaching his students to scrutinize the histories and constitutions of hundreds of city-states throughout Greece for clues to human behavior and the right political ideas. Political experience was not only academically important to him; it had been his profession. The experience of counseling a rising emperor who would control the fate of millions informed his observations and his insights into the possibilities of politics. Philosophy, for Aristotle, was not abstraction; it was a key to action.

Aristotle was no less fascinated than Plato by the struggle between democracy and the demagogue. Demagogues haunt the pages of Aristotle's writing on politics and, one imagines, his sessions with his great pupil, Alexander the Great. The very real question was how to control the hundreds of city-states within Alexander's domain. How were minor revolts and waves of dissent to be stopped from becoming a tidal wave swamping the empire? Aristotle counseled his students that democracy could succeed, but only if the people were well-informed, temperate, and dedicated to the rule of law. Aristotle is often cited as a hero by the American right. As Irving Kristol wrote, "Neoconservatives are admiring of Aristotle, respectful of Locke, distrustful of Rousseau."[75] In general, Aristotle believed history had more to teach than idealism, and defended the inherited order more than he endorsed the pursuit of political schemes like Plato's. At times, he defended harsh, anti-egalitarian institutions, even slavery, on the basis of a genetic theory of class superiority. He seemed to believe that stability, rather than justice, was the proper end of society. For all of these reasons, conservatives have cherry-picked his writing to support their ideas, while progressives have often ignored or derided him.

But Aristotle, like many great political thinkers, was complicated. There were repellent elements in his thought, to be sure. But he also outlined a persuasive and pragmatic case for democracy against other systems of government—a case made even more powerful in light of the conservative elements elsewhere in his writing. Aristotle believed in the people's potential, even if they wouldn't always choose well. He wrote in *The Politics:* "The principle that the multitude ought to be supreme rather than the few best is one that is maintained, and, though not free from difficulty, yet seems to contain an element of truth." Aristotle then offered a somewhat silly metaphor to explain the idea that the people's collective judgment, generally, is good: "For the many, of whom each individual is but an ordinary person, when they meet together may very likely be better than the few good, if regarded not individually but collectively, just as a feast to which many contribute is better than a dinner provided out of a single purse."[76] This proposition is a bit strained; it's a rare pot-luck that competes with the product of a master chef. But Aristotle had a point to make about democracy, and he would push his metaphors to the limit for it.

There was a strange, halting, stubborn quality to the philosopher's attempts to justify his radical idea that the people should be trusted with power but only if they have good judgment. Aristotle's commitment to the people was a matter of faith, not reason; the logical quality of his arguments on their behalf naturally suffered. Aristotle, perhaps sensing that his "feast" metaphor wouldn't convince skeptical students, tried another. "For each individual among the many has a share of virtue and prudence, and when they meet together, they become in a manner one man, who has many feet, and hands, and senses," he told his students. "[T]hat is a figure of their mind and disposition. Hence the many are better judges than a single man of music and poetry; for some understand one part, and some another, and among them they understand the whole." Again, by demanding too much of a metaphor, Aristotle violated common sense (what would his many-footed man-monster look like, exactly?), but the argument itself is more persuasive here. Yes, the sum of human knowledge is almost always greater than its parts; yes, by commingling the judgments of a thousand people, we end up with a wider and more resilient collective judgment than if the thousand were ruled by the judgment of one.

But Aristotle then backed down a bit, as if he realized that it was simply too audacious to offer an unqualified endorsement of democracy and the people that would apply across all nations and across the ages. After first offering an extended and more ambitious metaphor—that is, by combining the "qualities in good men" and the "scattered elements" of people ranging from the beautiful to the ugly, we will always end up with a more beautiful whole—the philosopher threw up his hands. "Whether this principle can apply to every democracy, and to all bodies or men, is not clear." Undaunted, he then tried, yet again, to solve the problem of democracy's universal applicability by likening the people in a democracy now to the members of a jury. "[T]he many may claim to have a higher authority than the few," he argued, "for the people, and the senate, and the courts consist of many persons, and their property collectively is greater than the property of one or of a few individuals holding great offices." This argument, unfortunately, was far less compelling than the earlier one; just because there are more brains in a room does not mean that their collective activity can be likened to property, and that more is better than less. At this point, Aristotle seems to have realized that the path of his argument had simply run out, and that he was teetering on a logical cliff. "But," he wrote, giving up: "Enough of this."[77]

Despite his obsessive, tortuous attempt to defend the people's role in democracy, Aristotle never converted his general approval of the people's judgment into applause for democracy itself. On the contrary, he was very clear to draw a distinction between the three "true forms" of government—kingly rule (the rule of the one), aristocracy (the rule of the few), and "constitutional government" (the rule of the many)—and their "corresponding perversions"—tyranny, oligarchy, and *democracy*.[78] Of the three perversions, Aristotle wrote, "democracy is the most tolerable."[79] He noted that Plato disagreed with him, placing democracy as "the worst."[80] That difference was the signal contradiction between teacher and student.

The demagogue stepped out of the shadows in Aristotle's work when the philosopher attempted to explain why the law falls victim to mass rule. "This," Aristotle argued, "is a state of affairs brought about by demagogues."[81] He described their rise in a chilling passage. "For in democracies which are subject to the rule of law the best citizens hold the first place, and there are no demagogues," he wrote. "[B]ut where the laws are not supreme, there demagogues spring up." The collapse of the independent force of law enables the demagogue to set up camp and invade the people's hearts. "At all events this sort of democracy, which is now a monarch, and no longer under the control of law, seeks to exercise monarchical sway, and grows into a despot; the flatterer is held in honor." The people, drunk on their own desires and made complacent by their relaxation of the law, essentially tyrannize themselves, with the demagogue simply a ready means to their own self-destruction. "The decrees of the demos correspond to the edicts of the tyrant," he explained, "and the demagogue is to the one what the flatterer is to the other."[82]

And how exactly does the demagogue increase his power? "The demagogues make the decrees of the people override the laws, by referring all things to the popular assembly," he wrote. "And therefore they grow great, because the people have all things in their hands, and they hold in their hands the votes of the people, who are too ready to listen to them."[83] The people, in a spasm of affection for the demagogue, make the laws disappear. It is not too far from this to Hitler's words in *Mein Kampf.* "Faith is harder to shake than knowledge, love succumbs less to change than respect, hate is more enduring than aversion," Hitler wrote, "and the impetus to the mightiest upheavals on this earth has at all times consisted less in a scientific knowledge dominating the masses than in a fanaticism which inspired them and sometimes in a hysteria which drove them forward."[84]

The controlling element—the bulwark between the mass emotion that demagogues like Hitler thrive on and upheaval—is the people's embrace of the law, defying any authority who would transcend the law. The two halves of Aristotle's theory—his faith in popular wisdom and his observation about the terrible consequences of a people turned against itself—united in the radical responsibility of the people themselves to defy the demagogue. The demagogue is a product of the people, and only the people can stop him.

◆

A CITY LEARNS

SEVERAL YEARS AGO, I VISITED THE PNYX IN ATHENS. IT WAS A startling place. At first glance, the flat span of hard mountain dirt and matted grass, perhaps the size of a football field, seemed far too small for its influence on history. The scholars say that 5,000 people regularly gathered there, but it was almost impossible to imagine so many people crowded into the small space. I strolled across the small hilltop toward the old *bema,* a stone platform that was used by speakers addressing the Assembly. This platform was in use from 500 B.C. to 400 B.C. and sits at the northern side of the grassy area. When I reached the *bema,* I turned around and noted how the Pnyx sloped down toward this side in such a way that a crowd could easily see over their neighbors' heads. I realized that a politician standing here would have spoken *up* to the assembled audience. Cleon would have been in power during this period (around 420 B.C.), and it was easy to imagine him in his element on that site, bellowing and gesticulating toward an adoring audience comfortably watching from the hill sloping down to him.

I walked across the grassy field toward the "new" *bema.* A sign said the Greeks had placed this platform after 400 B.C., a quarter-century after Cleon's death, on the southwest end of the Pnyx. This *bema* was originally just a large piece of stone, but was later cut into the natural rock of the hill as three enormous, foot-tall steps in front of an even larger four-foot-tall pedestal, cut from the same rock. I walked down the slight slope of the ground, about fifty feet away, and turned around. My gaze was approximately at the level of its base. I realized that a citizen standing here—in the audience—would have had to tilt his head up, at a slightly uncomfortable angle, to watch the speaker.

During this period, when the Athenians had begun to try to get the problem of demagogues under control, the explosive influence of demagogues may have been checked simply by the theater itself, minimizing demagogues' comfort and maximizing their alertness. I wondered: could the physical arrangement of the demagogues' platform have been a mirror for Athens' changing regard for their own worst enemy? At the very least, could the two *bemas* serve as a metaphor for how a thoughtful people tried to get a hold on democracy's dilemma?

As Aristotle suggested, we will always be vulnerable to the predations of the demagogue if we do not value the rule of law above all else. This is the only way freedom can save itself from itself. In part because of the delayed effect of the discussion Aristophanes desperately tried to provoke during Cleon's lifetime, the Athenians gradually began to learn from their mistakes. These lessons really took hold in the next century—the high period of Athenian democracy. Even when Cleon was in power, however, signs of a constitutional resurgence began to appear. Tellingly, it was Diodotus, not Cleon, who won the Mytilenean debate, saving the lives of the Mytileneans. A series of devastating wars launched by demagogues like Cleon made clear the geopolitical costs of the demagogues the Athenians had indulged. The Athenians then began attacking and controlling these demagogues—not through speeches or plays, but through their own political culture and through the rule of law. What followed was a series of self-restraints—as if the people, like a disenchanted lover, collectively took a deep breath and stepped back from their seducer.

The first self-restraint was cultural. Athenians began to cultivate among themselves the notion that they were distinctly intelligent and discriminating and therefore each shared the burden of maintaining society's self-control. Over time, this high self-regard served as a natural cooling mechanism to the demagogue's fire. Politicians began to communicate in more intelligent terms, and their audience deliberated more and reacted less. This attitude could certainly be criticized as self-important. As one scholar has written, the citizens developed the "conviction that Athenians were by nature more intelligent than other people."[85] But Athenians' high opinion of themselves had an important corrective effect; it meant that the people, rather than the demagogue, considered themselves in charge.

Culture enabled the second kind of self-restraint: the law. From these beginnings, the Athenians introduced practical measures to arrest the rise of would-be demagogues and teach the citizens an anti-demagogue *ethos*—in other words, a set of practices and a way of thinking that would intrinsically turn their minds to the rule of law, to stability, and to the greater good rather than the allure of strongmen. For example, in 427 B.C., the Athenians decided to exile demagogues.[86] Under this new mechanism, a politician could be turned out of the city simply for "having proposed a measure contrary to democratic principles and to Athens' laws."[87] The principle was breathtakingly broad—in a democracy, almost anything could be "contrary to democratic principles." It therefore clearly aimed to give the benefit of the doubt to the people making this judgment and to put any enemy of the people on the defensive. The measure was commonly used. Athenians would scratch the name of someone to be exiled on shards of pottery, which would then be counted before the demagogue was expelled from the city for ten years. Over the years, archaeologists have excavated more than 11,000 of these shards.[88]

Additional punishments were also implemented. In 410 B.C., about a decade after Cleon's death, the Athenians passed a law requiring all citizens to take an oath to these astonishing duties: "I shall kill by word and by deed, by vote and with my own hand, if I can, anyone who subverts the democracy of Athens, whoever holds public office after its suppression, and whoever tries to become a tyrant or helps to install one. And if anyone else kills such a person I will regard him as blameless before the gods and demons as having killed an enemy of the Athenian people."[89] Not only were Athenians bound to murder demagogues; they were to sanctify the act as "blameless before the gods and demons."

In the early years, these oaths had limited effectiveness, as the citizens were still seduced by demagogues and Athens was still rocked by turmoil. Six years after the harsh oath was introduced, an oligarchic coup nevertheless again took place, resulting in a horrific reign of terror. Over a period of thirteen months, more than 1,000 Athenians were killed either for their political views, or simply for their money and property.[90] But after the *demos* recovered power from the coup, they continued where they had left off, trying to consolidate the democracy. Rather than launching a new reign of terror against the perpetrators of the regime change, the ruling democrats acted instead with "unbelievable generosity," declaring a general amnesty for all of the supporters of the coup, with the exception of a few key perpetrators.[91] They did this because they understood that to do otherwise would poison the well, creating a political culture of revenge and, in all likelihood, resuscitating the cycle of regimes again.[92]

The Athenians, like Aristotle, had come to recognize that demagogues would prosper in proportion to an audience's ignorance. After Cleon's reign, Socrates observed that a demagogue could have power only with the ignorant. All Athenians were individually responsible for becoming more discriminating, more reflective, and less irrational, but the state also had a responsibility to educate the people about proper political practice and thereby enable them to protect themselves. This

required self-improvement, if you will, would in turn inhibit demagogues. The city ultimately reached a common recognition: "The
interests of the Athenians were in fact protected by the simultane-
ous sovereignty of the people and the law."[93] Athenians eventually
learned to eye demagogues through the lens of a ritualized critique.
Attendance at the Assembly and in the law courts gave the average
citizen experience in discerning between rhetoric and fact. Over time,
Athenians increasingly committed themselves to critically thinking
about and disciplining political oratory, as seen in a practiced "evils of
flattery" theme that Athenians began to use to flag down and shame
demagogues. Josiah Ober, the preeminent contemporary authority on
Athenian democracy, writes, "Athenians were aware of their own tendency to listen to the pleasant and not to the necessary and were willing to be chided for it."[94]

One example from Athens' most mature stage, in the mid-fourth
century B.C., occurred when the famed orator Demosthenes spoke to
Athenians after demagogues had instigated yet another ill-advised foreign conflict. In 348 B.C., Demosthenes told the assembled people: "But
now, by practicing demagoguery and pleasing you, [demagogues] have
brought you to such a state of mind that in the Assembly you are elated
by their flattery and lend a willing ear to their compliments, while in
your public affairs and practices you currently run the gravest risks."[95]
His point was to criticize the perverse reality of Athens: "Politicians had
prepared the *demos* to be difficult and fierce in the Assembly but lax and
contemptible in war preparations," when just the opposite should have
been the case.[96]

Any politician seeking to manipulate the people now found it more
difficult because he was forced by the audience's expectations to advise
them to watch out for demagogues. Demagogues were finally deprived
of the very fodder their burning passion required. In 337 B.C.—less than
a century after Cleon's death—the Athenians inscribed a decree on a
marble column showing a female figure called "Democracy" crowning
a bearded man meant to symbolize the *demos*. While the earlier decree
from 410 B.C. held the murderous enforcers blameless before "gods and
demons," the demagogue's assassin was now blameless before men and
the state. The text read: "If anyone should rise up against the Demos
for tyranny or join in establishing the tyranny or overthrow the Demos

of the Athenians or the democracy in Athens, whoever kills him who does any of these things shall be blameless."[97] Setting aside vigilante justice for a full-blown demagogue, less severe civil penalties also awaited anyone even taking steps toward these powers. The decree promised the confiscation of property and the deprivation of civil rights for any councilor who would hold a meeting "or deliberate about anything" if democracy was overthrown.

In 1979, the journalist I. F. Stone published a best-selling book titled *The Trial of Socrates*. Stone presented an unconventional thesis about the death of Socrates—that the jury convicted Socrates not for the purported formal crimes of corrupting the youth of Athens and for worshiping false gods, but for an underlying offense. By citing certain Homeric passages, by continuing to play a public gadfly role after the Thirty were deposed and democracy bloodily restored, by repeatedly seeming to take Sparta's side in philosophical debates, and by refusing to worship the civic gods and goddesses that Athenian citizens honored as keepers of the democratic spirit, Socrates was challenging Athenian democracy itself.[98] In other words, in issuing its verdict against Socrates, the *demos* may actually have been lashing out at the self-described gadfly as an anti-democratic force.

If we're convinced by Stone's thesis (and many have been), we can conclude that one stage in Athens' consolidation of its own democracy after the reign of demagogues was to lash out at anyone who challenged the democratic *ethos*—even a decrepit old man like Socrates. We obviously can't defend on moral grounds an action that seems more like the equivalent of a medieval cure for witchcraft than a productive political act. And it certainly means we should not sugar-coat Athenian democracy; like all systems used to organize political power, it was unforgiving to its enemies. But Stone's thesis suggests how very seriously Athenians took their democracy.

The irony is that Plato employed Socrates' trial to an opposite end and to an opposite extreme. Instead of viewing the trial as an attempted defense of democracy by democracy, Plato responded to the trial by building the most anti-democratic philosophy imaginable. If Plato's democracy was trying to defend itself, Plato saw instead only the murder of a beloved friend. His response helped lay the groundwork for authoritarianism rather than solve any problem of democracy. This is why it's so important to understand the struggle of great thinkers like Plato and Aristotle with the difficulties of democracy. We can see in their personal struggles the same mistakes we all can make in our daily political lives. In the cases of the great philosophers, however, their reactions can inspire ideas that go on to shape the world.

———

With the 337 B.C. decree resanctioning the assassination of demagogres, Athens had come full circle. The city was throwing everything—even property—into its effort to root out demagogues from the polity. In the end, Athenians had realized that if the *demos* were put on guard and made eternally suspicious of the demagogue's seduction, the state would survive. After all, the Thirty's reign of terror had backfired, creating among the oppressed and the exiled a force that would return to the city and overthrow the oligarchy, reestablishing Athens' democracy.[99] Over the centuries, this lesson about what we might call the people's "constitutional conscience" began to echo, reaching its full strength two and a half millennia later and a continent away, in humanity's greatest experiment with democracy: the United States of America.

PART II

DEMAGOGUERY IN AMERICA

If it be asked what is to restrain the House of Representatives from making legal discriminations in favor of themselves and a particular class of society? I answer, the genius of the whole system, the nature of just and constitutional laws, and *above all* the vigilant and manly spirit which actuates the people of America, a spirit which nourishes freedom, and in return is nourished by it.[1]

—James Madison, *Federalist Papers* No. 57

IN AMERICA TODAY, DEMOCRACY'S ANCIENT THREAT SEEMS FIRMLY at bay. Americans watch as presidents peacefully make the transition from one administration to the next. Even during the disputed presidential election between George W. Bush and Al Gore in 2000, citizens allowed the court system to determine the outcome. The military is unquestionably under civilian leadership. Politicians don't control private militias. In general, even those who hold and express strong opinions on controversial matters go about their daily business unbothered by government forces or the political opposition. Although there is some jockeying for position, the three branches of government are, in relative terms, equally strong and separate. And, despite the disquieting lack of civic knowledge and political engagement among broad sections of the American people, the essential anti-authoritarian and self-reliant character of our historic political culture endures and even grows year by year.

As these facts show, there's a reason America has not seen a national-level demagogue seriously threaten the Constitution. Demagogues, by definition, are leaders of the people. As Athens learned, if the people are not interested in the rule of law and prefer a strong man, then a demagogue will always be able to shove aside the law. No matter how beautifully designed the constitution or how wealthy the country, if ordinary people themselves are uninterested in holding authoritarians to account, they will readily hand the country over to a demagogue. But if the people embrace their rights and block anyone aspiring to unconstitutional powers, the demagogue will never have a chance.

This is the story of America—and, more importantly, of the American people. Most Americans, whether a meter maid in Manchester or a doctor in Dubuque, will tell you that they are wary of strong men, of the accumulation of power in single leaders, and of the kinds of mass waves of emotions perpetuated by demagogues. These basic, often unnoticed, second-nature attitudes and beliefs among Americans have served as the ultimate barrier to demagogues.

We in America, in other words, have much to be thankful for. This is not to say, however, that all is well in America. Our history reveals that eternal vigilance is indeed the price of liberty, and that we should never rest easy. Today, after the unsettling record of the recent presidential administration, is the right time to reflect on America's constitutional history and to consider how best to approach democracy abroad and democracy at home in light of our extraordinary past.

GEORGE W. BUSH: DEMAGOGUE?

THIS COUNTRY UNDERWENT A CRISIS OF CONFIDENCE DURING THE administration of George W. Bush. Polls conducted in the summer of 2008 showed that the vast majority of Americans—81 percent—believed the country was on the wrong track.[2] In recent years, legitimate frustration at Bush's constitutional overreaches, foreign policy deceptions, and stubborn political and ideological approach drove some critics to illegitimate historical comparisons. At Bush's second inaugural in Washington, D.C. on January 20, 2005, for instance, I saw two teenage girls swathed in soft scarves and coats against the freezing cold standing together and smiling at the crowds who passed. With proud, uplifted arms, each was holding a section of the *Washington Post* with a large, foot-high photo of Bush. They had drawn Hitler mustaches on Bush's face and a swastika on his forehead. This was an extreme but not isolated example of a trend. A recent Google search found "about 447,000" mentions of "Bush" and "demagogue" together.

While it's clearly important to hold government figures to a high standard and to call foul when necessary, we also must avoid generalizing the category of "demagogue" to include all nefarious public figures. The casual, broad usage of the term demagogue misunderstands the precise relationship with the masses that a politician must create and sustain to qualify as a demagogue and threaten democracy itself. George W. Bush was, in fact, not a demagogue, because he failed at least two of the four elements: He was not a man of the common people, and he did not inspire overpowering emotional reactions among them. While he occasionally styled himself as a man of the lower classes—a famous example being his habit of very publicly clearing brush at his Texas ranch—he never successfully defined himself, in any powerfully convincing way, as a man of the common people. Even though the Ivy League–educated businessman made attempts to seem like an ordinary Texan, these efforts did not convincingly create a mass leader persona, certainly not on the level of any true historical demagogue, whether Huey Long, George Wallace, or Hugo Chávez. On the contrary, Bush never hid his profound dependence on elites— the millionaire and billionaire donors and bundlers who comprised his "Rangers" and "Pioneers." Even if he had tried to become a true common leader, these connections would have undermined that persona.

Furthermore, Bush never triggered the kind of passion among the masses that a true demagogue does. Despite his attempt to exploit a quasi-populist image for political benefit, his grasp on public opinion was always slippery, even inept. He lost the popular vote in 2000. Even before 9/11, his approval rating was relatively low, as it was during the majority of his presidency. Beginning in January 2004, his approval rating consistently fell below 50 percent. From January 2006 onward, his approval rating rarely went above 40 percent, and in 2008, it fell below 30 percent—one of the lowest ever recorded for an American president.[3]

There is a lesson in the Bush presidency about the maintenance of our constitutional culture, however. The fact that large blocs of the American people seemed unbothered, for substantial periods of time, by the administration's flagrant constitutional overreaches—whether in circumventing the established legal process for wiretapping or in the treatment of prisoners at Abu Ghraib and the detention center at Guantanamo Bay—highlights the urgent need for increased civic education and political and legal activism about our constitutional rights and obligations. That large blocs of the people allowed the Bush administration seemingly to stir their emotions for political advantage—whether by confusingly changing the color-coded threat levels meant to describe homeland security risks in advance of the 2004 presidential election, staging redundant and divisive state-based referenda on gay marriage in 2004, or forcing the vote to authorize force in Iraq a mere three weeks before the 2002 mid-term elections—was equally unsettling.

At the same time, the tremendous agitation these abuses triggered among other blocs of people suggests that America's constitutional conscience is alive and well. While caricaturing Bush as Hitler substantially overstates the case, it's a symptom of America's historical, and sometimes overzealous, vigilance against those who would bully our Constitution. The fact that Bush's approval ratings were solidly mired in the low thirtieth percentile, dipping even into the twenties during his last months in office, indicates that, although he held the office of the presidency, he did not hold the American people.

———————

While the Bush years warrant a certain amount of pessimism, we should still be optimistic in a broader, historical sense about the sweep of American constitutional accomplishments and the strength of the country today. Success was not foreordained in the land of liberty. The growth of Americans' constitutional conscience took years to fully develop and, for a time, was touch and go. The story of Americans' struggle with the demagogue, then, is also the story of America herself.

———————◆———————

WATERING THE TREE OF LIBERTY

In 1780, a wealthy group of merchants, financiers, and political officers passed a new state constitution in Massachusetts. The new constitution dramatically increased the property qualification for office-holding. You could run for the state senate only if you owned a freehold estate of 300 pounds or a personal estate of 600 pounds; to be governor, you needed a freehold of 1,000 pounds.[4] In several property-poor Berkshire towns, not one single citizen qualified to hold statewide office. By the summer of 1786, Boston had piled more injuries on that insult. Aggressive entrepreneurial bankers had been lending to the desperately poor agrarians at usuriously high rates. Amid a general, devastating recession, farmers began defaulting *en masse*. Special debtors' prisons were built and quickly filled, so more were built. Financiers continued to grow wealthy, and the gap between the rich and poor—between the elite and the common—widened.

An unlikely demagogue—a Revolutionary War veteran and farmer who had never before been involved in politics—rose on the tide of the people's fury. With Daniel Shays as their leader, a group of farmers soon resolved to strike against the judges who met periodically in each town to imprison debtors. Through his identity as an anti-elite farmer, his passionate relationship with the common people, and his ambition to create a political force, Shays revealed himself as a demagogue to be reckoned with. Through the fourth rule—the unlawfulness he threatened against an intrinsically unjust regime—Shays became the rare beneficial demagogue, wielding the power of the people against a system that was holding them down and striking a blow that shook the Founding Fathers to their classically educated cores.

On August 29, 1786, Shays led a crowd of 1,500 men to the Northampton Courthouse and delivered a petition demanding that the judges adjourn. The judges, alarmed by the sudden mob, relented. Four days later, Governor James Bowdoin issued a proclamation condemning efforts "to subvert all law and government and introduce riot, anarchy and confusion, which would probably terminate in absolute despotism, consequently destroying the fairest prospects of political happiness that any people was ever favored with."[5] Bowdoin's ironfisted response met with nods of approval from elites throughout the Northern states, who thought the revolt, however tiny, might "light up the pass, and throw the whole union into a flame."[6]

They were partly right. By the end of the year, almost 9,000 militants—about one-quarter of the "fighting men" in rural New England—had joined Shays' uprising against the courts, the merchants, and the political class.[7] But the state proved too strong. After the Northampton uprising, the rebels quickly lost momentum. Bowdoin commissioned the former Secretary of War, Benjamin Lincoln, to summon a force of several thousand mercenaries against the "Shaysites," as they came to be called. Early the next year, Lincoln's forces briefly clashed with the rebels, killing four. From that point forward, the insurrectionists were in a permanent state of flight. During the subsequent months, they periodically reemerged for brief skirmishes with Lincoln's forces. All were ultimately apprehended by the summer of 1787, just when the Founding Fathers were convening in Philadelphia.

The significance of Shays' Rebellion lay not in the actual threat it posed to the government, but in the consequences it held for the Founding Fathers' plans for democracy. Shays' Rebellion never really involved more than a few thousand farmers and only led to a single actual military confrontation. Yet it truly panicked many of the Framers. In a letter to George Washington in 1786, the New York lawyer John Jay wrote, "Our affairs seem to lead to some crisis—some Revolution—something that I cannot foresee, or conjecture." Jay continued, "A State of uncertainty and Fluctuation must disgust and alarm such men, and prepare their minds for almost any change that may promise them Quiet & Security."[8] General Washington's mail was rarely cheerful the summer of Shays' Rebellion. "Having proceeded to this length for which they are now ripe, we shall have a formidable rebellion against reason, the principle of all government, and the very name of liberty," wrote General Henry Knox. "This dreadful situation has alarmed every man of principle and property in New England. They start as from a dream, and ask what has been the cause of our delusion? [W]hat is to afford us security against the violence of lawless men?"[9]

Washington generally regarded the minutiae of the everyday with the calm of a man who knows that his page in history is already written. But each day's post probably shook even this benevolent, methodical man. It's easy to imagine Washington fitfully waking in the middle of a humid August night to scrawl this response to Jay: "Your sentiments, that our affairs are drawing rapidly to a crisis, accord with my own. What the event will be is also beyond the reach of my foresight. . . . We have probably had too good an opinion of human nature in forming our confederation."[10] Some went as far as to suggest that Shays would actually overthrow the nation's government. A general named William Shepherd said the rebellion would "overturn the very foundations of our government and our constitution, and on their ruins exert the unprincipled and lawless domination of one man."[11] One wealthy creditor named William Williams said that Shays had designs to "conquer" Massachusetts and to become "the tyrant of America."[12]

Why did these ragged rebels terrify the Founding Fathers so much? Part of the fear was certainly simply about economics, with one class defending itself against another. America's wealthy merchants were absolutely panicked at the thought of losing economic control, and naturally employed political language to make their case. But there was a deeper issue related to democracy itself. Scholars like Bruce Ackerman, the Yale Law School professor, have referred to the Constitutional Convention as a "constitutional moment"—a discrete period of time with heightened sensibility about our ideals and their consequences.[13] At the time of Shays' Rebellion, the United States was entering such a constitutional moment, defined by an overarching mission even bolder than the Revolution: to design a hopeful new country from scratch. The Framers hoped to gather all their accumulated knowledge about human nature, the progress of history, and the lessons of classical political theory in a single document that would shape a great nation.

It was enough to make the men who gathered in Philadelphia understandably nervous about demagogues, with a notable exception. The third character in our story, after Plato and Aristotle, is the American farmer, philosopher, and statesman Thomas Jefferson. Jefferson believed the demagogue could best be defeated not through elaborate government controls, but through a more modest but profound avenue: the people themselves.

———

When Shays' Rebellion boiled over, Thomas Jefferson was in Paris. France was seething at the time (the French Revolution would erupt the next year), but considering the turmoil around him, Jefferson was strikingly relaxed about the rebellion back at home. Shays' Rebellion was the event that prompted one of Jefferson's most famous arguments. In a letter to Madison at the very beginning of the year of the Constitutional Convention, Jefferson expanded on his deep conviction that the people were the ultimate safeguard of the Constitution. The people were so essential to the chastening of authority and the maintenance of a healthy republic that Jefferson famously argued in favor of violence. "I hold it that a little rebellion now and then is a good thing," he told Madison, "and as necessary in the political world as storms in the physical."[14] He expressed his contrarian view of Shays' Rebellion: "The tumults in America," he wrote, "I expected would have produced in Europe an unfavorable opinion of our political state. But it has not." The reason was that the people ultimately sided with the constitutional process instead of attempting to undermine the state: "The interposition of the people themselves on the side of government has had a great effect on the opinion here."

Eleven months later, his opinion had strengthened. In a letter to his friend William Smith dated November 13, 1787, Jefferson famously wrote, "We have had thirteen states independent for eleven years. There has been one rebellion." About Shays' Rebellion, Jefferson was strikingly sanguine: "What signify a few lives lost in a century or two? The tree of liberty must be refreshed from time to time with the blood of patriots and tyrants. It is its natural manure."[15]

Jefferson could not be accused of supporting occasional violence out of either naïveté or idealism. A rigorous classical education informed his political observations. From the ages of nine to fourteen, he attended the Reverend William Douglas's Latin School in Virginia, where he learned "the rudiments" of Latin and Greek. While a student at the College of William and Mary, he learned to read Greek and Roman authors in the original, which he later called a "sublime luxury."[16] He also brought a wealth of practical experience to his observation of politics. He served in the Virginia House of Burgesses from 1769 to 1776, when he authored the brilliant and poetic Declaration of Independence. In 1783, Jefferson also drafted the constitution for Virginia, and he served as governor of Virginia from 1779 to 1781. In 1783, he was elected to the Continental Congress in Philadelphia, and set upon the path of helping the young nation eventually design a constitution. In 1784, Jefferson was chosen by Congress to serve as Minister in Paris. He set sail for the foreign capital, but always kept an eye on events back home.[17] During these years, he maintained an epic struggle with the brilliant and charismatic Alexander Hamilton, who believed that America should be an aristocratic monarchy just as strongly as Jefferson believed it should be a citizen-led democracy.

The battle to control the direction of the new nation helped to drive the formation of Jefferson's philosophy. His argument that a "little rebellion now and then is a good thing" was part of a broader stream of forceful commentary on constitutional events in America. While in Paris, Jefferson maintained an extensive and elaborate correspondence with friends in the United States who were drafting a constitution for adoption in 1789. He was particularly close to Madison, who went on to do more than anyone else to craft the actual Constitution. Perhaps Jefferson's remove afforded him the necessary intellectual distance and forcefulness he needed to shape the Constitution, which is what he did. Jefferson was eight years Madison's senior, and the slight, shy, intellectually powerful young Congressman would constantly look to Jefferson for guidance from Paris. Were it not for the paradoxical and hypocritical exclusion of African Americans (when Jefferson himself owned slaves and fathered children with Sally Hemings), his eloquent and expansive vision of participatory democracy would stand as an almost completely successful defense of the democratic principle.

After receiving a copy of the Constitution that had been passed in Philadelphia, Jefferson wrote Madison on December 20, 1787, that "The late rebellion in Massachusetts has given more alarm than I think it should have done." After all, Jefferson wrote, "a great deal more blood was spilt" in France and England's revolutions. He contrasted the "ferocious depredations of their insurgents" with the "moderation and the almost self extinguishment" of America's.[18]

It's clear that Daniel Shays the demagogue played a special part in Jefferson's thinking about democracy in America. Jefferson's underlying principle, like Aristotle's, was simple and uncompromising: So long as people are well-educated and hold deep constitutional values, if they are given power and trust, they will, in general, use it responsibly: "After all," Jefferson wrote, "it is my principle that the will of the majority should always prevail."[19] In this influential letter, Jefferson suggested Madison include in the Constitution an entirely new device that would establish forever his goal of giving the people ultimate power. Jefferson told Madison, "Let me add that a bill of rights is what the people are entitled to against every government on earth, general or particular, and what no just government should refuse, or rest on inference."[20] A bill of rights would give the people a check on the government itself—reserving to them both specific and general powers and never allowing the government to slip toward autocracy.

Jefferson's idea was not his alone, and the hard political battles for a bill of rights were fought primarily by others. The Framer George Mason had authored Virginia's Declaration of Rights in 1776, which became the model for the federal effort. Mason refused to sign the 1787 Constitution because it lacked a bill of rights. In large part because of his ardent activism and Jefferson's persuasion during the four years that followed, a bill of rights was finally incorporated into the Constitution in 1791. Jefferson's dream finally became a political reality.

Jefferson's ultimate goal was to empower the people, rather than the state, through a self-sustaining hunger for constitutionalism. "Where is our republicanism to be found?" Jefferson asked. "Not in the constitution, but merely in the spirit of the people."[21] As one Jefferson scholar has observed, Jefferson's constitutionalism "placed less emphasis on mechanics . . . than it did on the character of the people themselves."[22] Jefferson once quoted a poem to make the point:

> What constitutes a state?
> Not high-raised battlements, or labor'd mound,
> Thick wall, or moated gate;
> Not cities proud, with spires and turrets crown'd;
> No: men, high minded men;
> Men, who their duties know;
> But know their rights; and knowing, dare maintain.
> These constitute a State.

Jefferson's words about "high minded men . . . who their duties know" were similar to Thomas Paine's declaration that "A constitution is a thing *antecedent* to a government, and a government is only the creature of a constitution. The constitution of a country," Paine argued, putting similar faith in the people, "is not the act of its government, but of the people constituting a government."[23] The gift of freedom, in other words, came with strings. It required the people to take an active role, cherishing and caretaking democracy itself.

Jefferson's invocation of a constitutional state grounded on free individuals seems, at first glance, unqualified. But he did, in fact, include a critical catch with implications for governance then and for the promotion of democracy today: the people, Jefferson believed, couldn't realize their constitutional conscience solely on their own. They would need consistent assistance from the state through strong public education and the inculcation, by government, of an ethos of moral and, by implication, civic responsibility. Jefferson concluded one letter with an admonition about the connection between moral education and the citizens' commitment to their own liberty "Above all things," he wrote, "I hope the education of the common people will be attended to; convinced that on their good sense we may rely with the most security for the preservation of a due degree of liberty."[24] The state had an especially important role in Jefferson's constitutional scheme: to equip the people with the education necessary for them to govern themselves and keep their leaders on a short leash. The judgment of the people—in his day, of course, that meant only white, property-owning men—could be trusted if the nation enabled them to be trusted. But they would require excellent public schools and a wide access to colleges and universities.[25] It was, in short, a reciprocal relationship.

I graduated from the University of Virginia School of Law and, like any other graduate, firmly believe that the University's "Grounds" (never "campus") in Charlottesville is one of the most bewitching places in the world. Graceful columns and domes gently frame "Mr. Jefferson's University," as it is still called. Students stroll along the quiet lengths of Jefferson's "Academical Village," framed by columns that impart a dignity and historical sensibility to the University. Students readily embrace the Honor Code, a Jeffersonian institution generally prohibiting the supervision of most exams on the assumption that students—as free citizens in a free society—ought to take active responsibility for cultivating ethical rules. There is no better parallel than the Code for the spirit Jefferson sought to inspire in America's political society at large.

Jefferson's spirit infuses almost everything not only about the University but about Virginia itself. Virginia politicians, lawyers, and judges can barely get through a speech without citing Jefferson, perhaps because so many of them have attended the University of Virginia. This is surely how Jefferson would have wanted it. True to form, he gave extremely specific instructions for his gravesite, including the text he wanted engraved on his tombstone. The words he wanted are telling:

HERE WAS BURIED

THOMAS JEFFERSON

AUTHOR OF THE DECLARATION OF INDEPENDENCE

OF THE STATUTE OF VIRGINIA FOR RELIGIOUS FREEDOM

& FATHER OF THE UNIVERSITY OF VIRGINIA[26]

Taken together, these three accomplishments clearly signaled Jefferson's wish to be remembered for his commitment to constitutionalism. But it's noteworthy that Jefferson concluded his list for posterity with his founding of the great public institution of the University of Virginia.

Jefferson founded the University when he was nearly eighty years old, but still dedicated himself to it with incredible energy. In a report to the Commissioners of the University of Virginia in 1819, Jefferson said that among his primary goals in founding the University was "to form the statesmen, legislators and judges, on whom public prosperity and individual happiness are so much to depend."[27] A broader spiritual ambition overarched his practical goals. Jefferson's ambition, he wrote a friend in 1820, was as large as America's itself. "This institution of my native state, the hobby of my old age," he said, "will be based on the illimitable freedom of the human mind, to explore and to expose every subject susceptible of it's [sic] contemplation."[28] The constitutional conscience would be America's overseer and protector, but success would require constant education to push the freedom of the human mind to "every subject susceptible of it's [sic] contemplation." America would require intellectual freedom, political liberty, and eternal vigilance against authoritarianism to succeed; strong civic education would bond the three elements together for the life of the nation.

Jefferson's vision of a populist constitution would be only partially realized. He was too late for the first draft of the Constitution, where, for the most part, the enemies of the common people carried the Convention. In presenting the "Virginia plan" that went to great lengths to separate the people from the machinery of power and would become the template for the Constitution, for instance, Edmund Randolph warned the delegates that "our chief danger arises from the democratic parts of our constitutions."[29] Alexander Hamilton argued at the Constitutional Convention that "the people are turbulent and changing; they seldom judge or determine right."[30] Declaring that "nothing but a permanent body can check the imprudency of democracy," Hamilton proposed that America follow the English model of government, with chief executives and senators serving life terms.[31]

A number of leaders took a hand in lashing democracy down with punishing stays and constraints. They included Elbridge Gerry of Massachusetts; Connecticut's Roger Sherman, who first proposed the compromise of an elite Senate and a popular House of Representatives; Delaware's John Dickinson; Charles Pinckney of South Carolina, who said even the House of Representatives ought to be selected by state legislatures because "the people were less fit judges"[32]; George Washington himself; James Madison; and, especially, the greatest advocate of centralized government, Alexander Hamilton, who once even proposed that the presidency be an office held for life. In the design of these elitists, the people would have a voice, but little power, and that power would be checked on all sides by powerful balances, negatives, and vetoes.

This context helps explain some episodes often neglected by our traditionally sunny hindsight. These Framers prevented the people from directly electing the president, weakening the popular will as it passed through the Electoral College. These now-archaic "electors" were meant to provide an elite barrier between the popular will and the elective machinery of the state. Initially, the states voted, eight against two, against allowing the people directly to elect the members of the House of Representatives. They concluded that senators should be selected only by state legislatures, rather than the people. Randolph specifically argued that the "democratic licentiousness of the State Legislatures proved the necessity of a firm Senate," because the Senate would "guard the Constitution against encroachments of the Executive who will be apt to form combinations with the demagogues of the popular branch."[33] They created an independent, unelected judiciary as a check on the democratic excesses of legislative majorities, with Madison asserting that "the followers of different Demagogues" would be controlled by "provisions against the measures of an interested majority."[34] They even considered—and came within a hair of accepting—property requirements not only of voters, but also of the candidates for office themselves.

Over time, however, Jefferson's ideas would prevail. The states ratified the Bill of Rights in 1791, and the amendments gathered momentum and influence as the decades and centuries rolled on. But the American republic would endure several tests as Americans realized their constitutional conscience.

———

There was an obvious hiccup in the evolution of America's constitutional conscience: the Alien and Sedition Acts. These four laws were drafted by the Federalist Party, which supported a stronger central government during the war with France, purportedly to protect the United States from internal agents of foreign powers and to stop sedition. Congress passed the bills in 1798, and President John Adams signed them into law, immediately triggering a firestorm of controversy in the young nation. The laws allowed the president to expel foreign citizens suspected of treason and prohibited false or hostile words against the American government. In these respects alone, the bills were a shocking departure from the formal ambitions of the Constitution and the Bill of Rights. They egregiously subjected those hopes to the short-term political ambitions of a single party. The violations can perhaps be explained as the product of geopolitical anxiety and of concern about France as a mortal enemy of the republic, but they cannot thereby be excused.

Fittingly, Thomas Jefferson himself put an end to the disappointing episode in America's early constitutional evolution, and the debate he initiated revealed the vigor of America's emerging constitutional conscience. His party, the Democratic-Republicans, attacked the laws as unconstitutional infringements on the Bill of Rights. In 1798, collaborating with James Madison, and at the risk of being charged with sedition himself, Jefferson wrote a resolution for the Virginia government charging that the Acts were unconstitutional and urging "a change by the people" as "the constitutional remedy."[35] The constitutional eclipse shadowed America for only about four years; with the exception of the Alien Enemies Act, the laws expired or were repealed by 1802. In 1801, however, Jefferson would get the opportunity to practice what he preached. On March 4, the day he was inaugurated president, Jefferson declared the laws unconstitutional, and pardoned and released those who had been convicted under them.[36]

There is an instructive footnote to Shays' Rebellion: ultimately, most of the rebels' demands were addressed by the political process. Frustrated by a Massachusetts state legislature that paid itself stratospheric salaries, the farmers argued that voters should approve legislators' compensation. They asserted that the various fees that attended the process of the law—filing complaints, retaining lawyers—were unfair and prohibitively expensive. They resisted forced enrollment in militias that always were governed by far-away members of the elite. They said the debts the state legislature had undertaken were being paid off too slowly and at too high an interest rate, diluting the effective power of each taxpayer. High taxes required a greater money supply, but Boston refused to help through its monetary policy; the rebels therefore agitated for paper money.[37]

Less than a year after the rebels' defeat, almost all of their proposals were addressed through Massachusetts law.[38] And, while many defeated rebels were sentenced to brutal, sometimes capital, punishment by the standing regime, the state legislature, succumbing to petitions for leniency from more than twenty towns across Massachusetts, ultimately pardoned all fourteen rebels originally condemned to death, including Daniel Shays himself.[39] Most incredible of all, when the new constitution came before the Massachusetts legislature in the fall of 1788—only a year and a half after the final sputtering of the rebellion—more than twenty members in Massachusetts' legislature were former rebels.[40]

In other words, Shays was absorbed into the constitutional republic, as he himself had poked and prodded it to action. Revealingly, he described his role in the rebellion in democratic terms. In one conversation about his role, he shouted: "I at their head! I am not." When describing a particular siege of a courthouse, he said he "never had any hand in the matter; it was done by a committee."[41]

The fact is that Jefferson was right. Shays' Rebellion was more important as a prod for America's emerging constitutional conscience than as a threat to the nation. By expanding the rule of law to incorporate citizens who might otherwise attack the political structure itself, Americans were developing a home-grown solution to demagogues that echoed the Athenian answer from over 2,000 years before. Over time, Americans' constitutional culture would moot the harsh features of a system originally designed to limit demagogues. Today, for instance, the Electoral College is a historical oddity: its "electors" are not the deliberative elites that the Framers imagined would militate against a "victorious demagogue" attempting to seize the entire national government. Rather, they are usually ordinary political party activists unmindful of their historic charge. Elites in the Electoral College are no longer needed to prevent a demagogue from taking over the country. In the end, America arrived at a deceptively simple resolution of democracy's paradox: the people themselves.

———————

Less than two weeks before he died, Jefferson wrote that America's fifty years of constitutional success had been a "Signal of arousing men to burst the chains, under which Monkish ignorance and superstition had persuaded them to bind themselves, and to assume the blessings and security of self government. . . ." Ten days later, on July 4,

1826, Jefferson died—on the same day as his old nemesis John Adams, sponsor of the Alien and Sedition Acts. For the time being, at least, Jefferson had prevailed. His message to America, and his legacy for the world, was intact and secure.

———————◆———————

A PECULIAR INSTITUTION

ONE CANNOT FAIRLY TALK ABOUT JEFFERSON, OR ABOUT AMERICAN democracy, without considering slavery. Well in advance of the Civil War, de Tocqueville said slavery was the "most dreadful of evils" and blamed it for almost all of the "present troubles and future dangers of the Union."[42] Slavery's injury to America is an inexhaustible topic. It breached the basic commitment of the Constitution and of Americans to each other in shockingly formal ways. During the Constitutional Convention, for instance, the Founding Fathers decided to count slaves as full human beings for population purposes yet discount their value as citizens by defining a slave as three-fifths of a person. The Constitution determined that the slave trade would be phased out as an active institution yet made no provision for the millions of living slaves who were denied political and civil rights.

The contradictions were as stunning as Jefferson's own double life and represent the dualism of the American constitutional experience. Jefferson owned about 200 slaves.[43] In 1784, he sponsored a Congressional bill to outlaw slavery in any new state, which almost passed; but almost forty years later, in 1820, he said that the new state of Missouri should be allowed to have slavery. The contradictions are infuriating, leading the historian Joseph Ellis to describe Jefferson as an "American Sphinx."[44] In the words of one Jefferson critic,

On one hand, Jefferson wrote that slavery was an abomination. On the other hand, he seldom freed slaves. On the one hand, he argued that slaves could not be freed because they were like children. On the other hand, he saw to it that many slaves on his plantation became skilled craftsmen. . . . On one hand, Jefferson seems to have been revolted by the notion of amalgamation and made them favored members of his household. . . . The truth is that Thomas Jefferson can be cited to support almost any position on slavery and the race question that could exist.[45]

Perhaps Jefferson can only be understood as embodying the contradictions of America itself. Each nation's constitutionalism, like each nation, will have its own character, complications, nuances, and contradictions. There have been tremendous injuries to African Americans through *de jure* discrimination. The list includes the Supreme Court's *Dred Scott* decision in 1857, which found that slaves were less than full citizens and therefore subject to re-capture in states where slavery was illegal; the Civil War, where states separated from the Union in part to hold onto the legal regime of slavery; Reconstruction and Jim Crow, which put African Americans under a regime of *de jure* and *de facto* oppression; and Massive Resistance, during which states and their leaders politically and legally defied federal rulings and laws that countered or weakened Jim Crow.

During these dark passages in American history, majorities and pluralities of the American people committed themselves to racism, to cruelty, and to institutional discrimination. Racist demagogues emerged from these depths, especially in the first decades of the twentieth century. "Pitchfork Ben" Tillman, the brutally racist U.S. senator from South Carolina, first elected governor in 1890, once said, "We of the South have never recognized the right of the negro to govern white men, and we never will. We have never believed him to be the equal of the white man, and we will not submit to his gratifying his lust on our wives and daughters without lynching him."[46] Eugene Talmadge, a bombastic "wild man" white supremacist, was elected governor of Georgia in 1934. He once answered a heckler who asked if a man should be punished for beating his wife: "Depends on how hard you hit her." When he died, his funeral featured a gigantic Ku Klux Klan wreath.[47] Theodore Bilbo, a U.S. senator from Mississippi elected in 1934, said it was "practically impossible, without loss of life, to prevent lynchings of negro rapists"[48] and promised, during his Senate campaign, "Let me get into that Senate and I'll strike a match that will dim every blaze."[49] As recently as 1963, Governor George Wallace of Alabama pronounced in his inaugural gubernatorial address, "In the name of the greatest people that have ever trod this earth, I draw the line in the dust and toss the gauntlet before the feet of tyranny and I say segregation now, segregation tomorrow, segregation forever."[50]

These political leaders clearly met the four rules of the demagogue. They (1) fashioned themselves as leaders of the masses, (2) triggered great emotional reactions from the people, (3) exploited those reactions for political benefit, and (4) threatened or broke the rules. These modern demagogues were a product of racist and bigoted Americans. They were enabled by thousands of common American citizens, mostly from the southern states, who saw African Americans as inferior and were ready to hand over authority to leaders who championed this belief.

Yet then, as now, broad local pluralities and majorities of ordinary Americans were strongly committed to freedom, equality, and justice for slaves, their descendants, and African Americans in general. Committed communities of abolitionists and their followers changed laws, brought lawsuits, helped create social institutions such as the Underground Railroad, formed the Republican Party, and put their own lives at risk for the Union during the Civil War. John Brown, a charismatic but bloody demagogue, led a revolt against the oppressive system in Harpers Ferry; he lost his life but was rewarded with the thanks of history. In the wake of the Civil War, the Fourteenth and Fifteenth Amendments were passed to provide African Americans with legal and civil rights, which were, of course, denied throughout most of the southern and border states during Reconstruction and Jim Crow. However, in a curious twist on America's conflicted constitutional conscience, these same amendments would ultimately be used to expand rights not only to African Americans, but also to women and any insular minorities with a history of discrimination. The right of "substantive due process" was created by the Supreme Court to give individuals and groups more sway over a government that could otherwise oppress them.

In this way, America's constitutional conscience, like a vine, wrapped around even the knottiest problems. Those Americans who believed in expanding constitutional rights undertook a pitched battle with those who did not. Those who placed their own bigotry above their commitment to the shared constitutional experience readily supported racist demagogues and *de jure* and *de facto* discrimination.

Even today, well into the nation's third century, the constitutional-ism we have is far from perfect and is riddled with practical and philo-sophical contradictions, missteps, and pain. This constitutionalism is *ours*—it is American, shaped and defined by the ongoing struggle to reconcile the divisions that have riven the American people them-selves. Even though the U.S. Supreme Court has consistently found intentional *de jure* discrimination against African Americans illegal, it has also ruled that the laws themselves cannot be invalidated if only their effect is discriminatory. We therefore have a number of practices that operate systematically, if not intentionally, to discriminate against African Americans, including the effectively discriminatory practices of political redistricting, which can weaken African Americans' politi-cal power, and the underfinancing of many public schools, which can devastate the educational foundation of African American communi-ties. By undermining these citizens' ability to participate in our politi-cal system, these practices directly damage our democracy. As recently as 1972, a demagogue like George Wallace could still capitalize on these divisions within the populace and make the intentional infringe-ment of African Americans' rights a central plank in his platform. Fortunately, we have not seen such demagogues on a broad scale in recent years, but the underlying shortcomings of our constitutional conscience mean there always will be work to do.

"KING MOB"

IN THE *FEDERALIST PAPERS*, ALEXANDER HAMILTON WORRIED MOST about the "military despotism of a victorious demagogue." The ancient scenario of a general like Cleon who, by militating against a foreign enemy, would play to the passions of the masses and use the military to take over the government, was a real fear as the young nation got on its feet.

The first great contest in America's struggle with the demagogue arrived with a popular hero who seemed to emerge, fully formed, from the darkest recesses of the Founding Fathers' imagination. Andrew

Jackson, at first glance, was exactly what the Framers had feared most. He was an extraordinary and captivating figure—a military celebrity and a self-touted "common man" with a powerful bond with the common people of America. He presented a vivid character on the public stage, with flowing hair, leathery skin, a gruff and uncultured manner, and the clothes of a frontiersman. When he arrived in the capital at Philadelphia as Tennessee's first congressman in 1796, he was described as a "tall, lank, uncouth-looking personage, with long locks of hair hanging over his face, and a queue down his back tied in an eel skin."[51]

Jackson didn't only look rough; he seemed to possess the temperament and violence of a Cleon as well. Jackson had a tremendous temper, evident in his unnerving habit of dueling people who gave him offense, including a sitting governor of Tennessee. Even though he was a legislator at the time, Jackson killed a man named Charles Dickinson in a duel because Jackson believed he had insulted his wife.[52] He also directed a ruthless war against Native Americans, becoming alternately renowned, hated, and feared throughout the United States for the savagery of his conduct in the Indian–American Wars. Jackson applied his passion and his ambition to national causes, leading America to victory over England in the War of 1812 and achieving fame in the bloody Battle of New Orleans.

Jackson was as ambitious as he was audacious. In a rare miscalculation of his popular appeal, Jackson ran for president prematurely and unsuccessfully in 1824. Despite his loss, everyone recognized an unprecedented political force. Some, like Jackson's great nemesis Senator Henry Clay, worried that Jackson was the Framers' great demagogue, come at long last; Clay said that Jackson's election would "give the strongest guaranty that the republic will march in the fatal road which has conducted every other republic to ruin."[53] Jackson was elected president in 1828. One quaking Democratic senator described the new president in a way that would have chilled the Framers: "The people believed in General Jackson as much as the Turks in their prophet, and would have followed him wherever he chose to lead them. With this species of popularity it is in vain to contend. . . ."[54]

Three of the four defining elements of the demagogue clearly applied to Jackson. He was a man of the masses. He had a powerful emotional connection with them. He used this connection to political benefit and railed against distant elites. But did he satisfy the fourth condition? Did he bend, or break, the rules?

Jackson's enemies had no doubt about the answer to this essential question. The Virginia aristocrats who had controlled the presidency and whose principal concern was maintaining their grip on power saw Jackson as intrinsically dangerous. Even Thomas Jefferson was taken in by the myth, telling Daniel Webster, "He is one of the most unfit men I know of for such a place. . . . he is a dangerous man."[55] Elites saw in Jackson a creature out of the pages of Plato, the very embodiment of the cycle of regimes. As Arthur M. Schlesinger wrote: "[W]hile the newly enfranchised and chauvinistic masses regarded the military hero with wild enthusiasm, to the old aristocracy, raised on classical analogies, no figure could seem more dangerous to the Republic."[56] One commentator thought the movement Jackson had started threatened actual revolution: "What will be the character of this revolution, which is felt to be approaching? To what institutions will it give birth? Who must perish in the day of account? Who will rise on the storm? Who will resist the action of the ages?"[57] In large part because of the strong emotions and controversies that tended to follow the giant figure of this friend of the people, it was difficult for Jackson's contemporaries to see with any real clarity whether he actually threatened the rule of law. Jackson would have to defend himself.

When Jackson became president in 1829, some thought the Constitution would collapse. Their fears seemed perfectly realized during his famous inauguration, when the unkempt masses stormed the White House. As a melee descended on the mansion and people climbed in and out of windows, Jackson himself had to retreat down a back stairway to a boardinghouse. Supreme Court Justice Joseph Story said that the "reign of KING MOB" had started.[58]

With the hindsight of history, however, it's clear that the new president was in fact a product of the constitutional culture in which he was raised and so was unlikely to attack the constitutional system itself. Before he entered politics and military service, Jackson was a practicing country lawyer, schooled in the rule of the common law like any member of the bar. The English common law, dominant at the time in both Great Britain and the United States, held that the agglomerated decisions of judges, rather than a code devised from scratch and imperially handed down by government, would determine justice. Thomas Jefferson believed the common law enforced constitutionalism because it was built on this principle. "It is the will of the nation which makes the law obligatory," he wrote, "The law being law because it is the will of the nation. . . ."[59] In general, the common law's horizontal, democratic decision making operated indirectly, deriving legal judgments *from* the people, juries, and judges, rather than delivering the answers *to* them from on high. As Oliver Wendell Holmes, the great interpreter of the common law, wrote, "The first requirement of a sound body of law is, that it should correspond with the actual feelings and demands of the community, whether right or wrong."[60] The values and responsibilities that the common law inculcates in citizens, judges, and politicians must be taken into account in explaining why neither Great Britain nor the United States has seen a demagogue seriously threaten their respective democracies.

As an active lawyer, Jackson was also an active participant in the common law. By 1794, when he was only twenty-seven years old, he had participated in 476 court cases. In 1796, sixteen years before the War of 1812 and decades before his rise to the presidency, Jackson served as a member of the committee that drafted Tennessee's first constitution.[61] Granted, it wasn't the most democratic constitution, empowering justices of the peace with the right to choose all other county officials, for instance.[62] But the experience still gave Jackson personal expertise in the painstaking process of drafting an American constitution.

He also took part in the broad civic education that Jefferson said would be the curative for any tendency of the system to skew toward demagogues—interestingly, as an autodidact. In 1797, for example, during a trip to Philadelphia, Jackson bought copies of the English texts that founded the early American legal system, including Sir Edward Coke's three-volume *A Commentary upon Littleton,* John Joseph Lowell's *Essay upon the Law of Contracts and Agreements,* and Sir Geoffrey Gilbert's *The Law of Evidence.*[63] Fourteen years after purchasing these law books, Jackson supported one candidate running for governor in part because he said the opposing candidate and his colleagues were a "bunch of demagogues."[64] By education, by profession, and by experience, Jackson was already invested in the common American constitutional enterprise to such a degree that he could readily participate in the Athenian-style project of demonizing demagogues as anti-constitutional.

This perhaps helps explain why, as president, Jackson channeled the same political theory that Jefferson had announced a generation before, despite Jefferson's own skepticism about Jackson. When Jackson launched his famous attacks against the Bank of the United States—an unelected, elite board whose financial decisions impacted thousands of ordinary people—he fell back on democracy as his defense, criticizing the haughty disdain of the Bank's president, Nicholas Biddle, as inimical to the republic he wanted to help shape.[65] Similarly, when Jackson acted against nullification—the idea that a state could negate the federal government's actions—democracy provided his rationale. In his first address against nullification, he announced his principle: "the majority is to govern."[66]

"Jacksonian democracy" was born, under a single guiding star— the idea that democracy, as in some Newtonian law, should always expand. Voting increased throughout Jackson's presidency, both extending the franchise to new voters and reducing public corruption by newly accountable officials. The tenure of civil servants was limited through rotation. The mysterious machinery of the common law, previously understood only by lawyers, was codified. The election of judges was instituted. Funding to federal programs, such as roads and bridges, often used by the wealthy to benefit themselves, was cut.[67]

In the end, Jackson served two terms as president, left office peacefully, and retired to the Hermitage in Tennessee. He didn't become a demagogue, and the cycle of regimes didn't play out in America. We have no reason to suspect Jackson's sincerity when, after his presidency had ended, he wrote in a letter to Martin Van Buren: "You know I never despair. I have confidence in the virtue and good sense of the people. God is just, and while we act faithfully to the Constitution, he will smile and prosper our exertions."[68]

America had passed its first great test. We were saved, it seemed, from the demagogue.

◆

THE REIGN OF TERROR

THE BEST EXPLANATION OF HOW THE CONSTITUTION NOT ONLY survived but prospered during Andrew Jackson's tenure came, ironically enough, from the pen of a traveling Frenchman haunted by the personal trauma of democracy's self-destruction in his own backyard. The French sociologist Alexis de Tocqueville is the fourth character in our story of the fight to save democracy from its own worst enemy. De Tocqueville's writings about his travels in America in the 1830s have always ranked among the most trenchant observations of American political life. To understand their true depth we must understand that de Tocqueville—like Plato, Aristotle, and Jefferson before him— was another great thinker desperately working to resolve democracy's paradox.

De Tocqueville brought considerable personal anguish to his quest for the answer to democracy's dilemma. In the 1830s, France was still shuddering from its suffering during and after the democratic revolution of 1789. In that year, a group of lower-class revolutionaries calling themselves "*sans-culottes*" (meaning they did not wear the fancy breeches, or *culottes,* of the upper class) took over the government under a three-part slogan—*liberté, egalité, fraternité.* The world watched, transfixed, as the modern ideas of liberal political theorists including John Locke and Jean-Jacques Rousseau took political form in a country traditionally run by monarchies and barons.

France gave the world a particularly gut-churning iteration of the cycle of regimes. This revolution aimed at raw democracy—a perfectly horizontal political system spreading rights equally among all and completely flattening class divisions. Yet demagogues like Georges Danton, a charismatic populist who later led the dreaded Committee on Public Safety, quickly surfaced, whipping up the passions of the mob. These passions soon fell prey to the icy tyranny of Robespierre, who launched the Reign of Terror to enforce the metaphysical mandates of *liberté, egalité, fraternité* through a brutal framework of friend versus foe, enforced by the very physical instrument of the guillotine.

Alexis de Tocqueville was born in this crucible. As an aristocrat, he was by birth already an enemy of the mob. His ancestors belonged to an ancient Norman family and owned a fief in Normandy. His grandfather was a chevalier and his father a count. His mother and father, Hervé and Louise, were jailed in the Reign of Terror when his father was just twenty-one years old. Revolutionaries seized the couple at their estate and imprisoned them in Paris, where they watched as scores of wealthy family members were escorted to "the Barber"—the literally gallows-humor name for the guillotine. Alexis's parents escaped simply because of a fortuitous scheduling decision; they were placed in a late slot on the docket, and would have been executed had the cycle not turned on its own master. Robespierre was taken prisoner, the de Tocqueville family was released, and Robespierre himself was guillotined on July 28, 1794.[69]

The Reign of Terror was a textbook example of the "massacre" stage Polybius observed in the cycle of regimes. Only four years after the revolution in 1789, the Jacobins had revolted, Marie Antoinette was executed, the use of the guillotine against perceived opponents of the revolution was commonplace, and the prudish and terrifying Robespierre began his rise. This was the raw, unchained democracy of ancient Athens—the same state of affairs Aristophanes invoked by repeatedly using the Greek verb *tarattein* to describe Cleon's stormy politics. Louis-Antoine-Léon Saint-Just, a member of the Committee on Public Safety, said in the fall of 1793 to the revolution's enemies: "You have no more grounds for restraint against the enemies of the new order, and liberty must prevail at any price. . . . We must rule by iron those who cannot be ruled by justice."[70] Demagogues abounded on all sides of the complicated internal divisions, from Georges Danton to Napoleon Bonaparte. Roiled by popular leaders stirring them to campaigns of terror and assassinations, the young democracy rapidly evolved into a brutal regime policed by the Committee on Public Safety. Finally, the democracy was replaced by Napoleon's military dictatorship. The unification of politics and carnage during the Reign of

Terror led the historian Simon Schama to conclude, "In some depressingly unavoidable sense, violence *was* the Revolution itself."[71]

After the Reign of Terror ended, Alexis's father Hervé, whose hair had turned white after his experience at the edge of death, took an hour-long nap every afternoon from 3:00 to 4:00. This allowed him to escape in his dreams the deadly hour of 3:30 P.M., the time when aristocrats were summoned before the revolutionary tribunal to hear their death sentences. Louise never fully recovered; her nerves were shattered. Alexis was raised by a mother who was, by turns, "capricious, impatient . . . a victim of recurring migraine headaches, and afflicted with a profound, constant melancholy that must have been quite common among the survivors of the Reign of Terror."[72] One biographer writes, "The revolution darkened Alexis's youth," and that he "inherited his mother's often melancholy spirit, fits of anxiety, and fragile health."[73] The revolution reverberated through all aspects of Alexis's life. His wife's grandfather, for instance, was not as fortunate as Alexis's parents; he was guillotined along with his sister, daughter, son-in-law, another granddaughter, and the granddaughter's husband.[74]

Despite the wreckage democracy caused in its first wave through France, de Tocqueville thought it would inevitably return. It was coming, he said, because it was the "sacred character of the sovereign master's will." Not that this filled him with enthusiasm. On the contrary, he told French readers at the beginning of his classic *Democracy in America*, "The entire book you are going to read was written under the pressure of a sort of religious terror in the author's soul, produced by the sight of this irresistible revolution that for so many centuries has marched over all obstacles, and that one sees still advancing today amid the ruins it has made."[75] His imagery was antediluvian. "To wish to stop democracy would then appear to be to struggle against God himself."[76] His concern about whether the coming democracy would succeed or fail was particularly acute because France had already tried democracy once and had failed: "[F]rench democracy has overturned all that it has encountered in its way, shaking whatever it has not destroyed."[77] But those who hadn't been destroyed needed to prepare for another wave, like seaside residents boarding up their houses before a hurricane.

De Tocqueville's *Democracy in America* was a political document, an open letter of sorts urging France to adopt the right attitude to democracy, lest it self-destruct again. De Tocqueville expressly said that his aim was to tame raw democracy through a respect for the rule of law by the common people. Like Plato, he described democracy as a rough adolescent in need of both cultivation and discipline. "To instruct democracy, if possible to reanimate its beliefs, to purify its mores, to regulate its movements, to substitute little by little the science of affairs for its inexperience, and knowledge of its true interests for its blind instincts; to adapt its government to time and place; to modify it according to circumstances and men," he wrote: "[S]uch is the first duty imposed on those who direct society in our day."[78] In his view, democracy would have to be "instructed" and "purified" to avoid the cycle of regimes. De Tocqueville wrote, "Democracy has therefore been abandoned to its savage instincts; it has grown up like those children who, deprived of paternal care, rear themselves in the streets of our towns and know only society's vices and miseries."[79]

As both an aristocrat and a realist, de Tocqueville brought a hard-eyed sensibility to the enterprise of evaluating how America had tamed the unruly system of democracy and mastered demagogues. His purpose in writing *Democracy in America* was, in a sense, to "sell" to the French the democracy that was coming whether he, or they, liked it or not. At the time of his writing, in the 1830s, France was governed by the relatively peaceful monarchy of Louis-Phillipe I. But a new reformist movement was also starting to roil French society, so feelings about democracy were particularly uncertain. De Tocqueville sought to convince the uneasy public that democracy was not as bad as they thought, in part by explaining how America had stopped and dissolved the cycle of regimes. In France, he argued, democracy had taken place in form but not in content. He wrote, "[T]he democratic revolution has taken place without making the change in laws, ideas, habits, and mores that would have been necessary to make this revolution useful."[80] The political system revolved and changed, but because the citizens had failed to bring the aspirations of democracy into their hearts and minds, the cycle of regimes began spinning in the ashes. "There is one country where the great social revolution I am speaking of seems to have attained its natural limits; there it has operated in a simple and easy manner," he wrote of America with a wistful jealousy, "or rather one can say that this country sees the results of the democratic revolution operating among us without having had the revolution itself."[81]

Without having had the revolution itself, America had some-how arrived at the Holy Grail of democracy—liberty, equality, and fraternity (except for those, like women, African Americans, and Native Americans, who were excluded)—without all the blood. De Tocqueville wanted the French to understand that they could realize the aims of revolution without the human cost, if they embedded the "social revolution" in the "simple and easy manner" of the citizens themselves.

De Tocqueville pounded a simple thesis over and over in the sev-eral hundred pages of *Democracy in America*. It was *mores*—America's political culture—that caused democracy in America to succeed and that the French would have to emulate. He saw these mores as abso-lutely essential to the cultivation of constitutional values. He wrote, "I am convinced that the happiest situation and the best laws cannot maintain a constitution despite mores, whereas the latter turn even the most unfavorable positions and the worst laws to good account."[82] *Mores* were so important that they could even turn bad laws into good; they were, in a sense, alchemical.

What the word *more* means, exactly, is a famously nettlesome topic. The general essence is this: a *more* is a way of thinking, feel-ing, and judging that contains within it embedded cultural values. De Tocqueville described *mores* as "habits of the heart, but to the different notions that man possess, to the various opinions that are current in their midst, and to the sum of ideas of which the habits of the mind are formed."[83] He summed up: "I therefore comprehend under this word the whole moral and intellectual state of a people."[84] To chil-dren playing a game in a schoolyard, for instance, a *more* would be their collective sentiment that it is unacceptable to cheat. The *more* is the feeling and the idea underlying the rule, not just the rule itself. Americans, de Tocqueville argued, had a strong set of *mores* informing their practical ideas about democracy, stability, equality, and freedom. Taken together, these *mores* constituted America's constitutional conscience, which valued the rule of law above demagogues and anything else that would threaten the republic.

De Tocqueville dedicated substantial portions of his masterwork to divining exactly what drove America's *mores*, rendering American democracy distinctly constitutional. It's worth reminding ourselves of these traits because, like all habits, they are easily forgotten.

De Tocqueville believed, first of all, that Americans' passionate embrace of their rights explained the overall strength of America's constitutional democracy. A right is a simple but remarkable thing. It doesn't exist in physical form, per se; it's simply a claim one has against someone else or against government, and it matters only if fellow citizens or institutions recognize it. A right is therefore a product of *mores;* it exists only if people, collectively, recognize it. As de Tocqueville explained, rights were central to America's constitutional democracy. They allowed Americans not only to work together but also to stand individually. He explained Americans' embrace of individual rights through the idea of ownership and our belief that we should be able to own our own property and, by extension, determine on our own what we do with the things that we own. He employed a simple metaphor to explain the idea:

> When the child begins to move in the midst of external objects, instinct brings him to put to his use all that he encounters in his hands; he has no idea of the property of others, not even of its existence; but as he is made aware of the price of things and he discovers that he can be stripped of his in his turn, he becomes more circumspect and ends by respecting in those like him what he wants to be respected in himself.[85]

The American child's innocent notion of his own rights begins in a happy reciprocity that ends in a culture that could cradle America through difficult times. De Tocqueville explained: "The child puts to death when he is ignorant of the price of life; he takes away the property of others before knowing that one can rob him of his." Applying this lesson to grown people was straightforward: "The man of the people, at the instant when he is accorded political rights, finds himself, in relation to his rights, in the same position as the child vis-à-vis all nature. . . ."[86]

The aristocrat told a cautionary tale about rights in America, however, admitting that Americans were first given rights when it was "difficult for them to make bad use of them," because the "citizens were few and simple in *mores*."[87] The culture of rights took hold in America more easily because society was already predisposed culturally to constitutionalism, through the constitutions of the individual American states and also through the inheritance of English common law. In countries lacking such foundational elements, *mores* supporting constitutionalism would have a more difficult time taking root. Thus these lyrical but unsettling words: "One cannot say it too often: There is nothing more prolific in marvels than the art of being free; but there is nothing harder than the apprenticeship of freedom."[88] Just as Jefferson urged that arming citizens with civic education was necessary to protect the Constitution, de Tocqueville said the cycle of regimes could not be stopped unless the citizens themselves were equipped with the necessary *mores*.

The idea of the "apprenticeship of freedom" created a catch-22. If you needed practice for constitutionalism to work, what if you didn't have practice? To this dilemma, de Tocqueville gave an answer, but not a very satisfying one to those who would impose democracy and demand quick results. In a section titled "Would Laws and Mores Suffice to Maintain Democratic Institutions Elsewhere than in America?" written in the 1830s, well before the democratic revolutions across Europe in 1848, he wrote: "What I have seen among the Anglo-Americans brings me to believe that democratic institutions of this nature, introduced prudently into society, that would mix little by little with habits and gradually blend with the very opinions of the people, could subsist elsewhere than in America."[89] The apprenticeship of freedom happened "little by little" and "gradually blends." This didn't mean democracy must necessarily be slow; it just can't occur *all at once*. People have to learn how to take care of a constitution and have to commit themselves to chastening the ambitions of would-be demagogues.

De Tocqueville thought, in other words, that all societies could craft organic, authentic forms of democracy tailored to their own cultures. "The mores and laws of the Americans are not the only ones that can suit democratic peoples," he wrote. But if a country wanted to "escape from the despotism and anarchy that threatens them"—to stop the cycle of regimes—it would need to pay attention to America's constitutional conscience. "The Americans have doubtless not resolved this problem, but they furnish useful lessons to those who wish to resolve it."[90] Americans had completed the apprenticeship, with brilliant results. De Tocqueville was sharing the lessons of how to answer the destiny of democracy with France. America, and Americans, had led the way.

THE DEMAGOGUE AND THE DEVIL

AFTER JACKSON, DEMAGOGUES WERE CONSIDERED SO EVIL THAT they were best explained as the result of metaphysical forces. *The Demagogue: A Political Novel* was published in 1891—squarely between the eras of America's one great potential demagogue, Andrew Jackson, and its greatest real demagogue, Huey Long—by a journalist, satirist, and Confederate sympathizer named David Ross Locke. The potboiler followed the rise and fall of an ambitious, gifted, and ruthless young politician, Caleb Mason, in Ohio during the era of the Civil War. It also unintentionally revealed the lengths to which Americans were willing to go to keep the demagogue at bay. The book was clearly popular reading, chock-full of trite and cartoonish devices.[91] But despite bottom-of-the-barrel prose, or perhaps because of it, the book successfully described the demagogue as a radical political villain. The book's antagonist, evil to the core, exemplified the archetypal American demagogue whose success could be explained only as a result of pure evil. In America, the logic went, a good person would never take advantage of democracy.

At the novel's beginning, Mason is born into a poor, sickly household to a drunken father and a "slatternly" mother. The Mason family members are "the outcasts, the ne'er-do-weels [*sic*], of whom nothing was expected, and for whom nothing could be done."[92] The plot of Mason's rise and fall is cinematic. Mason ingratiates himself with Sarah, the daughter of the prominent wealthy Farmer Dunlap, in part by saving her life when she falls into a stream. Sarah's wealthy father becomes Mason's sponsor, giving him his first job as the printer of a local newspaper and funding his law school education. When Farmer Dunlap falls gravely ill, the doctor asks Mason to administer several drops of medication. But Mason kills the farmer, inherits his estate, jilts Sarah, and marries Helen, the daughter of a prominent local political figure. Mason quickly wins a seat in Congress, but his dirty laundry—the murder as well as his corrupt financial dealings—eventually undoes him. After a night spent sitting in a room tormented by the ghosts of all the people he has ruined, Mason kills himself.

A fascinating turning point occurs when the demagogue decides to kill Farmer Dunlap on his sickbed. The author describes his character in chilling, if purple, prose: "And he turned and looked the horrified old man squarely in the face, his cold gray eye growing colder, glittering with a ferocity that threatened death from active rather than passive interference."[93] When the mute farmer, realizing Mason's murderous intent, sits up and silently pleads with Mason not to kill him, the soon-to-be demagogue becomes even colder: "Caleb Mason stood there with his nostrils distended, his cold eye glistening, as handsome and as immovable as the demon that filled him."[94] The next moment, the farmer dies.

It's unclear whether Mason, the demon, or some unspeakable hybrid of both kills the kindly farmer. Yet Mason, from this point forward, is contaminated by his demon and becomes, by extension, irretrievably evil. Further developments reinforce Mason's inhuman character. After the demagogue receives all of Dunlap's assets, he goes to the funeral and comforts Sarah. Afterward, "a more light-hearted, joyous, jubilant man never bestrode a horse." Later, he sits at his desk "with a most gratified expression on his face."[95] Immediately after, he decides to reject Sarah in favor of Helen, the political daughter "as ambitious as Lucifer," to help forward his career.[96]

The events and descriptions in the novel are important. To construct a believable demagogue for the book's popular audience, the author needed to introduce the *deus ex machina* of a demon. The book is a consummate work of exaggeration and caricature, but these elements are instructive. The portrait of Mason reveals the significance of a particularly crucial political stereotype—the default set of attitudes about the demagogue as the *döppelganger* of democracy in the late nineteenth century. The plot that Jefferson had laid out, and that de Tocqueville had narrated, was unfolding. The people were taking responsibility for the stability of the republic and turning on their ostensible protector. It was all going according to plan.

———————

For a potent contrast, we look to the only other novel in English with the word demagogue in the title—a *British* novel published in 1911, *The Demagogue and Lady Phayre*, by a novelist who, in a curiosity of history, shared the last name of the author of *The Demagogue:* William John Locke. The book follows the rise of Daniel Goddard, a working-class labor activist, who from humble beginnings becomes a high-profile member of Parliament. The book's hero is as honest, straightforward, and full of integrity as Mason was deceptive, manipulative, and corrupt. In this book, the word demagogue actually becomes a term of praise. One character describes the hero as "The anomaly of his generation—a hot reformer with luminous common-sense—a popular demagogue with an idea of proportion—an original thinker—a powerful, eloquent speaker."[97] Later, the author describes Goddard walking through the streets of London and seeing the hopelessness and poverty of the working class: "The squalor and misery of it all touched the ever-responsive chord in his nature, awoke the demagogue in him to sympathy with the people."[98] After one character watches the hero connect with a crowd of working-class people, he erupts: "That's the genuine article, isn't it?" Another character answers, "He is a power among these people."[99]

The Demagogue and Lady Phayre reminds us of the difference between destructive and beneficial demagogues. "Demagogue" can actually be a term of praise in the rare instances when a demagogue, by applying the fourth rule—bending or breaking the rules—challenges a manifestly unjust system and achieves benefits for common people. The definition particularly made sense in the early years of the twentieth century, when England was undergoing great trauma to incorporate its working-class citizens into politics. That a labor leader who also was a man of the people would be pictured as both a hero and a demagogue is interesting but not startling. The usage is consistent with the Oxford English Dictionary's original definition of "demagogue" as a positive term: "In ancient times, a leader of the people; a popular leader or orator who espoused the cause of the people against any other party in the state."[100]

The positive use of the term has a long past in England. In 1651, the philosopher Thomas Hobbes equated the term simply with "powerfull Oratours . . . with the people."[101] In America, however, feelings about the need to defend democracy have been so powerful that leaders of the common people have almost never received the benefit of the doubt, no matter how unjust the policies they have attacked. In the end, as Socrates learned in Athens, a democracy's constitutional conscience can be a harsh and sometimes unfair judge.

◆

AMERICA'S ACHILLES HEEL

A cyclone just went through here and is headed your way. Very few trees standing.[102]

—Arkansas politician, about Huey Long

IN THE 1930S, AMERICA ENCOUNTERED WHAT APPEARED TO BE THE gravest threat yet to our constitutional democracy, a figure who, like Andrew Jackson before him, seemed to leap from the ancient pages of Plato and Polybius. America's Depression-era system was about to face a test with the ascension of Huey Long. Long is important to understand because he was, in a sense, a limit example of America's

fight to save democracy from the demagogue. The story of Huey
Long is also the story of the Achilles' heel of America's constitutional
conscience.

In 1935, *Redbook* magazine gave a dinner in New York City in
honor of General Hugh S. Johnson, the former director of President
Franklin D. Roosevelt's National Recovery Administration, who
was publishing his autobiography with *Redbook*. Around the tables,
sparkling with crystal and fine cutlery, sat many leaders of the New
Deal era—union leaders, radio executives, and government officials.
As the room hushed, Johnson stepped to the podium. The audience
burst into applause. Johnson then launched into his speech and began
attacking two prominent nationwide political figures: Huey Long and
Father Charles B. Coughlin. Coughlin was a charismatic Catholic
priest based in Detroit who commanded a daily radio audience of tens
of millions by combining a folksy demeanor, religious fervor, and an
anti-capitalism agenda. At the peak of his powers in the mid-1930s,
Coughlin received more mail than any other person in America (at
least 80,000 letters in an average week), received contributions of a
half million dollars a year, and had a clerical staff of 150.[103] To support
his agenda, in 1934 Coughlin had declared America's political parties
"all but dead" and announced his own movement, the National Union
for Social Justice.[104]

Coughlin and Long were "demagogues," Johnson yelled suddenly, and were pushing the American democratic experiment
toward a "licking or a dictator." He linked the pair to the evolving
fascist regimes abroad. "Between the team of Huey and the priest
[Coughlin] we have the whole bag of crazy or crafty tricks possessed
by . . . Peter the Hermit, Napoleon Bonaparte, Sitting Bull, William
Hohenzollern, the Mahdi of the Sudan, Hitler, Lenin, Trotsky, and
the Leatherwood God," he told the audience.[105] He went on to predict
the "great Louisiana demagogue" would be an "American Hitler" rid-
ing into Washington.[106]

The next week, Americans across the country walked into soda
shops and lunch counters and saw the front page of *News-week*
(the magazine's title at the time) emblazoned with a single word—
"Demagogues." The corresponding cover story bore the title: "Johnson

Lambastes Senator and Priest; Long Counters with Utopia; Coughlin Parries with Spirit of '76." The word dominated the American scene once again, as millions of citizens fixated on the specter of a democracy rapidly degenerating into a tyranny.

The events leading up to Johnson's attack had taken about a decade, beginning with Huey Long's assumption of the common people's burden. In 1924, Long, then in his late twenties, stood beneath the "Evangeline Oak" in Louisiana, made famous by the poet Longfellow. Huey Long looked strange, to say the least. His face was "a cartoonist's delight—exaggerated, comic, and yet impressive." He had a fleshy, bulbous nose that "tilted up impudently." His face was large, "inclining to jowliness," with a wide mouth, a cleft chin, and a dimple "that gave him when smiling a pixielike mien."[107] Seeming to strive, through a litany of public policy complaints, for a higher plane, this peculiar figure pronounced to the small crowd gathered under the shade of the great tree an eloquent vision of the future:

> And it is here under this oak where Evangeline waited for her lover, Gabriel, who never came. This oak is an immortal spot, made so by Longfellow's poem, but Evangeline is not the only one who has waited here in disappointment. . . . Where are the schools that you have waited for your children to have, that have never come? Where are the roads and the highways that you send your money to build, that are no nearer now than ever before? Where are the institutions to care for the sick and the disabled? Evangeline wept bitter tears in her disappointment, but it lasted through only one lifetime. Your tears in this country, around this oak, have lasted for generations. Give me the chance to dry the eyes of those who still weep here![108]

This speech and the surrounding event exemplified the style of politics Long would plot and employ over the coming years—brilliant oratory combined with an almost kinetic appeal to the underclass. Long aimed to divide Louisiana into supporters and enemies along lines based on class, and he was succeeding.

With this explosive approach, Long began rocketing through the ranks of American politics. After serving as Louisiana's governor, he was elected senator and began creating a mass movement aimed at supporting his rise as an alternative to President Roosevelt. His political success began in personal ambition, routed through the common people but poised to trample every boundary. His chief biographer, T. Harry Williams, wrote, "He was intensely and solely interested in himself. He had to dominate every scene he was in and every person around him. He craved attention and would go to almost any length to get it. He knew that an audacious action, although it was harsh and even barbarous, could shock people into a state where they could be manipulated."[109] In his gubernatorial campaign in 1928, Long sailed over the political divides that had structured Louisiana politics for decades. Protestants were supposed to be against Catholics, Anglo-Saxons against Creoles, and northerners against southerners. But Long's program deconstructed these divisions and established class— poor against rich—as the single dividing line of Louisiana politics. From an electoral beachhead in the small-farming, rural population of northern Louisiana, Long succeeded, winning more than 126,000 votes in his gubernatorial campaign—44 percent of the total—which was almost as many as his two major opponents combined. At age thirty-five, Long was elected governor.

During the career that followed, Long repeatedly demonstrated strength and even courage. In this sense, he was an unusual hybrid of both the destructive and beneficial demagogue—at once threatening the rule of law while benefiting the common people through public policy in a perfect storm of demagoguery. In the face of a nation of politicians who cooperated with hundreds of powerful and established corporate interests, Long had the courage or wherewithal to attack corporations in the name of the "redistribution of wealth." In contrast to dozens of earlier and contemporaneous "Dixie Demagogues," from Talmadge in Georgia to Bilbo in Mississippi,[110] Long not only avoided bigotry, he generally went out of his way to endorse equality of opportunity for Louisiana's black population.

His critics expected that he would do little in the way of enacting public programs. But during his governorship, the state expanded its public-health facilities and its treatment programs for the mentally ill, opened a major medical school, successfully pursued improvements at Louisiana State University, started night schools to promote literacy, provided free textbooks to public school students, developed a program of state-supported school buses, improved classroom facilities, exempted low-income families from most state property taxes, and provided increases in workmen's compensation. As the historian Alan Brinkley writes, "Long was, whether he realized it or not, helping to fulfill one of the first needs of any developing society: the creation of an infrastructure, the construction of the basic services and facilities without which more complex economic progress would be impossible."[111] This was the beneficial demagogue *par excellence.*

Long's programs established him as savior, voice, and mirror of the poor American *demos.* When he was elected to the U.S. Senate in 1930, his confident performances on the national stage generated a surge of nationwide popularity that would have terrified the Founders. "When Long appeared in the Senate chamber . . . he displayed no . . . restraint, proving so shameless in his pursuit of publicity, and so adept at getting it, that he was soon attracting more attention from the press and the galleries than most of the rest of his colleagues combined."[112] He was aided by a buffoonish style that mystified and enraged his elite critics, but that connected directly to the hopes and fears of the underclass he needed for political power. In 1931, Long prompted a firestorm of controversy when, wearing a pair of green silk pajamas and a bathrobe, he greeted a German naval commander on an official call. The German consul's office issued statements of outrage and protest, and the next day Long again met the commander, this time wearing a formal striped suit and tails. But he hardly felt regret about the incident. One scholar writes, "[T]he lesson he learned from the incident was less the importance of diplomatic niceties than the value of buffoonery in winning national publicity. . . . He continued in the following months and years to cultivate a reputation as a country bumpkin and clown."[113]

This approach allowed Long to connect intensely with the common people, a connection his critics were powerless to contest. Long's Share Our Wealth Society was perhaps the ultimate ideological means of appealing to a poor, Depression-ridden *demos.* Begun in Louisiana and then spread nationwide by Long and his long-time proselytizer,

Reverend Gerald L. K. Smith, the Society was only getting going when Long was assassinated in 1935. In *My First Days in the White House,* a little-known but fascinating book published posthumously in September 1935, Long detailed his plans for America and its *demos.* Equal parts demagoguery, serious policy planning, and utopian dream, the book traces the steps Long planned to take upon becoming president, which would result in a redistribution of wealth by an efficacious democratic government. Long's campaign platform, and the principle behind the Share Our Wealth organization, was to limit wealth for the extremely rich and to give money and property to the extremely poor. In the book, Long promised to close his inaugural address "extemporaneously" with the following words:

> I promise life to the guaranties of our immortal document, the Declaration of Independence, which has decreed that all shall be born equal, and by this I mean that children shall not come into this life burdened with debt, but on the contrary, shall inherit the right to life, liberty and such education and training as qualified them and equips them to take their proper rank in the pursuance of the occupation and vocation wherein they are worth most to themselves and to this country. And now I must be about my work.[114]

Specifically, each man was to be able to possess no more than $3 million in holdings and make no more than $1 million annually. Any greater earnings or possessions were immediately to be seized by the government and redistributed to the lower classes. The overall purpose of his plan, President Long tells Congress, was to "give hope and encouragement to the ambitions and aspirations of 125,000,000 more people rather than to excite the greed of fifty-eight."[115]

Huey Long was a quintessential demagogue, fulfilling all four rules perfectly. First, he fashioned himself as a man of the common people. Second, he triggered tremendous emotional responses from them. Third, he used these responses for political power, as governor, U.S. senator,

and erstwhile presidential candidate. And finally—and most importantly—Huey Long, by his very nature, tested boundaries and broke
rules. The "Kingfish" (his preferred nickname) was what the Founding
Fathers feared most: a national-level demagogue, comfortable with testing, manipulating, and even breaking laws, who had a hammerlock on
the passions of the masses and ambitions to rule the country.

According to his chief biographer, Long made a habit of "incredible
actions," finding lines and crossing them. "If he disliked existing rules,
he was quite ready to make up his own. These are qualities that make
an ordinary person the opposite of endearing—but in a politician they
are called genius."[116] These patterns led Long to establish a tyranny
in Louisiana—a one-man rule where Long routinely threatened his
political opponents and rammed bills through the legislature. He even
controlled the state government while in the U.S. Senate. He was not
above using the implements of state-controlled violence in service of
his political aims. In one of many examples, Long launched a series
of raids on gambling houses in 1928 using the National Guard. The
actions clearly fell under the jurisdiction of the courts and the police,
but contrary to established procedure and law, Long didn't secure warrants through a judge. Instead, relying on a state militia under his sole
command, he instructed the adjutant general of the National Guard
to send hundreds of men on raids.[117]

As a U.S. senator, Long continued to exercise an iron grip on
affairs back home in Louisiana. His handpicked successor, Governor
O. K. Allen, on Long's instruction, once imposed "partial martial law"
in a disputed grand jury investigation of voting fraud; militia soldiers
watched over the jury room as votes were counted.[118] Another time, at
Long's direction, Allen imposed martial law in Baton Rouge because
Long said there was a plot by Standard Oil to assassinate him; more
than 800 troops massed in the state capitol grounds.[119] He was so sub-
servient to Long's demands that Long's brother Earl Long once said,
"A leaf once blew in the window of Allen's office and fell on his desk.
Allen signed it."[120]

This was the destructive demagogue. The historian Arthur M.
Schlesinger, Jr., wrote that Long "was not a nice man"[121] and that
he exhibited "flippant brutality." "The yes men and hoodlums who
clustered around him were bound to him by fear or by greed, not by
affection."[122] Long "was a man propelled by a greed for power and a

delight in its careless exercise."[123] Julius Long said of his estranged brother, "The only sincerity there was in him was for himself"[124] and "There has never been such an administration of ego and pomposity since the days of Nero."[125] As for his political method, it consisted of "the comic impudence, the gay egotism, the bravado, the mean hatred, the fear."[126]

Contemporaneous news stories featured equally believable descriptions of friendliness and meanness, beneficence and anger, republican sentiment and ruthless self-promotion. Long combined aspects of the destructive and beneficial demagogue in a single, titanic political character. For instance, an article in *The Saturday Evening Post* titled "Paradox in Pajamas," published in October 1935, a month after Long's death, found profound contradictions in Long. The writer noted Long's contradictory identities—that the "young zealot" of Long's youth wasn't the senator, that the senator wasn't the Long "who addressed political rallies at creek forks," that this Long wasn't the one who stood "bukk nekkid" while he "laid down the law to a group of political fuglemen in a hotel suite."[127] Posthumously, the article recounted the contrast between Long's focus on people in conversation "as though seeking to hypnotize a subject" and his "tendency to fly into violent and momentarily quite ungovernable rages without so much as an instant's notice."[128]

The grand sum of all these contradictions was, for the author, Long's alternating savagery and kindness to the erratic driver of his limousine during a rough ride.[129] After coaching the nervous driver after a swerve by crooning, "Take it easy, son; ju-u-ust take it ea-ea-asy," Long exploded, "Get the hell out of this car before I kill you like you just tried to kill me!"[130] A *New York Times Magazine* story reported that "Huey Long thinks that 'Dr. Jekyll and Mr. Hyde is the greatest book ever written'; he said so in his senatorial office with a grin of impish satisfaction. One thought of Huey Long swashbuckling in Louisiana, and the same man talking amusingly and rather persuasively in Washington, and one could understand his liking for the theory of a dual personality. It permits him to do so many contradictory and extraordinary things."[131]

Over time, Long's crazy-like-a-fox maneuvers gave him unparalleled power in Louisiana and a reputation for tyranny. T. Harry Williams writes, "He was stigmatized by many epithets and classified by various labels—despot of the delta, Caesar of the bayous, the first American dictator, the first great native Fascist, an American counterpart of Hitler or Mussolini."[132] A compilation of essays in *Huey P. Long: Southern Demagogue or American Democrat?* includes Louisiana author John Kingston Fineran's description of Long as a "tinpot Napoleon" and the Southern political scientist V. O. Key, Jr.'s pronouncement that Long's "control of Louisiana more nearly matched the power of a South American dictator than that of any other American state boss."[133] *The New Republic* published two opposing essays in February 1935, one entitled "Bogeyman" by Hodding Carter and the other, "Or Superman," by Reverend Smith, Long's supporter and proselytizer. In his piece, Carter mocked Long's legal accomplishments as "legislative travesties," his Share Our Wealth Society as a "group of zealots," and the possibility of Long in the White House as a "preposterous belly-laugh."[134]

These attacks failed to diminish Long's popularity. Like Cleon sailing unscathed through the arrows of Aristophanes' critiques, Long only became more powerful as his enemies savaged him. He was impeached as Louisiana's governor, only to defeat the charge and ascend to the U.S. Senate, where he became more and more popular even as his critics attacked him as a bumpkin and buffoon.

Scholarship is mixed on whether or not Huey Long could have posed a serious challenge to F.D.R. in 1936. It's clear, however, that he intended to; *My First Days in the White House* left laughably little mystery about his plans. For his part, Roosevelt considered Long to be a very real threat. As president, Roosevelt used a wide range of powers to undermine Long, instructing his top administration officials to withhold all patronage from Long's supporters: "[D]on't put anybody in and don't help anybody that is working for Huey Long or his crowd! That is 100 percent!"[135] But Long's power only grew, leading some Democrats to fear the Louisianan was "getting ready to pounce upon their party and absorb all or a large part of it in 1936."[136] The threat of a Long insurgency was real and destabilizing. As the *New York Times* reported, "If the [Share-Our-Wealth] clubs can be tied together and imbued with the announced purpose of their creator, a force will be let loose that the more sober cannot contemplate serenely."[137]

In the final analysis, Long probably wouldn't have become president in 1936, but he certainly would have altered the course of national politics that year. At the time when he was killed, he doubted he could win the presidency outright, but he was still formulating a plan to lead a third-party insurgency that would forge the forces of radicals like Father Coughlin; Congressman William Lemke, who had created a powerful "nonpartisan league" and would later be the Union Party's candidate for president; Gerald L. K. Smith; and Dr. Frances Townsend, who had cultivated a citizens' movement around an "Old Age Retirement Plan."[138]

By collectively drawing votes from Roosevelt, Long thought this ticket might help elect a Republican administration, whose failures would leave the country eager for a "strong man" and a triumphant Long candidacy in 1940.[139] Internal polls taken by the F.D.R. administration reflected Long's appeal. Without any campaigning, the polls found, the Kingfish would still attract from three million to six million votes, not only in the South but also in the eastern industrial centers that could decide the election.[140] Headlines immediately after Long's assassination revealed his potential impact on the presidential race: "Radical Party Wedge Goes With Huey Long: Roosevelt Democrats No Longer Fear Leftist Cut Into Vote."[141]

Tellingly, some of Long's contemporary critics clung to their faith in the Founders' aging safeguards against nationwide American demagogues. The journalist J. Hodding Carter described Long as an "impossible irony of Democracy." He saw the Founders' innovative institutional safeguard—the old-fashioned, even quaint Electoral College—as the final barrier between the people and democratic disaster: "[I]f the electoral college is abolished and the depression isn't, stranger political disasters could befall a tragically ignorant people groping for surety."[142] For the first time since its creation by the Constitution, the Electoral College might have been called upon to play the anti-demagogue role for which it was designed.

———————

One has to wonder: If Long had *not* been assassinated, what would have followed? We know that the American people successfully had cultivated a constitutional conscience strong enough to inhibit a demagogue from taking over the government. Even if the destabilizing forces of the Depression had helped Long reach the presidency and the cycle of regimes had begun to turn, the American people most likely would have checked Long. This isn't to say that Long would not have been able to do some real damage. Laws certainly would have been broken, and perhaps violence would have occurred. But America was very different from Germany, where ordinary Germans never did check Hitler. In short, it's virtually impossible to imagine Huey Long becoming president and the American people failing to check any movement toward actual tyranny.

Despite a tremendous amount of publicity toward and anxiety about the political leaders testing American democracy in the 1930s, they saw very limited national political success. In that decade, Father Coughlin, William Lemke, and Dr. Townsend all collapsed when it came to actual political success. The historian David Bennett credits the "built-in safeguards in the great democracy against a successful bid for power by any combination of radicals." The principal safeguard was "traditional American conservatism at the polls. No matter how much they applaud the extremist when he speaks on the radio or in the auditorium, many Americans become suspicious when they enter the voting booth. Perhaps this is simply a natural timidity, but perhaps it is something more."[143]

The "something more" was Americans' constitutional conscience. On Election Day in 1936, the Union Party, which Coughlin, Lemke, Smith, and Townsend were all supporting, basically imploded. Despite all the uprisings and demagogues of this singular decade, F.D.R. won with the most lopsided margin in American political history. Bennett describes Father Coughlin's reaction after this run-in with America's constitutional conscience: "When he first heard the results, Father Coughlin sat stunned in his Royal Oak [Michigan] office, the tears streaming down his cheeks. It was beyond comprehension."[144] But it was *not* beyond comprehension to any student of America's constitutional values, which could be as brutal toward those seeking to swamp the proper boundaries of authority as the Athenians were toward Socrates.

Then there was the matter of Long himself—what he believed and what he would have attempted. In an essay published in 1969, Long's lieutenant Gerald L. K. Smith, who H. L. Mencken once described as "the gustiest and goriest, the deadliest and damndest orator ever heard of on this or any other earth—the champion boob-bumper of all epochs,"[145] gave a surprising account of Long's relationship to his own power. Smith wrote, "Mr. Long's definition of practical statesmanship was: 'The ability to campaign as convincingly as a demagogue with much of the drama of a demagogue while possessing an inner self-respect dedicated to Constitutional procedures and a high regard for national tradition.'"[146] This "inner self-respect dedicated to Constitutional procedures" may have been either a joke or a canard. But it isn't hard to see as the truth. As a governor and U.S. senator from a state with a tradition of corruption and a Napoleonic code dramatically different from the legal regimes in other states, Long certainly established one-man rule in his state. As president of the nation, though, would he have attempted to subvert the U.S. Constitution itself? Or did he share the same constitutional conscience as most Americans?

Did Long really want to be a dictator? Long once admitted, in a fascinating interview, that he himself reflected on democracy's struggle with the demagogue—unsurprisingly taking his own side. "There are all kinds of demagogues. Some deceive the people in the interests of the lords and masters of creation, the Rockefellers and the Morgans. Some of them deceive the people in their own interests."[147] Another time, he went further, telling an interviewer, "What this country needs is a dictator," qualified only by "his impish grin." But then he also said, "I don't believe in dictatorships, all these Hitlers and Mussolinis. They don't belong in our American life."[148] He applied his reasoning to Louisiana: "There is no dictatorship in Louisiana. There is a perfect democracy there, and when you have a perfect democracy it is pretty hard to tell it from a dictatorship."

"When you have a perfect democracy it is pretty hard to tell it from a dictatorship." These words were spoken by a perfectly legitimate candidate for the presidency of the United States describing his own best accomplishments in his home state. It's tempting to liken Long to Cleon lecturing the crowd about how they were responsible for his predations. Fascinatingly, Long actually cited Plato in describing himself: "It is all in Plato. You know—the Greek philosopher. I hadn't read

Plato before I wrote my material on the 'Share the Wealth' movement, and when I did read Plato afterwards, I found I had said almost exactly the same things. I felt as if I had written Plato's 'Republic' myself."[149]

Long was murdered by Carl Weiss, a young and idealistic doctor and the son-in-law of Judge Benjamin Pavy, one of Long's "bitterest enemies."[150] Long had responded to Pavy's repeated challenges by proposing a gerrymander bill in the legislature that essentially would have drawn Pavy out of his district, removing him from power.[151] While there have been generations of speculation about Long's death, some of it approaching J.F.K.-style conspiracy theories about whether Long's guards actually killed him, Long's great biographer T. Harry Williams concluded that Weiss killed Long as a martyr kills a tyrant. Weiss was immediately shot by Long's guards. He was later found to have thirty bullet holes in the back, twenty-nine in the front, and two in the head.[152]

Weiss, Williams concluded, was a "sincere and idealistic young man who agonized over the evils that he believed Huey Long was inflicting on his class and his state."[153] Weiss was on a political mission. "He went into the capitol that Sunday night to remove a tyrant."[154] A friend of Judge Pavy went further: "Carl was a deep student of political theory," he said. "I am convinced that this intensive study of the Louisiana political situation convinced him that the form of government in the state under Senator Long's dictatorship was so terrible and such a miscarriage of justice that his broodings finally unbalanced his mind." In conclusion: "I believe that, thus mentally unbalanced on this subject, he saw as a martyr to liberty the man who would assassinate Senator Long."[155]

The tempting conclusion is that Long's assassination was a political attempt—raw, untrained, chaotic, out of the constitutional order, but still political—by a citizen to respond to the terrifying increase in Long's power. That conclusion runs a serious risk of classifying an assassination as a political tactic, which of course it should never be. Assassination can never be a legitimate political act, especially within a constitutional system in which citizens are invested with common respect for a common rule. But we can at once analyze this reaction to

Huey Long while condemning it as immoral, illegal, and a grotesque violation of American ideals. Demagogues like Long operate within the fourth rule, bending and breaking rules at will. They naturally inspire hatred among those whom they quash on their rise to power and who view, with anger and terror, their constitutional consequences. If Long had never tested those boundaries, if he had not flaunted and exercised his tyrannical power in Louisiana so shamelessly, and if he had not openly toyed with the realms of constitutional authority as a national figure, he might well have lived.

◆

AMERICANS FIGHT BACK

THE *IN EXTREMIS* POLITICS OF LONG AND THE UNIQUE AND confusing combination of the beneficial and destructive demagogue shook the nation. During the traumatic decade of the 1930s, many Americans obsessed about the same dark fantasy that had haunted the Founding Fathers: the cycle of regimes playing out in America. In 1935, on the crest of Huey Long's rise (and before his assassination), the popular novelist Sinclair Lewis completed a novel titled *It Can't Happen Here.* Like Aristophanes before him, Lewis was driven by an urgent need to wake up his countrymen; writing at a white-hot pace, he finished the book in a mere eight weeks. The novel paints its characters in broad, satirical brushstrokes, following the rise of a populist Democratic U.S. senator named Berzelius "Buzz" Windrip who, in 1936, defeats incumbent President Matt Trowbridge (a stand-in for F.D.R.) on waves of economic malcontent. Through speeches laden with emotional appeals, as well as a raft of propaganda designed by a Goebbels-like personal aide, Lewis's protagonist becomes a homegrown fascist tyrant, aided by a violent personal army of thugs called not Brownshirts but "Minutemen."

Lewis's obvious motivation in writing the book was to trigger in Americans a new wave of reflection about the problem of demagogues. It's clear from the writing that Lewis was eyeing Long with deep alarm. His narrator says in the beginning pages of the novel: "Why, there is no country in the world that can get more hysterical—yes, or more obsequious!—than America. Look how Huey Long became absolute monarch over Louisiana. . . ." To Lewis, the American people's own involvement in—and implicit approval of—unconstitutional trends was the fulcrum of America's pivot to disaster. "Listen to Bishop Prang and Father Coughlin on the radio—divine oracles, to millions. Remember how casually most Americans have accepted Tammany grafting and Chicago gangs and the crookedness of so many of President Harding's appointees? Could Hitler's bunch, or Windrip's, be worse?"[156]

Lewis believed Americans were "hysterical" and that their vulnerability to demagogues led to the worst of America's political patterns, from open corruption to violence. The book was therefore part of the culture of self-critique and self-improvement that underlies our constitutional conscience. The paroxysm of self-doubt about our democracy that followed Nazi Germany's rise was essential to the improvement of our constitutional values—upgrading them, if you will, to the modern world, where radio and television afforded manipulative leaders entirely new opportunities to become demagogues. The art form has proven durable. Seventy years later, in 2004, the contemporary novelist Philip Roth wrote a novel titled *The Plot Against America,* which imagined the popular and charismatic pilot Charles Lindbergh defeating F.D.R. for the presidency in 1940 and rapidly enacting an anti-Semitic and totalitarian platform. The novel was a best-seller, proving the drama of the cycle of regimes can still draw an audience.[157]

Like Roth's novel, Lewis's novel struck a chord with Americans. In 1935—the same year Long was assassinated—Lewis's novel sold 235,000 copies. Hundreds of thousands of people wondered whether "it" really could "happen here," bought the book, and resolved that it would not.

In 1937, two years after Long's assassination, President Roosevelt himself took a step toward demagoguery, and the reaction he provoked provides the most overwhelming evidence that Americans were in the midst of consolidating their constitutional values in a decade when democracy was undergoing its most profound tests abroad.

It's difficult to charge F.D.R. with demagoguery. Though F.D.R. provoked enormous enmity among his political enemies in his day, history shows that his enemies, for the most part, were wrong—wrong on the issues, wrong on the direction of American history, and wrong for the poor and oppressed Americans whose lives were immeasurably improved by F.D.R.'s governance. Yet, all the same, in 1937 F.D.R. did try to exploit his tremendous and passionate popularity among the masses not only to bend a constitutional rule, but also to break it. And he did so in furtherance of his own agenda. The saving grace is that the American people themselves rebuked F.D.R.

In the mid-1930s, F.D.R. was engaged in a constant battle with a Supreme Court largely appointed by a series of Republican presidents, including Calvin Coolidge and Herbert Hoover. From January 1935 to May 1936, the Supreme Court voided more than a dozen New Deal laws, and federal judges issued about 1,600 injunctions against New Deal laws. Al Smith, the Democratic presidential nominee in 1928, commented that the courts were throwing the New Deal's "Alphabet Soup" out the window "three letters at a time."[158] Roosevelt was infuriated. With his landslide victory in the November election in 1936, he decided to attack the Court itself and prepared a plan that he would introduce in Congress on February 5, 1937. The plan would allow the president to introduce one new member of the Court for every member who was over the age of 70. The president and the administration pitched the plan to the public on the flimsy rationale that it would increase the efficiency of a court ill-equipped to handle the workload of a modern judiciary. But everyone knew the real objective was to allow the president to defeat what he regarded as an obstructionist and separate branch of government.

The public's reaction was swift and stinging. The mail flooding congressional offices ran a stunning nine to one against the proposal. One senator received 1,000 telegrams in one day, and his staff couldn't open all of the letters. Another senator received 30,000 letters and telegrams.[159] The public attacked F.D.R. for "perverting the Constitution, undermining judicial integrity, and destroying judicial independence."[160] One critic responded in an address to the Women's Patriotic Congress on the charge that F.D.R. had a "power complex" like Mussolini's, that "this is precisely the judgment which the people of the U.S. have reached." The critic explained, "[T]hey know that a constitutional president cannot even aspire to dictatorial powers unless he harbors in his breast a willingness and an intention to overthrow the Constitution."[161]

But F.D.R. fought on. On March 4, at the Mayflower Hotel in Washington, D.C., he dedicated a major speech to the proposal. He also made a Victory Dinner speech in Newark, New Jersey, to defend the idea, attacking the Court for obstructing his laws to raise wages, reduce labor hours, abolish child labor, and eliminate unfair trade practices. F.D.R. attempted to seize the ground of democracy for himself rather than for the Court: "If we would keep faith with those who had faith in us, if we would make democracy succeed, I say we must act—NOW!"[162] But the speeches failed. A Gallup poll showed that opposition to the bill dropped only one point from 48 to 47 percent, and support was at 41 percent.[163] F.D.R. dedicated a Fireside Chat on March 9 to the proposal, likening the three branches of government to three horses in front of a plow, and said the American people were "in the driver's seat." If they wanted the "furrow plowed," they should "expect the third horse to pull in unison with the other two."[164]

None of it worked. When the bill finally came to a vote on July 22, it lost by an astonishing seventy to twenty votes. Vividly, the *Jackson (Miss.) Daily News* wrote that the proposal was "dead as a salt mackeral [*sic*] shining beneath the pale moonlight. As dead as the ashes of Moses, the world's first law giver."[165] In the words of one scholar, "No issue in the years before World War II shook the country as did President Roosevelt's proposal to enlarge the membership of the Supreme Court. No less amazing was the manner in which most of the electorate rose up in wrathful protest. . . ."[166] What happened during the court-packing crisis is simple—F.D.R. ran into the buzz saw of America's constitutional conscience and had to turn back.

◆

A RED-BAITER AND AN AMERICAN CAESAR

FIFTEEN YEARS AFTER THE RISE AND FALL OF HUEY LONG AND THE defeat of F.D.R.'s court-packing scheme, two demagogues launched meteoric rises that captivated millions of Americans, not to mention the world. They both fell, victims of America's constitutional conscience.

In 1950, Joseph McCarthy, then an obscure senator from Wisconsin, stood before a bank of television cameras, holding behind his back a secret weapon: a list of communists purportedly burrowed deep within the federal government. He never showed the list to anyone, but the cameras carried his message. He became an immediate sensation. McCarthy had never demonstrated a particular concern with communists before. In the *Congressional Quarterly*, McCarthy is listed as making comments on about 215 topics from 1947 to 1949. Only two clearly involved communism.[167] He was a product of his own ambition, and the path to power ran straight through the masses. He had consciously chosen anti-communism as a cause at a famous dinner in early 1950 at the Colony Restaurant in Washington, D.C. At that dinner, McCarthy had brainstormed with four friends about a cause he could adopt to gain greater prominence and ensure his electoral victory in 1952. He rejected various options as not "sexy" enough. Finally, when one of his friends, Father Edmund A. Walsh, the dean of Georgetown University's School of Foreign Service, said, "How about communism as an issue?" McCarthy "pounced upon the suggestion." "The government is full of communists," he declared. "The thing to do is hammer at them."[168]

From 1950 forward, McCarthy never diverged from his new purpose. His hearings became the center of the universe for many Americans—those riveted by the communist threat and those who thought our constitutional values were deeply threatened by the new star chamber. McCarthy ruined reputations with glee, delighted in creating blacklists, and reveled in his intense celebrity. He was clearly a demagogue: (1) He was a man of the people, (2) he created great passions among them, (3) he was using those reactions for his own political benefit, and (4) he happily broke the rules, victimizing American citizens and bending the Bill of Rights. And he seemed to have the people's favor. By January of 1954, McCarthy's approval rating was 50 percent with the American people. Only 29 percent felt unfavorably about him.[169]

But within that same year, the people turned on the demagogue. By early 1954, McCarthy had enjoyed a three-year surge. Americans, panicked about the Soviet threat and deeply concerned about internal stability, had shelved their deepest constitutional concerns and admittedly allowed a demagogue to threaten and outright attack the Constitution. But their patience was wearing thin in reaction to McCarthy's constitutional abuses, his hubris, and his lengthening list of victims. In the spring and summer of 1954, the Army–McCarthy hearings were televised. Senator after senator attacked McCarthy. The famous last straw was laid when McCarthy impugned the character of a young lawyer at Joseph Welch's law firm for belonging to the National Lawyers Guild (a purported communist outfit). Welch pleaded, "Little did I dream you could be so reckless and cruel as to do an injury to that lad. . . . Let us not assassinate this lad further, Senator. You have done enough. Have you no sense of decency, sir, at long last? Have you left no sense of decency?"[170]

The word "decency" was apt, recalling Americans to their essential values. The nation began to wake up. Doubts about McCarthy grew, and his popularity quickly waned. After the Army–McCarthy hearings, when the Senate—the more senior body of Congress itself, appropriately the people's branch of government—finally challenged the demagogue, his unfavorability rating rose 16 percent, to 45 percent; his favorability rating fell to only 34 percent.[171] McCarthy was censured that same year by the Senate on December 2. The people's branch of government had revolted against a presumed leader of the people, and the demagogue, rather than overtaking the regime, was overtaken by it.

McCarthy's political career and his demagoguery quickly deflated. He died a mere two and a half years later, a victim of alcoholism, ignominy, and a growing recognition among Americans of his danger.

The same year that McCarthy launched his crusade in the Senate, General Douglas MacArthur returned home from Korea to a hero's welcome. There was something ancient about MacArthur. One adjutant who served under him when he commanded West Point wrote that he was "both a patrician and a plebeian." He explained: "I could close my eyes and see him in his toga, imperiously mounting his chariot, and the next minute clad in homespun, sitting on the narrow sidewalk of Pompeii and chatting informally with a slave."[172] This account not only recognized MacArthur as a timeless figure who brought the deepest stirrings of the ancient world into modern American life; it also revealed his deep connection with the people.

MacArthur, the general who accepted Japan's surrender in 1945, oversaw America's occupation of Japan from 1945 to 1951, and commanded America's forces in 1950 and 1951, is perhaps best known for his public wrestling match with President Harry S Truman in 1951. America had never seen such a public confrontation between an unelected military leader and an elected president, and it seemed to many that the Constitution, for once, might really be threatened.

The controversy about MacArthur was not new. Twenty years earlier, after MacArthur commanded troops that removed protesting veterans from the nation's capital, F.D.R. had told an aide that MacArthur was "one of the two most dangerous men in the country"—the other being Huey Long.[173] When Harry Truman flew to Korea in 1950 for a vaunted meeting, MacArthur was commanding American troops in an offensive against North Korea. MacArthur's strategy involved what Truman thought were unnecessarily provocative steps toward China, a North Korea ally already heavily involved in battle with American troops. At the meeting the general's very dress seemed to challenge the elected constitutional leader. MacArthur's shirt was unbuttoned and he was wearing a hat that Truman said in his memoirs "had evidently seen a good deal of use."[174] But Truman was in a bind. He wrote: "If he'd been a lieutenant in my outfit going around dressed like that, I'd have busted him so fast he wouldn't have known what happened to him."[175] That MacArthur was a general to a president—not much different from a lieutenant to a captain—seemed to escape the general. MacArthur didn't even salute the president; he merely shook his hand. In the face of MacArthur's popularity with the American public and Truman's own desire not to pick a fight he wasn't sure he could easily win, Truman found himself essentially powerless to take any direct action against the insubordination he perceived, even though the general was under his chain of command. The episode spoke volumes about MacArthur's status vis-à-vis the elected president.

Truman fired MacArthur in part because of MacArthur's unilateral escalation of the Chinese conflict. The action unleashed passions never before seen in America. Richard H. Rovere and Arthur M. Schlesinger, Jr. wrote, "It is doubtful if there has ever been in this country so violent and spontaneous a discharge of political passion as that provoked by the President's dismissal of the General. . . . Certainly there has been nothing to match it since the Civil War."[176] Of the first 78,000 telegrams the White House received, opponents of the recall outnumbered supporters twenty to one; the White House, either exhausted or fearful (or both), stopped keeping track of the proportion.[177] When the general addressed Congress, he was interrupted by applause thirty times in his thirty-four minute speech.[178] Afterward, the legislators "were sobbing their praise." One shouted, "We heard God speak here today, God in the flesh, the voice of God!"[179] That afternoon, MacArthur drove down Pennsylvania Avenue under the trails of Air Force jets, watched by a crowd of a half-million.[180] He then traveled to New York City, where the largest crowd in New York City's history gathered along Broadway under a blizzard of tickertape. An astonishing *seven million* people thronged along the boulevard to watch an unemployed general ride down Broadway, in the first salvo of his war against the unpopular president who had fired him. For seven hours, MacArthur traveled a nineteen-mile course.[181]

Shortly afterward, MacArthur began preparing to formally enter politics; millions were ecstatic. But many were also deeply concerned. From 1951 to 1952, MacArthur made a series of speeches across the country assailing Truman's war policy in Korea and apparently attempting to set himself up as a future president. The people began to stir against him. In Seattle, several civic leaders left the hall where he was speaking, and the city's Democratic congressman called him a demagogue.[182] The *New York Post* said he was a "desperate, demagogic Republican politician fighting a dirty political war."[183] MacArthur sided with Senator Robert Taft of Ohio against Dwight Eisenhower in the Republican nomination fight that year and lost, because Ike successfully set himself apart from MacArthur.[184] When Eisenhower won the nomination, MacArthur's star began truly to fall.

In retrospect, MacArthur's decline began when he ran, head-long, into Congress. In May of 1951, the general appeared before a joint inquiry of the U.S. Senate's Armed Services and Foreign Relations committees. At the hearings, conducted by Senator Richard Russell, the Senate carefully dissected MacArthur's grounds for opposing President Truman. The rigorous, rational questioning laid bare for the media, and for the people at large, the dangers of endorsing the military leader's overt defiance of an elected president. Over forty-two days of testimony, the committee revealed that MacArthur had no broader plan for winning a world war that could have begun in the Pacific. One senator asked him, "If we go into all-out war, I want to find out how you propose in your own mind to defend the American nation against that war." MacArthur answered, "That doesn't happen to be my responsibility, Senator. My responsibilities were in the Pacific."[185]

MacArthur's political force was deflated by administration witnesses who demonstrated that Truman's plan, and the underlying intellectual framework of George Kennan's more modest theory of "containment," deserved respect, at the very least, if not an outright embrace. MacArthur, on the other hand, appeared not to grasp the link between the broader geopolitical threat posed by the Soviet Union and apparently local strategic issues in Asia. Truman, Congress concluded, was better positioned to make the geopolitical judgments that attended military decisions in the Pacific. Americans decided the authority of the commander-in-chief had better stay where it already legitimately was—in the president's hands.

Like McCarthy, MacArthur tested the limits of America's democracy. But he was different from the senator in one important respect. A deeper look at MacArthur reveals that even this supposed "American Caesar" probably shared most Americans' commitment to the Constitution. It was under MacArthur's Mandarin-like oversight, after all, that the Japanese constitution was written. Truman appointed MacArthur Supreme Commander for the Allied Powers in 1945, and he enjoyed complete autocratic powers in Japan from 1945 to 1951. MacArthur could have suspended Emperor Hirohito's functions, dissolved the Diet (the legislature), prohibited political parties, and disqualified whoever he wanted from public office.[186] For anyone with an untrammeled lust for power, the temptations to tyranny would have been both unimaginable and obvious.

Yet MacArthur evidenced instead a concern for Japan's long-term stability, to which he thought constitutional values would be a great contributor. One reporter said his attitude was "Olympian." He was, she wrote, "thinking in centuries and populations."[187] Under MacArthur's oversight, the prime minister appointed a committee to draft a constitution. This new document borrowed liberally from Japan's regressive Meiji Constitution, which had been drafted in the late 1800s and which formally ranked women as inferior beings, vested power in eleven industrial families, and established peasants as sharecroppers.[188] The new constitution got rid of the most repressive elements, yet retained just enough to make the Japanese consider the constitution at least partly their own—for instance, the new constitution retained the emperor, though denying him the vote. MacArthur himself said the new constitution was just "an amendment to the old Meiji one."[189]

The new document blended elements from America's Constitution with Great Britain's unwritten one. It established three separate branches of government and a prime minister. It also prohibited "war as a sovereign right of the nation."[190] The relationship to Japan's original constitution, as well as broader rights for the people, helped ensure the new constitution's acceptance. In 1946, Emperor Hirohito announced a national holiday in celebration of the document. Around Japan, women wore their best kimonos, and sake toasts to the new constitution abounded.[191]

Over a half-century later, the document still holds. Japan is a peaceful and relatively liberal country. The citizens embrace their constitution. It seems hard to believe that the general who supervised this transition—who planted the seeds whereby constitutional values would be cultivated—himself would have desired the cycle of regimes. In any event, he was rebuked by the very people he would have needed to subvert the American regime. The general's ambitions were contained by America's constitutional conscience. Alexander Hamilton's concluding fear in the *Federalist Papers*—about the "military despotism of a victorious demagogue"—never came to pass.

———

Through the twentieth century, other demagogues would fall as well, from the racist Alabama governor and presidential candidate George Wallace, who was shot and paralyzed in 1972, to the Louisiana

Congressman and Ku Klux Klan Grand Wizard David Duke, who lost his campaign for the U.S. Senate in 1990. To date, we still haven't seen the figure the Framers feared the most—the demagogue who would overturn the Constitution. Constitutionalism helps explain these victories. Certainly, the checks and balances in American politics have helped stabilize our system from attack, even if some of them, such as the Electoral College, have been mooted by Americans' constitutionalism. But our constitutional conscience must be given its due. As the preceding stories so amply reveal, constitutionalism has played—and continues to play—an essential role both in strengthening America's legitimate government and in denying those who would do it harm.

PART III

THE MODERN STRUGGLE

An American foreign policy, to be successful, must quicken the public pulse. Americans have a missionary streak, and democracy is our mission. The new sticker should read "pro-democracy."[1]

—Ben Wattenberg, *First Universal Nation*

GIVEN AMERICA'S EXTRAORDINARY SUCCESS IN CULTIVATING constitutionalism at home, you would be excused for imagining that a concern with constitutionalism would also drive our foreign policy—particularly in countries where demagogues lie in wait. But exactly the opposite has been the case in recent years. Rather than appreciating that the people and their values are the beating heart of any healthy democracy, recent leaders repeated Plato's mistake. They dreamed up a castle in the air, cut loose from the brick-and-mortar, Aristotelian foundations of common sense and popular values. They neglected the essentials for a thriving democracy—political culture, the people's own regard for themselves, and a habituated hostility to authoritarian leaders. And so, instead of solving the cycle of regimes, they helped to replicate it.

But most curious of all was how these leaders made Plato's mistake by *employing* democracy rather than *rejecting* it. Plato, remember, despised democracy, and employed every philosopher's instrument in his tool chest to block the people from political power. The people who made our foreign policy during the George W. Bush presidency shared Plato's faith that elites, once put in charge, could solve most of the problems purportedly created by ordinary people. But where Plato sought to remove democracy from our ambitions, the neoconservatives instead placed democracy at the heart of their goals. Perhaps more importantly, these dreamers applied Plato's logic to the idea of America itself. They reconstituted America not as the learned and practiced cultural inheritance Jefferson planned and de Tocqueville explained, but rather as a metaphysical destiny. America, to them, became the idea toward which history was aimed. Democracy the idea became America the idea, and both fused into an intoxicating notion not only of American empire, but American destiny.

This has been an American story, to be sure, and we can have some sympathy with the neoconservatives as patriots fully invested in the classic enterprise of American exceptionalism. But the tragic irony is that, just as with Plato, their metaphysical treatment both of democracy and of America itself repeated Plato's mistake. Authoritarianism—not democracy—whispered in the eaves of their castle in the sky. They neglected the essence of any real constitutional democracy: the people. And the people, in Iraq and elsewhere, weren't happy about it. Demagogues, like Moqtada al-Sadr, naturally arrived again.

IGNORING IRAQIS

TO UNRAVEL THE MYSTERY OF HOW DEMOCRACY WENT SO FAR OFF track in Iraq in the early years, enabling the quick ascendancy of Moqtada al-Sadr from cleric to firebrand to demagogue, we must take a close look at what we did—and did not—do. In the space of less than a year, the Bush administration invaded a sovereign nation, removed a brutal—but stable—one-party system and dictatorship, and installed a fresh and fragile democracy. On March 16, 2003, days before the launch of the Iraq War, Vice President Dick Cheney told Tim Russert on *Meet the Press*, "[I] really do believe that we will be greeted as liberators." The planners of the war, assuming democracy would take root fairly rapidly in Iraq, paid far too little attention to the people of Iraq—who, after all, would ultimately decide whether democracy lived or died there.

The catalogue of cultural facts that our policymakers ignored is nothing short of astonishing. They simply didn't seem to understand that prior to the 2003 invasion, Iraq's history had already been dominated by pain and violence, with many of its leading political figures bathed in blood. Any reasonable person would have been challenged to summon much objective optimism about the prospects for easily creating a successful democracy in Iraq, as its people were well-practiced in widespread outrage at a foreign oppressor. After World War I, Lawrence of Arabia promised Britain's wartime Arab allies that

Arab countries would be independent. British planners, who cobbled Iraq together from three former Ottoman provinces, instead decided to run the country as a protectorate, breaking Lawrence's promise altogether. But the country was immediately too discordant for calm external governance.

In 1932, Iraq became an independent constitutional monarchy; in only four years, insurgents staged the first coup in the Arab world. After that, in the words of one writer, "the violence never really stopped, with coups, ethnic pogroms and massacres among political parties."[2] The constitutional monarchy was overthrown again in 1958 and, in the years that followed, military regimes regularly replaced each other. In 1968, the Ba'ath party, which had begun during World War II as a native effort to support the Iraqi Nazi Party, took over, with Saddam Hussein as its head of security. Saddam formally assumed the presidency in 1979 and launched a brutal regime, including genocide against the Kurdish minority in the north and the savage suppression of the country's majority Shi'a ethnic group.[3]

For the first bloody years after the U.S. invasion, Moqtada al-Sadr was the natural mirror of a people with this chaotic, angry history. As a descendant of the prophet Mohammed, he wore the customary black turban that commands reverence from millions of people. Sadr's father, the Grand Ayatollah Mohammed Sadiq al-Sadr, was the most powerful Shiite cleric in Iraq in the late 1990s, more famous even than his son would become. In 1999 Sunni troops loyal to Saddam Hussein murdered the Grand Ayatollah and two of his sons—Moqtada's brothers. Moqtada, in his twenties, was seared by the assassinations; the Shi'a masses eventually elevated him as their avenger. Sadr's popularity stemmed both from his personal history and from his powerful connection with the common people of Iraq.

Before the Iraq invasion, many analysts predicted that it would be difficult for the United States to create a friendly democracy in Iraq, contradicting Vice President Cheney's confident assertion that Americans would be "greeted as liberators." In 1999, one conservative analyst forecast the course of events pretty much as they happened.

"Given the hardships the Iraq population has suffered since the 1991 war, a post-Saddam regime could be even more virulently anti-United States than he is."[4] It was easy to anticipate the rise of a powerful demagogue from the fundamental facts of Iraqi society: "[I]n a post-Saddam Iraq, Shiite influence would likely rise. . . . Although the Shiites currently lack political influence, Saddam's fall could alter that and threaten Iraq's outnumbered Sunnis."[5] Another expert expanded on the insight, in a darker direction: "How will such a new ruler cope with inevitable bloodletting as thousands of Iraqis who have suffered under Saddam's rule kill intelligence agents and Ba'ath Party officials?"[6]

Another report in 2003 *specifically* predicted the difficulty of setting up a constitutional government in Iraq: "The constitution must lay the basis of a democratic polity. Yet this is no easy task given the lack of a tradition of constitutionalism or the rule of law."[7] This analyst proceeded to argue that the Iraqi system depended on "patrimonialism," in which "personalized power is exercised through small circles of kinsmen."[8] This system was defined by a lack of participation or accountability, meaning that the Iraqi people had been acculturated precisely to *anti*-democratic habits: "The ideology is the sacredness or even the power of an individual, and coercion is the principal instrument of rule. The system does not aim at inclusiveness, but operates through opportunistic alliances which shift with the expediency of the moment."[9]

Even after the Iraqi occupation, American policymakers seemed determined to ignore the lessons of history. Shortly after taking up residence in Baghdad, Coalition Provisional Authority (CPA) director Paul Bremer requested a "warts-and-all" briefing with the staff of the CPA. During the meeting, Bremer heard from officials that the electrical and educational systems were completely broken. He soon announced his plans to issue a disastrous "de-Ba'athification" order. In short order, Bremer instituted a number of actions that helped undermine the development of the constitutional conscience that would have served as a bulwark against Sadr. He disbanded the military, putting 400,000 Iraqi men into the street without jobs and without paychecks.[10] He failed to work sufficiently closely with the moderate clerical community, which was far more open to a constitutional form of Islam than the Americans knew. He enacted other anti-Ba'athist measures that prohibited thousands of experienced civil servants from working in the government, simultaneously undermining the effectiveness of the state while creating a hotbed of resentment among the populace—a remarkable double-whammy.

The missteps were especially evident in the way that experts were deployed to try to effect a transition to democracy. Larry Diamond, a Senior Fellow at the Hoover Institution in California and the editor of the *Journal of Democracy*, was tapped by the Bush administration to supervise democracy efforts in Iraq during the first three months of 2004, the year after the invasion. But Diamond found his expertise futile in the actual governance of the country. In his book *Squandered Victory*, Diamond describes the situation when he arrived in Iraq. He recounts hearing about a plan to "establish the infrastructure of democracy" in *six months*, with "tens of millions of dollars." At the beginning of this process, Bremer gave the planners an astonishing instruction. "We have 175 days left," Bremer announced, "and then we're out of here. We have to get this done."[11]

The plan included items like training Iraqi political parties; building the production facilities for mass media; and recruiting, staffing, and training a new electoral commission. However, the six-month plan was missing one major item. In contravention of even the most basic lessons from Aristotle, Jefferson, and de Tocqueville, the people were simply not given a major role. "Gradually I realized that Bremer and his most trusted CPA advisers simply did not grasp the depth of Iraqi disaffection, suspicion, and frustration, even among many of our partners and philosophical allies within the Iraqi political class," Diamond writes. This lack of penetration into the basic social reality of everyday Iraqi life led to an elite, top-down approach. "Thus they simply imposed a transition plan on the Iraqi people and political class, rather than engaging in an open, broad-based dialogue that might have generated wider consensus."[12]

There are many other examples of the depth of American leaders' failure to work with the people, who are necessary to stop a demagogue—a leader of the people—from destabilizing democracy. In June 2003, for instance, to meet the requirement of the regime's Transitional Administrative Law (TAL) of "receiving proposals from the citizens of Iraq as it writes the constitution," an "Outreach Unit" was established with the mission of spreading information about the constitution to the public and analyzing the public response through surveys. It was given a staff of fifty; but before June, the United States had not even prepared office space even though it had only two months to complete its mission. As one expert, Jonathan Morrow of the U.S. Institute of Peace, writes, "The attempt to conduct a serious national constitutional dialogue in such a short period of time was probably unprecedented." The problem, Morrow writes, was there was "no serious attempt at educating the public on constitutional issues, so that non-elite Iraqis had little chance to understand even the simple questionnaire."

The Outreach Unit ultimately received about 150,000 submissions, from a country of almost thirty million people. These included only 10,000 from Sunni Arab regions. In the end, partly because of the severe time constraints on the Outreach Unit and partly because the unit was run mostly by Shi'a replicating the internal divisions in Iraq, the constitution never fully took the views of the public into account. Worse, the opportunity to address the widespread desire for "transparency and participation in constitutional matters," expressed during focus groups, was missed. The Iraqi public concluded that the process did not take the public itself into account.[13]

The pattern of ignoring the people's role in democracy's success continued in the CPA's negotiation with Iraq's major Shi'a cleric, the Ayatollah al-Sistani. "According to yet another staffer, no one knew what Sistani really thought, so we should just follow our instincts," Diamond recalls. Relevant policymakers had not even read Sistani's work, which would have revealed a deep commitment to basic tenets of democracy, albeit filtered through a Shi'a religious lens: "Amazingly, no one considered the most obvious interpretations, derivable from the serious study of Sistani's writings and philosophy: a sincere belief in the political legitimacy of a social contract between rulers and ruled."[14]

All of this led to awkward mistakes with the first constitutional document, the Transitional Administrative Laws (TAL). The CPA drafted the TAL with minimal Iraqi input and began holding public meetings. But Sistani's forces—alienated from the process and from the TAL itself—began agitating against this ostensible instrument of democracy. Shortly after the TAL was released, Sistani's forces put out a leaflet that said:

IN THE NAME OF ALLAH MOST COMPASSIONATE MOST MERCIFUL
You Enthusiastic Iraqis
You who are concerned about the unity, independence, and stability of Iraq and are interested in keeping the rights of the Iraqi people from different sects and ethnicity.
Let us explain to you the tragedy of [the TAL.]
This law paves the way to divide Iraq and deepen sectarianism in its future system and makes Iraq [fall] into a stage of instability and violence, which cannot be estimated, but by our Maker.
This law was made in coordination with the occupying power; we can see the fingerprints of that power clearly on its articles and sources.
This law was made behind doors under pressure of the occupiers on many of the Governing Council members so as to finish it before the election campaign of Bush.
The occupiers didn't allow to show the TAL to the Iraqi people to be discussed through public seminar and the media before assigning it; many Iraqis didn't know anything about it till it passed.[15]

The complaints in the flyer were quite rational and democratic. Together, they exposed how extraordinarily important it would have been to begin where the people were. But, as one critic told Diamond, "The Iraqi people are absent; they gave no consent to this."[16]

The planners moved ahead anyway, concluding that public opinion could be manipulated through advertising. A communications and advertising offensive was launched to sell the TAL with the help of London- and Dubai-based advertising firms. An American policymaker said, "The CPA decision makers weren't interested in snappy communication; they wanted to win the argument and beat the Iraqis into submission with the rightness of their cause and the power of their logic."[17] The deepest irony, Diamond explains, was that democracy was being sold in an undemocratic way: "For the fourth or fifth time—I was losing count—the United States was finding itself on what appeared to be the *less* democratic side of an argument with Iraqis over transitional procedures."[18]

With such missteps, experts on the scene unsurprisingly began to capture troubling trends among the people that augured poorly for a quick and smooth transition to democracy. Brian Katulis and Tom Melia, two consultants who worked for the U.S.-based National Democratic Institute in the early months after the invasion, uncovered these trends in dozens of focus groups. Some citizens expressed hesitant enthusiasm about democracy, which was underlined by emerging constitutional values. One Sunni man in Baghdad said, "Democracy is like raising a little child. When he grows up and becomes an adult, he needs some time, so he can get more strength and confidence in himself."[19] A Shi'a woman in Diwaniya said, "We don't want the foreigners' democratic system. We want the Islamic democracy, which is of course the respect of the social rights and another's opinion."[20]

Others—notably including several from Moqtada al-Sadr's city—opposed democracy directly. A Shi'a man in Sadr City said, "[Democracy] is a door that will be opened that you can't close again, so we are afraid of it."[21] A Shi'a woman said, "[Democracy is] anyone can do anything they want. You don't be afraid from God or anyone. It is not good."[22] Katulis and Melia concluded in a *Washington Post* op-ed in August 2003—only a few months after the invasion and before Sadr began his reign and the occupation began truly to falter—that the Iraqis had a "deep skepticism" about the information they heard, reflected in a tendency to be "unenthusiastic about political leaders." They recommended that the United States begin where the Iraqi people actually were, by setting up better feedback mechanisms to hear "average Iraqis," by framing "all initiatives as responses to Iraqi desires," and by educating Iraqis about democracy through "massive civic education campaigns."[23]

The process immediately began to bear rotten fruit. In September 2003, regarding the decision to use a convoluted system of caucuses rather than national elections under the supervision of the United Nations, an Iraqi political scientist (and head of the Iraq Foundation for Development and Democracy) said: "If you continue down this road . . . I will have nothing to do with it." Why? He predicted ominous consequences if the *demos* was uninterested in the democracy: "You will alienate the Kurds, who are disenchanted with their two leaders. You will alienate the Sunnis, who fear [that] a list of cronies will be imposed on them. You will alienate Baathists, who will be completely marginalized." He continued darkly: "You will alienate all the progressive people, who want democracy. If all these people boycott the process, you will have *more* organized opposition. You will have more problems than you can imagine."[24]

The irony is that some of the ideas that caused democracy to stumble so badly in the initial years in Iraq stemmed from a good-faith attempt to respond to the greatest cycle of regimes in modern times: Adolf Hitler's ascent from the constitutional democracy of Weimar Germany. In a perverse accident of history, well-intentioned but misguided attempts to *stop* demagogues ended up *producing* demagogues. To tell that story, we must go back to the beginning—to the years just after the bloody first World War, and the hopeful but naïve democracy of Weimar Germany.

THE CYCLE BEGINS AGAIN

ON JANUARY 19, 1919, ORDINARY GERMANS WENT TO THE POLLS to elect delegates to a constitutional convention. In addition to the psychological aftereffects of its crushing defeat in World War I and the harsh peace of the Versailles Treaty, Germany was experiencing the heavy presence of international occupiers determined to prevent Germany from ever repeating the bellicose policies that led to world war. And yet, despite the tragedy of the past, spirits were high among constitutional reformers as activists prepared to tear Germany free from its bloody past and become a modern, liberal nation.

After they were elected, the delegates decided the convention could not be held in the capital city of Berlin, which they thought was still too fraught with post-war tension. They decided instead to convene in the city of Weimar, traditionally a "symbol of classical, humanistic German culture."[25] At the convention, the delegates drafted a document that protected freedom of speech and of the press, provided for equality between women and men, gave voting rights to all citizens at least twenty-one years old, recognized the right to collective bargaining, and gave the state responsibility for the unemployed, women, and children.[26] The Weimar Constitution finally put into law ideals that liberals and democratic socialists had been pursuing in Germany since the mid-nineteenth century.[27] However, thousands of Germans, seething after the Versailles Treaty, resented the Weimar Constitution as an imposed structure rather than the result of an organic process.

The constitution was formally adopted on August 11, 1919, and the convention—and the world—looked forward to a new era for freedom and democracy across the globe. Ever since Bismarck began assembling the loose collection of provinces into a state, Germany had adopted a belligerent stance toward the world. But with the new constitution, Weimar Germany gradually transformed. After an interim period of political chaos, lasting until roughly the mid-1920s, Germany changed from the brooding, maniacally ambitious nation of Friedrich Nietzsche and Richard Wagner into the cheerful, rambunctious country characterized by Kurt Weill and Bertolt Brecht's *The Threepenny Opera* and Thomas Mann's *Magic Mountain*.[28] The artistic, complex Jazz Age society of Germany in the late 1920s was not bound to turn into a fascist wasteland.

Five years after the Weimar Constitution was approved, and five days before Christmas in 1924, a young Austrian was released from prison in Landsberg, Germany, to a strange situation: He was forbidden by the government to speak in public. Adolf Hitler had been imprisoned for several months for leading a putsch—an attempt to overthrow the government—at the Buergerbraukeller, a beer hall in Munich. At the time, Hitler still led the nascent National Socialist

Democratic Party, a "weird assortment of misfits" that, when he had taken it over four years earlier in 1920, possessed seven marks and fifty pfennigs in its entire treasury.[29] Hitler had seen an opportunity in the porous, immature party, and he had rapidly moved to take over its propaganda apparatus. In the early months of that year, he created a twenty-five point platform that relentlessly curried favor with the masses—the workers and the peasants—who composed the bulk of German society and were the key to political power.

The crazy-quilt ideology ran a wide gamut, from point 11, which would abolish any income not derived from labor, to point 12, which would nationalize trusts, to point 18, which would impose the death penalty on profiteers.[30] In his mad manifesto, *Mein Kampf,* Hitler described the pseudo-democratic platform: "On February 24, 1920, the first great public demonstration of our young movement took place." He recounted the scene with relish: "In the Festival of the Munich Hofbräuhaus the twenty-five theses of the new party's program were submitted to a crowd of almost two thousand and every single point was accepted amid jubilant approval." Writing from prison, Hitler remembered with evident pleasure how he increased the popularity of the Nazi Party's platform: "With this the first guiding principles and directives were issued for a struggle which would do away with a veritable mass of old traditional conceptions and opinions and with unclear, yes, harmful, aims."[31]

Four years later, after Hitler was released, he followed the plan laid out in the inaugural Nazi Party doctrine. He hewed closely to the people, exhorting them from dispassion to ecstasy, all in the service of his personal ambition and grotesque ideology. However, he had difficulty gaining traction. The Nazi Party's vote had fallen from nearly two million in May 1924 to less than one million in December 1924, and the party was on the verge of collapsing.[32] Yet despite the party's flagging fortunes, Hitler still perceived political opportunity in the people themselves. After the Beer Hall Putsch, he had resolved to pursue only constitutional power. "Instead of working to achieve our power by armed coup," he said, "we shall have to hold our noses and enter the Reichstag against the opposition deputies. If outvoting them takes longer than outshooting them, at least the result will be guaranteed by their own constitution. Sooner or later we shall have a majority, and after that—Germany."[33] Despite these ambitions, the mid-1920s were lean years for the Nazi Party. William Shirer wrote that, "One scarcely heard of Hitler or the party except as butts of jokes. . . ."[34] In 1928, the Nazi Party received only 810,000 votes out of 31 million that were cast. The prime minister of Bavaria even lifted the region's ban on the party, telling a newspaper, in language startlingly reminiscent of Plato, "The wild beast is checked. We can afford to loosen the chain."[35]

The celebration was premature. Everything soon changed at a breathtaking pace, in large part because of how ordinary Germans responded to a sudden wave of economic distress. In 1929, the American stock market crashed, plunging Germany into immediate economic turmoil. Hitler quickly responded, tailoring the Nazi Party's platform to address the concerns of millions. The new platform refused to pay reparations to the Allied Powers, repudiated the much-despised Versailles Treaty, promised to eliminate corruption, and pledged to provide every German with a job. The Nazis' populism was suddenly effective. In 1930, the party quickly improved its vote share from 200,000 to a stunning 6,409,000. It had become the second largest party in Parliament.[36] Over the coming years, the German people continued to reward Hitler for his demagoguery. Hitler's party "threw themselves into the campaign with more fanaticism and force than ever before."[37] On July 31, 1932, the Nazi Party received more than 13 million votes, winning 230 seats in Parliament and making it the largest party in the Reichstag.

From there, the demagogue's path was clear and unimpeded. On January 30, 1933, President von Hindenburg appointed Hitler chancellor. The first step of Hitler's plan was finished—his connection with the people had enabled him to join the legitimate government. Now he would overthrow it. The history that followed is well known. Hitler's henchmen staged the Reichstag Fire on February 27, allowing Hitler to arrest his political opponents on suspicions that they had plotted the attack and to consolidate his control over the army. From there, the ostensible democrat would establish, in the space of a few short years, a total dictatorship.

None of this should have been a surprise, because Hitler had told everyone that the masses were central to his political vision. He needed the people because he wanted to subvert the fledgling democracy of Weimar Germany and install himself as a supreme leader—a plan painstakingly detailed in *Mein Kampf.* In his manifesto, he explained clearly that mastering the masses was the path to the revolutionary political power he sought: "An agitator who demonstrates the ability to transmit an idea to the broad masses must always be a psychologist, even if he were only a demagogue. Then he will still be more suited for leadership than the unworldly theoretician, who is ignorant of people. *For leading means: being able to move masses.*"[38] The German people were the linchpin of Hitler's quest for legitimate domestic political power, dictatorship, and world domination. He mocked the "unworldly theoretician" for not understanding the masses; only a "psychologist" (the term Hitler preferred for himself, rather than being "only a demagogue") could move the masses, nations, and the world.

Hitler's opportunity came because the German people were not committed to constitutionalism and the rule of law over other, more immediate satisfactions—including a vengeful response to the punitive reparations imposed by the Allied Powers, the perceived internal menace of Jews, and the need for the German nation to rise again. As the political scientist Daniel Goldhagen observed in his popular 1996 book, *Hitler's Willing Executioners,* something within the people actually drove the rise of Hitler: culture. After considering a variety of hypotheses to explain how ordinary Germans could be so complicit in assisting—indeed, could take action to explore and promote— Hitler and the genocide of Jews, Goldhagen arrives at a simple and unsettling conclusion: the massacre stage of the cycle of regimes was enabled by cultural factors rooted in the hearts and minds of ordinary Germans:

> The one explanation adequate to these tasks holds that a demonological anti-Semitism, of the virulent racial variety, was the common structure of the perpetrators' cognition and that of German society in general. The German perpetrators, in this view, were assenting mass executioners, men and women who, true to their own eliminationist antisemitic beliefs, faithful to their cultural antisemitic credo, considered the slaughter to be just.[39]

Culture is difficult to describe, precisely because it is ubiquitous. Indeed, "to be an anti-Semite in Hitler's Germany was so commonplace as to go practically unnoticed."[40] But like oxygen, this invisible substance fed the fire of Nazism.

Enabled by culture, anger against the Allies, and economic distress, ordinary Germans were more than willing to hand over their Weimar freedoms to the demagogue. A documentary interviewing Nazi Party members several decades after the fall of Hitler emphasizes the point. "I once paid four billion Reichsmark for a sausage and bread. It really was a collapse," said Emil Klein, a Nazi Party member from 1921 to 1945. "People said, 'It can't go on like this.' Then the debate began for the need for a strong man. And the call for a strong man got louder and louder. Because democracy achieved nothing."[41] In the words of one German scholar, "A less divided society, and one with a more expansive commitment to democratic principles, could have made the constitution work."[42] Ordinary Germans were revolting against democracy itself and its perceived economic failures, and they were clamoring for a demagogue. Hitler and the Nazis, after all, were openly campaigning against the Weimar system. Germans, many of them resentful of the modern constitution simply because it had been imposed on them, were handing over their democratic rights to a man they knew would be a strongman and most likely a tyrant. As central as Hitler was to creating the Third Reich, it was the people who enabled and supported his ascent to power.

A PHILOSOPHER-KING?

And there is a law of Destiny, that the soul which attains any vision of truth in company with a god is preserved from harm until the next period, and if attaining always is always unharmed.[43]

—Plato, *Phaedrus*

So far, we have explored the stories of four great thinkers who grappled with the personal costs of democracy's dilemma—Plato, Aristotle, Thomas Jefferson, and Alexis de Tocqueville. Each sought to come up with an answer to the demagogue problem, but they arrived at dramatically different conclusions. On one side of the divide is Plato, who thought the answer lay in an elite metaphysics that would disregard the role of practical experience and common wisdom in stopping the cycle of regimes. On the other side are Aristotle, who believed most of the people can be trusted most of the time; Jefferson, who thought the people, rather than elites, needed to be empowered with a radical sense of responsibility for the future of the republic; and de Tocqueville, who understood that the extraordinary accomplishment of America's constitutional culture provided the ultimate bulwark against homegrown demagogues. The ideas of Leo Strauss, our fifth character, played a critical role in the exertion of American power in the last quarter of the twentieth century and the first years of the twenty-first. Strauss joined Plato on the wrong side of the democracy divide, repeating the great philosopher's political goals and replicating his errors.

Strauss was born in 1899 in a rural town north of Frankfurt in Germany to a Jewish family that observed religious rituals, but which he described as having "very little Jewish knowledge."[44] As a teenager, Strauss was an intellectual, but not particularly ambitious. He described to one interviewer his ultimate goal, formed when he was sixteen: to "spend my life reading Plato and breeding rabbits while earning out my living as a rural postmaster."[45] He pursued Plato rather than the rabbits, receiving a Ph.D. at the young age of twenty-two in Hamburg.

Strauss continued his post-doctoral work in the towns of Freiburg and Marburg, where he first met the great philosopher Martin Heidegger. At the time, Heidegger was just beginning his masterwork, *Being in Time*, and was about a decade away from his own seduction by Adolf Hitler and Nazism. In 1925, Strauss, fascinated by his own ethnic and religious ancestry as a Jew, moved from the countryside to Berlin to work at the German Academy of Jewish Research. In 1931, as the Nazis were about to rise to power and as Hitler began to persecute the Jews, Strauss received a rare grant from the Rockefeller Foundation to perform research in France and England.[46]

Strauss used his time in France and England not just to perform academic research, but to continue trying to help European

Jewry—joining and leading the nascent Zionist movement. When Strauss's fellowship money ran out, he experienced an agonizing moment. Upon hearing the horrible stories of anti-Semitic violence in his home country, Strauss decided he could not return to now-Nazi Germany. So, like so many other Jews, he escaped across the ocean into the arms of the New World.[47]

Strauss arrived on the busy streets of Manhattan with a rare academic position; he began teaching American students at the New School for Social Research.[48] He became an American citizen in 1944, the year before the war ended and the Nazis were defeated.[49] Strauss remained in New York for about fifteen years, studying classical political philosophy and gradually gaining admirers and even adherents. He was then recruited west, to Chicago, where from 1948 until the 1960s he would teach hundreds of students enrolled in the University of Chicago's famously conservative Committee on Social Thought. Strauss returned to Germany only once—in 1954. It was to deliver a lecture on Socrates.[50]

Democracy's demagogue problem played a heavy role in Strauss's thinking, and he threaded a passionate anti-Hitler sentiment through otherwise dry and carefully worded narrations of philosophical texts. Strauss's biographers, from the most critical to the most sympathetic, have recognized that the decline of Weimar Germany was the most impactful event on Strauss's life. Shadia Drury, a professor of political theory and one of Strauss's harshest critics from the left, still credits Strauss with a political theory responsive to the demagogue problem, "The scenario described by Plato, whereby democracy gives way to tyranny, mirrors the scenario where Weimar sets the licentious stage for Hitler to emerge victorious," she writes. "Strauss understood both Weimar and America in terms of Plato's analysis of how democracy gives way to tyranny."[51] Two defenders of Strauss, writing from the right, agree: "[Strauss's] experience as a young Jew in Weimar Germany had led him to doubt the viability of liberal democracy—both in Germany specifically, and more generally—as it was defended on the basis of the principles of the Enlightenment."[52]

The demagogue lurked between the lines of even the most seemingly neutral parts of Strauss's writing. For instance, in harshly condemning the sociologist Max Weber's argument for a "value-free" social science, Strauss wrote, "To see this more clearly and to see at the same time why Weber could conceal from himself the nihilistic consequence of his doctrine of values, we have to follow his thought step by step." Strauss saw the path as so dangerous because of his own experience with democracy's demagogue problem: "In following this movement toward its end we shall inevitably reach a point beyond which the scene is darkened by the shadow of Hitler."[53]

There is a distinct fury here at nihilism, which Strauss held at least partly responsible for Hitler's seizure of the Weimar Republic. But notably, Strauss concentrated more on Hitler than on the German people. Much later, in 1979, Strauss wrote of Heidegger, "Heidegger, who surpasses in speculative intelligence all his contemporaries and is at the same time intellectually the counterpart of what Hitler was politically, attempts to go a way not yet trodden by anyone."[54] Demolishing inherited ways of thinking so radically—with the force and totality that implied—was, for Strauss, the philosophical equivalent of Hitler's political radicalism. That his mind leaped to Hitler for an example speaks volumes about the etiology of Strauss's own worldview, built around and against democracy's dilemma.

Strauss also blamed his professional home—the academy and the institutions of political science—for their impotence against the demagogue. In a book on the Greek philosopher Xenophon's little-read essay *Hiero or Tyrannicus,* Strauss condemned contemporary political theory for ignoring the dangers of Nazism: "[W]hen we were brought face to face with tyranny—with a kind of tyranny that surpassed the boldest imagination of the most powerful thinkers of the past—our political science failed to recognize it." Importantly, Strauss thought Plato had discovered the correct answer and blamed his contemporaries for their ignorance: "It is not surprising then that many of our contemporaries, disappointed or repelled by present-day analyses of present-day tyranny, were relieved when they rediscovered the pages in which Plato and other classical thinkers seemed to have interpreted for us the horrors of the twentieth century."[55]

———————

Strauss can be very difficult to read. But the difficulty is central to understanding his approach. His obscurantism infuriates his critics, but his followers find the mystical, incantatory quality of his writing intoxicating, in the same sense that Plato described the pursuit of truth. This only enhanced his magnetism to the cult-like following that surrounded Strauss at the University of Chicago. Anne Norton, a former Strauss student and prominent critic, describes the group of Strauss students and aficionados who gathered around Allan Bloom, a Strauss protégé who later mentored a preeminent policymaker and architect of the 2003 Iraq War, Paul Wolfowitz:

> Secrets entail a bond. The students of Bloom were bound together by what they refused to acknowledge in public, by what they would not say there but said readily in private and among themselves. The secret was a bond not because it was held silently but because it was revealed privately and only to a few. The hidden word binds a sect of people to one another. This is, I suspect, what animates both secrets and the rumors of secrets among the Straussians.[56]

As with Plato, the form and the content in Strauss can interweave, inculcating in the reader, and in his followers, a quasi-religious fervor—either you understand or you don't.[57]

Strauss's foes view him as the ultimate manifestation of his famous thesis in a book called *Persecution and the Art of Writing*—that writers who have strong political opinions in times when they might be persecuted for these very opinions often hide their political arguments through "esoteric" techniques.[58] These critics find Strauss's dense prose a thicket of hidden intent. They spend a lot of energy ferreting out the hidden despotism in the brambles of Strauss's dense analyses of Plato, Maimonides, and Aristophanes.

Strauss's defenders respond just as forcefully. They argue that, aside from a certain patriotic, pro-market philosophy that was very much at the surface of his writing, Strauss had no real political agenda. He therefore shouldn't be connected, at least in any direct way, to current political events. Francis Fukuyama (hardly himself a neutral observer, as I discuss below) writes, "More nonsense has been written about Leo Strauss and the Iraq war than on virtually any other subject. . . . If you were to ask Dick Cheney, Donald Rumsfeld, or President Bush himself to explain who Leo Strauss was, you would probably draw blank stares."[59]

But political theory's impact on history is such that we rarely cite the thinkers who most directly impact us, even though their ideas are often given form through the actions of ordinary political actors. Many of the citizens who reacted against F.D.R.'s court-packing plan probably did not have Jefferson in mind; the journalists who criticized McCarthy or MacArthur were not consciously citing de Tocqueville.[60] Strauss's ideas were important precisely *because* a very small number of people were taken in by their intricacy and intensity; studied them obsessively; absorbed them; propagated them in the intellectual framework that itself was often between the lines of articles and essays circulated to a small, but influential, readership; and, often enough, put them into play when they themselves, or their students, mentees, and disciples took up power in the Reagan and the second Bush administrations.

Many of Strauss's students, and students of theirs, went on to shape and direct American domestic and foreign policy in the latter half of the twentieth century. A partial list of people who may either be considered "Straussians" in that they were students of Strauss himself or of his students (like Allan Bloom), or were explicit expositors of Strauss's views would include Paul Wolfowitz, deputy secretary of defense in the George W. Bush administration; Douglas Feith, undersecretary of defense in the same administration; William Kristol, former chief of staff to Vice President Dan Quayle and founder of *The Weekly Standard;* Robert Kagan, a co-founder of the Project for a New American Century and prominent author; Gary Schmitt of the American Enterprise Institute, another co-founder of the Project for a New American Century; Abram Shulsky, head of the Pentagon's Office of

Special Plans leading up to the Iraq War; Charles Krauthammer, a prominent columnist at the *Washington Post;* Benjamin Wattenberg, a PBS commentator at the American Enterprise Institute; Richard Perle, chairman of the Defense Policy Board Advisory Committee during George W. Bush's presidency; Zalmay Khalilzad, George W. Bush's ambassador to the United Nations; and Alan Keyes, a commentator and perennial presidential candidate.[61]

After a generation of producing scores of articles and essays in journals like *Commentary* and *The Public Interest* in the 1960s and 1970s, the neoconservatives enjoyed two eras of political dominance. The first was in the Reagan administration, when they filled the apparent intellectual vacuum in the American left against the Soviet threat, converting a conservative administration into an activist and idealistic neoconservative one. The promotion of democracy first became a priority for the neoconservatives during Reagan's administration, when the National Endowment for Democracy was founded.

The movement retreated during the pragmatic and cautious administration of George H. W. Bush, who thought Reagan's idealistic ambitions imperiled America's moral and material assets. As Derek Chollet and James Goldgeier recount in *America Between the Wars,* democracy again became a major American goal during the administration of Bill Clinton. Clinton's aides saw democracy as so central to their foreign policy that they even sought to place it as the center of a new, George Kennan–esque doctrine of "democratic enlargement." Yet *realpolitik* challenges on the ground in places like Somalia and Bosnia set back the democratic movement during the latter years of the Clinton administration.[62] The movement found its third governmental home in the administration of George W. Bush—particularly after the president and Vice President Dick Cheney reacted to 9/11 as a time for the broad exertion of American might and a chance to remake the world in America's image. This "unipolar moment" was the opportunity Strauss's followers had been waiting for.

Some neoconservatives resist owning up to Strauss's influence. Wolfowitz, for instance, has energetically dismissed Strauss's influence on his thought. "I mean I took two terrific courses from Leo Strauss as a graduate student," he has said. "One was on Montesquieu's spirit of the laws, which did help me understand our Constitution better.

And one was on Plato's laws. The idea that this has anything to do with U.S. foreign policy is just laughable."[63] But power does not need to be exerted directly for it to be power. In Saul Bellow's *Ravelstein,* a fictional account of the life of Allan Bloom, Wolfowitz appears as a minor fictional character, Phil Gorman, who as an assistant secretary of defense frequently calls his mentor with tidbits of news from inside the Beltway. Bellow writes about Gorman, "Ravelstein [the Bloom stand-in] had given his boys a good education, in these degraded times—'the fourth wave of modernity.' They could be trusted with classified information, the state secrets they naturally would *not* pass on to their teacher who had opened their eyes to 'Great Politics.' "[64]

We will probably never know the exact facts of the intellectual relationship between Wolfowitz and Bloom. But we can imagine Strauss's ideas flowing through these conversations like a faint but authoritative harmony, organizing thoughts, pace, and moments—just as a Mozart symphony replaying in the mind of an undergraduate studying in a dark library can subtly influence the way she interprets the stacks of textbooks surrounding her.

―――――――

Strauss responded to Hitler with a Platonism of his own. Strauss believed that virtue, rather than freedom, should be the goal of America and the world. But he thought the linkage between virtue and greatness was authority—philosophy had to run through the circuitry of power to achieve greatness, which would necessarily involve powerful men, the type of people the neoconservatives wanted to be. This orphan of Weimar Germany wrote that the people must consent to be governed, but only that. He wrote, "The few wise cannot rule the many unwise by force. The unwise multitude must recognize the wise as wise and obey them freely because of their wisdom."[65] After they agreed to this bare-bones contract, they were free to go on about their lives, because they were being governed. This contrasts dramatically with the spiritual obligations and rewards for the layman recounted by de Tocqueville. However, Strauss sounded a cautionary note, and you can almost feel the disappointment in his voice when he wrote: "But the ability of the wise to persuade the unwise is extremely limited.

Therefore, it is extremely unlikely that the conditions required for the rule of the wise will ever be met."[66]

Much ink has been spilled about Strauss's elitism—the yearning for authority that limns the lines, which recalls the chaos he saw spreading around his lost fatherland.[67] Like Plato, he condemned the people for their ignorance and thought their failures could be corrected only by a superior class—in Strauss's case, made up of "gentlemen," rather than Guardians. Eerily, Strauss viewed the demagogue not as a result of the people, but simply as a natural force filling a vacuum of authority. The demagogue arises because no wise man who can command the loyalty of the masses can be found. "What is more likely to happen is that an unwise man, appealing to the natural right of wisdom and catering to the lowest desires of the many, will persuade the multitude of his right: the prospects for tyranny are brighter than those for rule of the wise." Against this dark vision of an "unwise man," much like Plato's demagogue who has seen only the eighth order of truth in the heavens, Strauss described how the people, misled, abandon wisdom in politics: "This being the case, the natural right of the wise must be questioned, and the indispensable requirement for wisdom with the requirement for consent."[68]

In Strauss's vision, these inevitable events meant that in the future a wise elite would need to force down the masses—the progeny of the people who failed him so miserably at home in Germany. Ordinary people barely figure in this account of politics. Recall Aristotle's argument that we should look to the collective judgment of the people for wisdom because "the many are better judges than a single man of music and poetry; for some understand one part, and some another, and among them they understand the whole."[69] Strauss would have none of this. Discussing Rousseau's concept of the "general will," in which a city thinks and acts together, he wrote, "The absorption of natural right by the positive law of a properly qualified democracy would be defensible if there were a guaranty that the general will—and this means, for all practical purposes, the will of the legal majority—could not err."[70] Strauss's logic built momentously, in an incantatory vault to the condemnation of democracy itself. Democracy was "defensible," he wrote, only "if the 'general will' 'could not err.'" But no: "The general will or the will of the people never errs insofar as it always wills the good of the people, but the people do not always see the good of the people. The general will is therefore in need of enlightenment."[71] The people do not even understand what's good for them, and they never will. They must therefore be controlled.

Thus, in a fell swoop, Strauss removed political power from the people and placed them under an overarching power. His solution was a Platonic conception of democracy in which the people are disciplined by the heavy hand of an elite who knows what's best for them: "Both the people as a whole and the individuals are then equally in need of a guide; the people must be taught to know what it wills, and the individual, who as a natural being is concerned exclusively with his private good, must be transformed into a citizen who unhesitatingly prefers the common good to his private good," he wrote. Note that neither the people nor the citizenry are capable of wisdom on their own—they must "be taught" or outright "transformed." How would this happen? Through wise elites, like Strauss himself (or Plato's Guardians): "The solution of this twofold problem is supplied by the legislator," Strauss explained, "or the father of a nation, i.e., by a man of superior intelligence who, by ascribing divine origin to a code which he has devised or by honoring the gods with his own wisdom, both convinces the people of the goodness of the laws which he submits to a vote and transforms the individual from a natural being into a citizen."[72]

Strauss has been attacked by his many detractors for an idealization of authority,[73] and rightly so. You can see here how hopefully he imagined a democracy shepherded by a "father of a nation" who is a "man of superior intelligence." The alchemy that occurs, when men are transformed from "natural beings" into the vaunted "citizens," only gilds the elect.

The fact is that Strauss just did not like democracy very much. Describing Socrates' views in the *Republic*, he said "democracy is not designed for inducing the nonphilosophers to attempt to become as good as they possibly can," and scoffed, "for the end of democracy is not virtue but freedom, i.e., the freedom to live either nobly or basely according to one's liking."[74] This was the decadent chaos he remembered from Weimar Germany: the pornography and jazz, the clothes and the inattention to the political manifestations of creeping anti-Semitism. These concerns far outweighed, for him, our modern fetish with equality. Elsewhere, Strauss dismissed the modern liberal democratic notion that "every man has the right to political freedom, to being a member of the sovereign, by virtue of the dignity which every man has as man—the dignity of a moral being."[75] Incredibly, this would mean a level playing field, politically, for people of all kinds and qualities. His writing pulsed with dismay: "Accordingly, the uneducated could even appear to have an advantage over the educated. . . ."[76] To Strauss, the fusion of equality, moral stature, and political power led directly to the horrors of the demagogue-led French Revolution, based on the "assertion that virtue is the principle of democracy and only of democracy. One conclusion from this assertion was Jacobin terror which punished not only actions and speeches but intentions as well."[77] The "terror" colored Strauss's intellectual concerns here as powerfully as Hitler's Nazism. His political theory, in many ways, was a desperate attempt to save people from themselves.

Nazi Germany clearly seems responsible for the harshness between the lines in Strauss's writing, which several commentators have attributed even more directly to Carl Schmitt—a philosopher who became a strong advocate of Nazism but whose writing about the interconnections between force, violence, enemy-and-friend distinctions, and ordinary politics resonates today.[78] In passages like the following, however, it's as easy to credit Hitler as Schmitt for driving Strauss's logic: "All violence applied to a being makes that being do something which goes against its grain, i.e., against its nature," Strauss observed, seemingly arguing against violence. But he then, like Polybius and Plato millennia before, buckled to what he saw as the ineluctable logic of history. "But the city stands or falls by violence, compulsion, or coercion. There is, then, no essential difference between political rule and the rule of a master over his slaves."[79]

This was a startling and not at all intuitive account of life in "the city"; the analogy of government to a slave-master is flatly preposterous. Yet we're left to wonder about the twisted influence of the German experience on Strauss's mind. He watched as a particular exercise in political power ran tragically awry, pulling into its vortex major intellects like Heidegger and Schmitt. Schmitt's admiration of the "political"—the force that dominates all human interactions and that, he argued, one must comprehend and master if one is to move capably in the political world—opened the door to his own Nazism. In writing that "the city stands or falls by violence, compulsion, or coercion," Strauss himself echoed the demagogue, though he certainly would have rejected this view. If political vision, and the quest to implement one's ideas, necessarily involves violence, then people can become a means to an end, rather than the ends themselves. Rather than escaping the cycle of regimes, then, Strauss risked repeating it.

Despite the ingredients of authoritarianism and violence in Strauss's recipe for saving democracy, it's worth noting that Strauss also attacked the role of idealism and even theory in politics. He wrote, "The intrusion of theory into politics is likely to have an unsettling and inflaming effect. No actual social order is perfect."[80] Strauss was fascinated by the conservative British philosopher and politician Edmund Burke, who had an opposite reaction from de Tocqueville to the French Revolution. Whereas de Tocqueville wanted to build up democracy with a people who shared strong and deep constitutional values, Burke essentially wanted to jettison the democratic project for aristocracy—a nation run by elites. Strauss approved: "[I]n judging the political leaders whom [Burke] opposed in the two major important actions of his life, he traced their lack of prudence less to passion than to the intrusion of the spirit of theory into the field of politics."[81] Why was "the spirit of theory" so dangerous for Burke as well as for Strauss? The words should ring eerily today in the ears of the neoconservatives who supposedly were channeling Leo Strauss in the planning and execution of the Iraq War: "The science of constructing a commonwealth, or renovating it, or reforming it," Strauss wrote, is an "experimental science, not to be taught *a priori*."[82]

Strauss would have been horrified by the utopian aspect of plans to construct a democracy from scratch in Iraq. He *specifically* argued that the "science of constructing a commonwealth" is "not to be taught *a priori*." It is, rather, "experimental"—the kind of science where you learn and grow. Strauss's authoritarian leanings still had their own bounds. He was more interested in the authoritarian element in Plato than the elaborate inner workings of the metaphysical infrastructure.

He had seen the danger of worshiping perfect abstractions in Hitler's Germany. Even though he hated the decadence and disorder of mass politics, he hated Nazi Germany more.

It took a few decades and a political movement freed by America's sole superpower status to corrupt Strauss's teachings beyond even his wildest imaginings. By then, it was too late for experiment. For a few shining moments, we entered the realm of pure ideas. But in that rarefied air, Plato's noble steed would stumble, the ignoble steed buck, and the chariot plummet. In the end, the whole glorious enterprise crashed back into the earth—where it belonged all along.

THE NEOCONSERVATIVE *PÈRE ET FILS*

It is the fundamental fallacy of American foreign policy to believe, in face of the evidence, that all peoples, everywhere, are immediately "entitled" to a liberal constitutional government— and a thoroughly democratic one at that.[83]

—Irving Kristol, 1978

After Saddam Hussein has been defeated and Iraq occupied, installing a decent and democratic government in Baghdad should be a manageable task for the United States. But not according to some realists.[84]

—Lawrence F. Kaplan and William Kristol, 2003

MUCH HAS BEEN MADE OF THE EVOLUTION IN CONSERVATIVE POLITICS from George H. W. Bush to his son, George W. Bush. In this narrative, made especially popular by the *New York Times* columnist Maureen Dowd,[85] the son rebelled recklessly against the father's cautious foreign policy, attempting to replace what he saw as the effete failures of his father's policy with a muscular, brash politics that was all his own. The Iraq War that began in 2003 plays a prominent role in this story. George H. W. Bush made the decision not to invade Baghdad and replace Saddam Hussein because of the enormous cost of running a country from afar; his son made exactly the opposite decision, deciding to shoulder that burden. We can tell a similar story about the evolution from Irving Kristol to his son Bill Kristol and about the replacement of the "neoconservative" by the "neocon."

The central figure in the movement known as neoconservatism was Irving Kristol, a self-fashioned intellectual who found Stalinism as horrible as Strauss found Nazism, yet who also stopped shy of endorsing the forcible installation of democracy. Irving Kristol's parents were Eastern Europeans who arrived in America in the 1890s. His father was a garment worker and later a clothing subcontractor; his mother gave birth to Irving in Brooklyn in 1920. Irving enrolled at CCNY, the City College of New York, when he was sixteen years old. Instead of paying much attention to classes or his professors, however, he dove into the roiling sea of extempore debate among the students.

Kristol combined wryness and tremendous self-confidence with a gregarious, common-man intellectuality familiar to anyone who has lived in New York City. The 1930s were a fervent time to be a student at CCNY, but they were especially exciting to the curious, charismatic young Irving. Fascism was taking hold in Italy and communism was surging in the Soviet Union. Germany had turned to the Nazis. Kristol recalled those days vividly. He lovingly described the lunchroom as "an especially slummy and smelly place." Students ate cheap, home-made, satiating lunches: "hard-boiled egg sandwiches, cream-cheese sandwiches, peanut-butter sandwiches, once in a while a chicken sandwich."[86] A dozen alcoves circled the central lunchroom aisle. In Kristol's words, "Around this central area there was a fairly wide and high-ceilinged aisle; and bordering the aisle, under large windows with small panes of glass that kept out as much light as they let in, were the alcoves—semicircular (or were they rectangular?), each with a bench fitted along the wall and a low, long refectory table in the middle."[87] Alcove No. 1 teemed with socialist students who hated and feared Stalin's method in the USSR. It was bordered by Alcove No. 2, which housed *pro*-Stalinist socialists.

The sometimes cheerful, sometimes angry clashes among students who were trying to decide where the world should go at this momentous period launched the intellectual movement that would grip America's foreign policy seventy years later, after the Soviet Union and after the Cold War. But the beginnings were innocent. Kristol wrote, "The first alcove on the right, as you entered the lunchroom, was Alcove No. 1, and this soon became most of what City College meant to me." He described the milieu as sometimes playful, sometimes intense: "It was there one ate lunch, played ping-pong (sometimes with a net, sometimes without), passed the time of day between and after classes, argued incessantly, and generally devoted oneself to solving the ultimate problems of the human race. The penultimate problems we figured could be left for our declining years, after we had graduated."[88]

An astonishing pool of raw talent somehow ended up in Alcove No. 1, the intellectual hothouse where the seed of neoconservatism first germinated. The list of the students sharing sandwiches in Alcove No. 1 included the Stanford sociologist Seymour Martin Lipset, "a kind of intellectual bumblebee," the Harvard sociologist Daniel Bell, who had a "kind of amused fondness for sectarian dialectics," the Harvard literary critic Nathan Glazer, the Berkeley political scientist Philip Selznick, and Melvin Lasky, the editor of *Encounter,* where Kristol would go on to publish many of his seminal essays.[89]

The denizens of Alcove No. 1 were less popular than the *au courant* socialists in Alcove No. 2 and were therefore, by nature and by experience, contrarians. Kristol recalls that they had only thirty "regulars" and could gather an audience of fifty to one hundred, if they were lucky.[90] Alcove No. 2, by contrast, could mobilize, when it tried, four or five hundred students out of CCNY's 20,000 students to a rally or a protest. These students had sympathy with Josef Stalin and, Kristol recalls, would go to lengths to justify his show trials and his purges. He found them a "dreary bunch" filled with "sectarian snobbery." The worst was their attempt to justify the "self-glorification of Josef Stalin."[91]

Over the decades, the intellectual movement that took root in Alcove No. 1 blossomed into neoconservatism. Kristol's project, as he described it later, was to re-imagine a "new" conservatism. Conservatism, historically speaking, sought to defer to and conserve inherited values from the past. It was skeptical about grand "liberal" projects. But it was also musty and inert, annoyingly avoiding grand goals and constantly lagging behind the times. With so much going on in the world—so much to defy—Kristol felt that a reinvigorated conservatism, one that could take on projects and move forward in the world, was needed. As he wrote about the neoconservatism that emerged in the 1960s and 1970s, "What is 'neo' ('new') about this conservatism is that it is resolutely free of nostalgia. It, too, claims the future—and it is this claim, more than anything else, that drives its critics on the Left into something approaching a frenzy of denunciation."[92]

Given his profound connection with what would be launched in the early twenty-first century under the name of "neocons," it's very important to be clear about one thing: Kristol's movement did not begin in response to a problem of *democracy*. It was a response instead to *totalitarianism*. The original contrarians in Alcove No. 1 were soldered together by the heat of their certainty, their defiance, and their moral fervor. Neoconservatism began in a Herculean effort to steer America away from the shoals of Stalinist corruption, totalitarianism, and moral decay—the movement cannot really be understood any other way. The temper and goals of the movement were therefore defined and shaped in contrast to the ideological and political movement of Stalinism. Democracy and problems of the masses, while they were important to the neoconservative project as elements of the human condition, were not driving factors in its creation. This is very different from the projects of figures as diverse as Plato, Alexis de Tocqueville, Leo Strauss, and, as we will see, Hannah Arendt. For them, democracy's paradox was so powerful that you could shape a life around it—so powerful that you always kept democracy's ancient enemy somewhere in the back of your thoughts.

Perhaps this is why Irving Kristol's political theory featured a certain balance and modesty. The Iraq War is sometimes alleged to have originated in his ideology. Yet, when you actually read what he wrote, Kristol presents a very different perspective on democracy than one might otherwise think. In 1978, he wrote, "It is the fundamental fallacy of American foreign policy to believe, in face of the evidence, that all peoples, everywhere, are immediately 'entitled' to a liberal constitutional government—and a thoroughly democratic one at that."[93] He blamed "Wilsonian slogans" introduced after World War I for the fact that "American foreign policy began to disregard the obvious for the sake of the quixotic pursuit of impossible ideals."[94] Kristol even went so far as to borrow directly from the *realpolitik* playbook of a Henry

Kissinger or Hans Morgenthau, albeit with typical coyness. "Is it not a betrayal of the democratic idea to imply that some dictatorships are better than others—that some dictatorships may claim a degree of political legitimacy that even liberal democrats ought to respect?" he asked rhetorically. "We really do not know how to cope with such a question."[95]

Elsewhere, Kristol moved from a flirtatious embrace of dictators abroad to a sophisticated understanding of the causes of successful democracy at home, with a typically neoconservative shudder at the state of contemporary morality. In a lecture he gave at New York University in 1970, when the protest against the Vietnam War was at a fever pitch and people were rioting in the streets, Kristol looked to America's constitutional accomplishments as a baseline for evaluating the riots. He pronounced that "moral earnestness and intellectual sobriety" were the "elements . . . most wanted in a democracy."[96] And, in arguing for a return to the "republican morality" that the Founding Fathers envisioned, Kristol invoked precisely the "character of the people," in contrast to "procedural and mechanical arrangements"[97]: "[W]hen one says that in a democracy the people are the ruling class," Kristol said, "one means that the character of the government and the destiny of the nation are in the longer run determined by the character of the people rather than of any particular class of people."[98]

Kristol's political activism was born in the shadow of Soviet communism, but he shaped his ambitions for America with an awareness of the dangers of overweening metaphysical ambitions and a belief that America's constitutionalism could light a path to the future. In other words, this purported father of the neocons and supposed begetter of Iraq saw a constitutional conscience as the heart of American democracy. This is important not because it tells us something about Kristol, but because it reveals the chasm between neoconservatism and the neocons while suggesting how the latter could go on to make such dreadful errors with democracy.

Irving's son, Bill Kristol, is an omnipresent and disarming presence in the American political world. He has a friendly, bemused demeanor, often mocking Republicans as much as Democrats, which can have a disarming effect on progressive critics. He regularly appears on the Sunday morning talk shows, usually on the strength of a couple of major mainstream *bona fides.* Having served as chief of staff to Vice President Dan Quayle during the 1980s, he speaks confidently on matters of practical politics and governance. As founder of the popular conservative magazine *The Weekly Standard,* Kristol can also serve as a standing journalist. In 2008, the *New York Times* made Kristol a regular columnist on its Op-Ed page, firmly installing him as a fixed star in America's political firmament.

But underneath all this, Bill Kristol is really an ideological heavy-weight—someone who sculpts the underlying ideas of the policy debate, pushes them into politics, and then launches them into American domestic and, especially, foreign policy. He's also the chairman of the Project for a New American Century, a group he founded in 1997 and dedicated to "a few fundamental propositions: that American leadership is good both for America and for the world; and that such leadership requires military strength, diplomatic energy and commitment to moral principle."[99]

These seemingly innocuous principles in fact provided a wellspring for a torrent of radical thought. In a book titled *The War Over Iraq* that he co-wrote with Lawrence Kaplan, published in 2003 by Encounter Press—the in-house press for conservatives edited by Melvin Lasky, his father's old alcove-mate—Bill Kristol argued that the United States should invade Iraq and establish a democracy there as a venture that would be "in accord with American principles."[100] The authors wrote that their book "offers a roadmap for a more hopeful future. The wisdom of regime change, the merits of promoting democracy, the desirability of American power and influence—these issues extend well beyond Iraq. So we dare to hope that this work will prove useful even after Baghdad is finally free."[101]

The sheer number of mistakes in this short book deserve quoting at length to convey how little the authors comprehended what would follow the invasion and how Iraq's new democracy would be challenged from within. They wrote: "According to one estimate, initially as many as 75,000 U.S. troops may be required to police the war's aftermath, at a cost of $16 billion a year. As other countries' forces arrive, and as Iraq rebuilds its economy and political system, that force could probably be drawn down to several thousand soldiers after a year or two."[102] As of this writing, the war has lasted for over five years. It initially required a steady force of about 130,000 troops, with a "surge" in 2007 and 2008 of an additional 30,000 troops. It has cost not $16 billion a year but almost that amount *per month*. And the Bush administration's own planning foresaw a "Korea-style" occupying force that could include 50,000 to 75,000 troops for the next ten years or more—not "several thousand" after a "year or two." The authors confidently asserted a stunning hypothesis: "After Saddam Hussein has been defeated and Iraq occupied, installing a decent and democratic government in Baghdad should be a manageable task for the United States."[103] In asserting that "installing" the democracy would be "manageable," the authors argued that the nature of the Iraqi people would make democracy easier, rather than harder. In trying to rebut one critic's charge that democracy cannot successfully be imposed by military forces, the authors wrote, "Really? What about Japan, Germany, Austria, Italy, Grenada, the Dominican Republic and Panama?"[104]

Setting aside the mixing of apples and oranges (the first four countries were defeated in a world war, the fifth is a tiny, homogeneous country, and the last two literally banana republics), the authors continued: "Furthermore, Iraq, more perhaps than any other nation in the region, is ripe for democracy." What was their evidence? "[O]ne need look no further than northern Iraq, where, under an umbrella of American air patrols, the Iraqi opposition already presides over a thriving democracy. Iraq possesses some of the highest literacy rates in the region, an urbanized middle class, and other demographic measures that typically conduce to democracy."[105]

This was either sophistry or ignorance, but either way it was an appalling act of intellectual neglect regarding the people who would ultimately sustain any democracy in Iraq. "Northern Iraq" was not a fluid region whose practices one could foresee spreading easily to the rest of Iraq; it was already virtually a separate nation, often called Kurdistan, with a population independent from and hostile to Saddam's Sunni Ba'athist regime. Yes, Iraq had certain indices of democracy. But it also had many other indices—chiefly, the harsh and enduring enmities between different ethnic groups, the prevalence of powerful clerics, the history of violence, and the relationship to Iran—that would naturally conduce to the cycle of regimes.

The authors argued, however, that an additional factor meant democracy would easily take hold. "Indeed, the exile umbrella group, the Iraqi National Congress, is already working on the shape of Baghdad's postwar government."[106] Here they betrayed their intellectual provenance. A whiff of Strauss's elitism hung over the idea of a constitution drafted by wealthy and sophisticated exiles such as Ahmed Chalabi and the other Iraqi National Congress members, not to mention the notion that they would return to a shower of garlands from their plebeian countrymen.

But the biggest error was the most astonishing. Kristol and Kaplan concluded that the war in Iraq would definitely increase America's power in the world. They argued that the "strategy of focusing on regime change to foster democracy" would help increase America's "security and economic interests."[107] With brio, they concluded: "For the United States, then, a straightforward argument from self-interest follows naturally: The more democratic the world becomes, the more likely it is to be congenial to America."[108]

Contrary to Kristol's and Kaplan's confident predictions, the effort to bring democracy to Iraq brought about instead a collapse in global public support for the United States. Since 2002, favorable ratings toward this country are lower in twenty-six of thirty-three countries for which trends are available, and people in nearly every country were less likely to support American-style democracy. In a poll published in 2007, a majority of respondents in every country surveyed except Israel, Ghana, Kenya, and Nigeria favored withdrawing troops from Iraq. The image of America "remains abysmal in most Muslim countries in the Middle East and Asia" and continues to fall among America's traditional allies.[109]

DEMOCRATIC DOMINION

In calling for democratic change in the Middle East, the neoconservatives had come full circle. In the late 1970s leading neoconservatives such as Jeane Kirkpatrick had passionately criticized the Carter administration for pushing the shah of Iran to make his regime more open and democratic. . . . Now, two decades later, the neoconservatives were proposing for the entire Middle East the same sort of democratic reforms they had once found objectionable when applied to the shah's Iran.[110]

—James Mann, *Rise of the Vulcans*

AT GEORGE W. BUSH'S SECOND INAUGURATION IN WASHINGTON, D.C., on January 20, 2005, the president announced one of the most expansive conceptions of American power in the history of our republic. When he took the podium on a bright, freezing day in Washington, Bush described a new foreign policy for America. "Across the generations we have proclaimed the imperative of self-government, because no one is fit to be a master, and no one deserves to be a slave," he said. He then hearkened back to the Founding Fathers, connecting the Framers with the present day: "Advancing these ideals is the mission that created our Nation. It is the honorable achievement of our fathers. Now it is the urgent requirement of our nation's security, and the calling of our time." The president completed with a ringing declaration. "So it is the policy of the United States," he said, "to seek and support the growth of democratic movements and institutions in every nation and culture, with the ultimate goal of ending tyranny in our world."[111]

Ending tyranny in our world. It was a Platonic ambition for a decidedly non-Platonic time. With this pronouncement, the brash Henry V–type president seemed to have discovered a cause suitable to his rebellious personality and what he judged to be the post-9/11 climate. The idealization of democracy came only after a series of accidents and historical events helped drive Bush to ambitions that, as an opponent of nation-building during his 2000 campaign, he couldn't himself have foreseen. The journalist Jacob Weisberg has divided the Bush presidency into six doctrines. The first Bush doctrine, "unipolar realism," was decidedly different from democracy installation; it was a commitment both to American power and to a skepticism about grand, idealistic projects that would last from March 2000 through September 10, 2001. The second was "With Us or Against Us," which went from 9/11 to May 31, 2002. The third, which Weisberg calls the "preemption doctrine," went from June 1, 2002, to November 5, 2003, thus including the first months of the Iraq War.

Democracy entered the picture only with the fourth doctrine—"Democracy in the Middle East"—which lasted from November 6, 2003, the day of a landmark speech by Bush about democracy promotion at the National Endowment of Democracy in Washington, D.C., to January 19, 2005, the day before Bush's second inaugural address. The fifth and penultimate version, Weisberg says, was "Freedom Everywhere," which went from January 20, 2005, to November 7, 2006. This policy was introduced in ringing terms in Bush's second inaugural speech.

The sixth and final stage of Bush's foreign policy, Weisberg argues, was "the absence of any functioning doctrine at all." The disarray of the final phase was created by the failures and conceptual errors of the prior two stages. When Bush's team sought first to spread democracy and then to spiritualize freedom as destiny, they did so in a way that ultimately undermined their goals. Democracy's demon was haunting the halls once again.[112]

In his November 6, 2003, speech at the National Endowment for Democracy, Bush pronounced a radical new vision of democratizing the world. The United States, he announced, "has adopted a new policy," which he described as "a forward strategy for freedom in the Middle East."[113] The speech's ambition was extraordinary:

> Sixty years of Western nations excusing and accommodating the lack of freedom in the Middle East did nothing to make us safe—because in the long run, stability cannot be purchased at the expense of liberty. As long as the Middle East remains a place where freedom does not flourish, it will remain a place of stagnation, resentment, and violence ready for export. . . . Therefore, the United States has adopted a new policy, a forward strategy of freedom in the Middle East. This strategy requires the same persistence and energy and idealism we have shown before. And it will yield the same results.[114]

In this historic passage, a torrent of action flowed from a single, intensely consequential word: "therefore." "Freedom does not flourish" in the

Middle East, Bush said, damaging our interests there. *Therefore,* we had a "new policy." He was not describing an experiment or a gradual approach. "Freedom," without any qualifications or even increments, would absolutely lead to an increase in our security.

We can see the influence of neocons like Bill Kristol here. How democracy would increase our security was not discussed or even really at issue, because the underlying equation of democracy = security = imperialism, was, like Plato's truth = beauty = justice, beyond reproach. As Weisberg puts it, "Here finally was the grand vision Bush had been looking for. Democratizing the Arab world was a clear, moral goal, the ambitious work of a consequential presidency. Like compassionate conservatism, it was a form of social evangelism, a mission inspired by faith but secular in application."[115] Just as Plato said that truth could be found only in the transcendental plane visible only to philosopher-kings, so democracy naturally became metaphysical to a group of leaders already high on their own idea of America.

In formulating his vision, Bush was strongly influenced by Natan Sharansky, a former Soviet Jewish dissident whose own life was a moral crusade for democracy. Sharansky was imprisoned by the Soviets and, upon release, immediately went to work on the cause of freeing Soviet Jewry. A tendentious but charismatic man who shuttled between Israeli and American colleagues to proselytize for democracy, he found a receptive audience in George W. Bush and the neocons. In the post-9/11 world, they were on the hunt for a foreign policy to match their own evangelical fervor and perfervid desire to tailor a national security response proportionate to the trauma of the Al-Qaeda attacks.

Sharansky's story, and his absolutism, suited perfectly. In a 2004 book titled *The Case for Democracy: The Power of Freedom to Overcome Tyranny and Terror,* Sharansky made the case against a world without "moral clarity": "[T]he principles that guided me as a dissident in the struggle against tyranny continue to guide me today. I believe that all people are capable of building a free society. I believe that all free societies will guarantee security and peace. And I believe that by linking international policy to building free societies, the free world can once again secure a better future for hundreds of millions of people around the world."[116] Like Plato and Strauss, Sharansky channeled his own frustrations with the failures of democracy into a set of ideas to fix the world and his own activism.

On the strength of these principles, Sharansky negotiated with leaders from Jimmy Carter to Ariel Sharon to promote democracy in the Middle East, even arguing that Israel had a duty to increase democracy among Palestinians. He was delighted when George W. Bush made democracy promotion a purported keystone of his Middle East strategy. Sharansky wrote, "The parallel between the president's words and my own ideas was so strong that a *Washington Post* writer questioned whether I had become one of Bush's speechwriters."[117]

Sharansky's story was powerful, his prose magnetic. But his passion created blind spots. Dismissing critics who try to change the question of "*how* democracy can best be established in a particular place" into an "erroneous assertion that democracy should never be established there at all," Sharansky wrote the following: "Of course, free elections can bring nondemocrats to power, as was the case in Nazi Germany in 1933. But what followed the Nazi ascension to power does not prove that democracy is dangerous." He explained: "It proves that democracy must *always* be protected. For it was not a democratic election that made Germany a threat to the world but rather the destruction of Germany's free society and the eventual suspension of its democracy."[118]

This reasoning completely elided the problem of the cycle of regimes and the responsibility of the people for ending it. Democracy, to Sharansky, had become something that needed to be "protected from" someone like Hitler. But he got the order of events wrong. True, it *is* much more difficult for citizens to oppose a demagogue once the demagogue has seized the state government and can launch a reign of oppression. This is what Sharansky meant when he wrote that the "destruction of Germany's free society" made Germany a threat to the world. But at this point the cycle of regimes has already turned, the demagogue has become a dictator, and Polybius's massacres are around the corner. What Sharansky neglected was the people's complicity in Hitler's rise. Hitler's rise to a dictatorship was enabled by a combination of ordinary Germans' rage and distress, Germany's democratic system, and the absence of a general constitutional conscience. In his rapture to the metaphysical power of democracy, Sharansky seemed to forget the people's fundamental role and responsibility for maintaining democracy. Such thinking, when employed by a powerful government more absorbed by the goal of quasi-empire than the cultivation of constitutionalism, can wreak havoc, as it did in Iraq.

———————

Most great political theory is formulated during times of revolution and turmoil. These human events concentrate the mind and raise the most profound problems for resolution. The original neoconservatives were trying to escape Stalinism, empower market liberalism, and create a "new conservatism" that would not be dominated and defined by the past but that could update itself, rewriting, in a sense, its DNA. Throughout all of this, the communist Soviet Union darkly loomed, ominous and puissant. The "neocons," on the other hand, were shaped by the Cold War, yes, but only in its imminent decline. They refused to update their ideology to a new world where the Soviet Union had collapsed, in part from the weight of its own internal contradictions.[119]

The contrast between the two eras can be seen everywhere in the evolution from neoconservative to neocon. One of the most influential sources for Reagan-era neoconservatism was Jeane Kirkpatrick's famous essay "Dictatorships and Double Standards," published in 1979 in *Commentary*. Kirkpatrick offered a bold and harshly pragmatic thesis of the Carter administration's purportedly dovish impulse to try to force all oppressive regimes to change their human rights practice. Kirkpatrick argued instead that the United States should draw a distinction between totalitarian systems like the one that prevailed in the Soviet Union and noncommunist dictatorships, which she asserted were open to positive social change that would ultimately redound to America's national security interests. In other words, while we should maintain the Cold War with the Soviet Union, we could work with (and thereby elect, not try to depose) dictators.[120] That argument was animated by anti-communism, not a pro-democracy sentiment. After the fall of the Soviet Union, Kirkpatrick unsurprisingly said that America should "give up the benefits of superpower status and become again an unusually successful open republic."[121] Old-style neoconservatives like Kirkpatrick were pilloried by the new post–Cold War neocons for, in the words of one commentator, "a reworked paleoconservatism dressed up in the language of realpolitik and unilateralism."[122]

And so it was that the basic tenets of neoconservatism, cut loose by the neocons from a material dialectic of ideas and combined with an unabashed nationalism, were freed to soar into the ether. America became destiny, the response to 9/11 became metaphysical and missionary, authority became idealized, the people were ignored, and democracy became a cause rather than an achievement. Amid the formulation of their cause, the neocons weren't actually even responding to democracy's demagogue problem; they had forgotten it even had one. They introduced democracy ungrounded in the people, and the demagogue problem was reborn.

There was one essential additional element in the neocon metaphysics of democracy: the idea of American empire. In the late 1980s and 1990s, neoconservatives sought to fuse their democracy promotion ideal with an ideal role for America as the only superpower in a post–Cold War world. The United States, through democracy, would become, in the words of the neocon columnist Ben Wattenberg, an "imperium of values."[123] This new quasi-imperial ambition entailed a distinct kind of unilateral domination. As one scholar explains, "Most neoconservatives were crusaders." These crusaders wanted a foreign policy that would fit into the gilded frame of a religious mission: "It was axiomatic for them that America needed a foreign policy mission that served its most expansive international visions. The United States was obliged to wage an economic, political, and military crusade for world democracy."[124] In the years after the fall of the Soviet Union, Joshua Muravchik, a leading neocon, published a book with the American Enterprise Institute titled *Exporting Democracy*, with the subtitle *Fulfilling America's Destiny*.[125] His goal, he wrote, was for a "Pax Americana unlike any previous peace, one of harmony, not of conquest." This ambition was downright Platonic; a perfect democracy would render a perfect world. Even though Muravchik envisioned a world where America's relative power would diminish as other nations copied our form of government, we would "stand triumphant for achieving by our model and our influence the visionary goal stamped by the founding fathers on the seal of the United States: *novus ordo seclorum,* a new order for the ages."[126]

The fusion of democracy, the "imperium" ideal, and "movement conservatism" began in the successful effort of the Reagan administration to push Ferdinand Marcos out of power in the Philippines in the mid-1980s, so that Corazin Aquino, who had been elected to replace Marcos, could take power. After months of shuttle diplomacy by people including Wolfowitz and his deputy, Lewis "Scooter" Libby (who would go on to become Dick Cheney's chief of staff during the Bush administration), Marcos was shipped out of the Philippines on an American Air Force plane.[127] The success of the effort effectively converted the promotion of democracy into a cause of the political right rather than the left.[128] During this period, Wolfowitz, then an assistant secretary of state, argued, "The best antidote to communism is democracy."[129] He was now willing "to forsake the status quo in pursuit of democratic ideals."[130]

After the fall of the Soviet Union and the end of the Cold War, these ambitions expanded to fill the vacuum, and the neoconservatives became neocons. Their intentions certainly were good; the neocons wanted a world of freedom, and they wanted a proud, safe, and strong America. The flaw was not in their motivation; it was, instead, in their idea and its execution. Where Strauss and the neoconservatives answered democracy's demagogue problem with a highly qualified political theory of nobility, elitism, and skepticism, the neocons shifted instead to a political theory of democratic determinism and a foreign policy of arrogance.

Contrary to those who suspect an esoteric, Straussian cabal of pulling the strings on our foreign policy from behind a curtain, neocon wizards were chanting their spells in plain view. Charles Krauthammer, for instance, is familiar to many because of his frequent television appearances. In print, he's a brilliant prose stylist, combining clipped, dry, devastating quips and phrases, an unyielding ideological passion, and severe logical analyses of his opponents' positions.

Krauthammer couldn't be further entrenched in the country's political establishment. He's a *Washington Post* columnist, a fixture in the commentariat circuit, and a Pulitzer Prize winner.[131] Yet he is also the expositor of a mystical theory of American power, a metaphysical brand of democracy, and a missionary sense of American dominion.

Raised in Canada, Krauthammer brings an outsider's passion to the analysis of politics. He first entered politics through a highly unusual avenue: professional psychiatry. He received an M.D. from Harvard Medical School in 1975 and practiced for the next thirteen years, specializing in diagnosing and researching bipolar manias.[132] Perhaps not coincidentally, he has a knack for making his opponents seem a bit crazy. Krauthammer quit medicine to join Jimmy Carter's administration in 1978. In 1980, he continued helping Democrats, working as a speechwriter for Vice President Walter Mondale. But when Carter and Mondale lost their bid for reelection, the disenchanted Krauthammer began drifting to the right. In 2006, the *Financial Times* said Krauthammer was the most influential commentator in America, adding "Krauthammer has influenced U.S. foreign policy for more than two decades."[133]

Much of the debate about what to do with American power took place in another Alcove No. 1, of sorts—in the neoconservative journals that few people ever read but where writers like Krauthammer make their strongest cases. It's remarkable how unabashed the neocons are when writing in these journals, as opposed to more popular venues. For example, in the 1990/1991 winter edition of the journal *Foreign Affairs,* which commands a small but mainstream audience of foreign policy professionals, academics, and general readers, Krauthammer wrote a now-famous article titled "The Unipolar Moment," in which he argued against the thesis that, after the Cold War and the fall of the Soviet Union, America's "unipolarity is unsustainable."[134] The last paragraph of his article—his peroration—rang clean and true, even to readers who might strongly disagree with him:

We are in for abnormal times. Our best hope for safety in such times, as in difficult times in the past, is in American strength and will—the strength and will to lead a unipolar world, unashamedly laying down the rules of world order and being prepared to enforce them. Compared to the task of defeating fascism and communism, averting chaos is a rather subtle call to greatness. It is not a great task we are any more eager to undertake than the great twilight struggle just concluded. But it is just as noble and just as necessary.[135]

This language about America's role in the world was strong and the ideas bracing—America, he wrote, needed to be "unashamedly" "laying down the rules," and we needed to do so because of a "subtle call to greatness."

But this was a relatively demure neocon, well-suited to the genteel readers of *Foreign Affairs*. For the raw version, you had to enter the neocons' new Alcove No. 1: the tiny journals that they wrote, read, and circulated among themselves, where they worked out their own schemes unbothered by the klieg lights of the Sunday morning shows. Just a year before the *Foreign Affairs* article, Krauthammer had published a much more direct article in Irving Kristol's magazine *The National Interest* titled, "Universal Dominion: Toward a Unipolar World." In this article, published just after the end of the Reagan administration, when neoconservatives were beginning to express great frustration at the realist-dominated foreign policy of George H. W. Bush's administration, Krauthammer described his great ambition for American foreign policy in terms at once stark and soaring: "After having doubly defeated totalitarianism," he argued, "America's purpose should be to steer the world away from its coming multipolar future toward a qualitatively new outcome—a unipolar world whose center is a confederated West."[136]

The unipolar world, in Krauthammer's vision, would be oriented around common markets—America's economic ideology spreading through cultural and political networks to simultaneously connect with and control societies that otherwise might challenge us. The vision, however, would not be realized on its own. Krauthammer criticized Francis Fukuyama's argument in "The End of History" that common marketization was a historical force ineluctably sweeping us up, for assuming that marketization was "either here or inevitably dawning."

Krauthammer wrote, "It is neither. The West had to make it happen, and for that, the United States has to wish it."[137] For America to
"wish" it, we must set our aims properly, which would require a heart-
in-mouth ambition: "[W]e are dealing with goals here, not reality. If
the new age dawns and some new national purpose is to be offered to
a skeptical American people, I suggest we go all the way and stop at
nothing short of universal dominion."[138]

A sort of nervy literary adrenaline powered Krauthammer's writing. It was as if the argument for "universal dominion" would collapse
without the momentum of the ideological surge underneath it. What
exactly was the purpose of this universal dominion? According to
Krauthammer, it was to accelerate the ripple effects from an ideological hub, generating waves of marketization in the world. The ostensible
ambition, therefore, was not power—it was markets. But was it really?
Europe could just as easily help build markets in the world. On second
reading, Krauthammer's idea was rather obviously driven by the pursuit of American greatness, inevitability, and the expansion of power.
This heady pursuit drove the ideas—not the other way around.

Ironically, this sense of American destiny and American cause
led Krauthammer to critique one aspect of the democracy enterprise
itself—the dimension relating just to people. "A great power under-
takes great battles," he pronounced, "because no one else can."[139] But
it was precisely for this reason that Krauthammer said the minute
details of democratization were beneath America's stature. "But with
the great battle won," he wrote, referring to the end of the Cold War,
"the question of whether to engage in the mop-up work is a very different one."[140] "Mop-up" work was a boring, tedious, workmanlike
aspect of democracy—boring because it was about governance and
results, not destiny and nobility. You can clearly see an element of
Strauss here in the neocons' yearning for a lost, ineffable greatness that
only they could see, while at the same time dismissing any effort that
failed to hit those elevated notes.

But most interesting was how Krauthammer's crusade for a self-
justifying American greatness based on American power initially led
him, over a decade before 9/11 and Iraq, to reject democracy promotion itself. He wrote, "I have been closely associated with the pro-
democracy internationalist school during the 1980s. I have some

doubts, however, whether in the radically changed post-communist world that we are postulating, the democratic crusade should be the central plank of an American foreign policy."[141] The reason was that democracy, quite simply, wasn't a "great struggle" in this neocon's eyes. True, it *resembled* a great struggle. But Krauthammer was careful to keep his focus on the Straussian goal of greatness:

> In its spirit and ultimate goal, this idea of a super-sovereign West is not far from that of the pro-democracy crusade. But its approach is radically different. It focuses on the center, not the periphery. It is based on the assumption that unification of the industrial West is the major goal of the democratic crusade, rather than the conversion, one by one, of the Third World states.[142]

In other words, democracy suited foreign policy only if it was a subset of, and subsumed into, the goal of a super-sovereign West with America as its queen bee. The proper goal of policymakers was the exhilarating expansion of American power.

This makes more sense of Iraq. The projects of Bill Kristol and Krauthammer, different as they were with respect to democracy, shared one crucial thing: they were both, almost literally, crusades. After 9/11, the neocons reified America and democracy into a fused metaphysical ideal, not a cultural and political reality that was the artifact of millions of ordinary people living their lives. They established America as a new kind of imperial power in the post–Cold War era. And they aimed for a spiritual cause—"greatness"—that dwarfed historical and cultural impediments. Constitutionalism was doomed from the start. As we've seen, constitutional democracy proceeds from minutiae such as beliefs, attitudes, culture, and the way people constrain, interrogate, and punish their leaders. It's painstaking, prosaic, quotidian work, with little glory. How could America cultivate constitutionalism among another people with such care if the imperial power was uninterested in constitutionalism itself?

In the end, the neocons hollowed out the neoconservatives' original ambitions for a "new" conservatism and committed the great Athenian sin—hubris. When the Cold War was still on, Krauthammer was more skeptical about whether America should be involved in the laborious process of "mop-up work" required by democracy promotion. When the United States stood alone as the world's sole superpower, however, Iraq was a project worth supporting, without hesitation or a backward glance at history. The neocons, after all, had bigger fish to fry. Dreaming big for themselves, for America, and for their own idea of "greatness," they took statecraft into a metaphysical realm. In the end, they violated what the foreign policy expert Michael Lind has described as the cardinal rule of American foreign policy: "The purpose of the American way of strategy is to defend the American way of life by means that do not endanger the American way of life."[143] By draining our strength internationally and undermining our ability to create stable, constitutional democracies, efforts like the Iraq War—with a terrible irony—ended up making the world less safe for Americans.

As the change from Irving to Bill Kristol and the thinking of individuals like Krauthammer dramatically reveal, after the Cold War ended, there was an evolution from *neoconservative* to *neocon*. This perverse progression mirrored the chain of unintended consequences seen in the story of Strauss—where the attempt to prevent a demagogue like Hitler from ever rising again, in the end, instead helped produce conditions favorable to new demagogues. In contrast to the original neoconservatives' relatively coherent ideology, "neocon" is instead a brand, a political movement, and a style. It is affect, not character. The fact is that to be a "neoconservative" without the history of revolting against Stalinism or liberalism simply makes no sense. You simply cannot be a neoconservative if you were not once liberal—there is no "neo." The original neoconservatives were rebelling against weak opposition to Stalinism, as a corruption of the progressive project brought to an unimaginable extreme. In their second turn—after they left Democrats like Henry M. "Scoop" Jackson, the U.S. Senator from Washington state who challenged Jimmy Carter in 1976 for president on a get-tough foreign policy platform, and turned to Ronald Reagan—the neoconservatives were still responding to actual events, such as the perceived weakness of Democrats on Vietnam and military issues and problems of the welfare state. Their policies still bore the imprint of actual experience and were therefore at least somewhat chastened by a sense of consequence and history. But after the Cold War ended and during the presidency of George W. Bush, the neoconservatives became neocons, and their politics became, at best, like a lofty dreamer who simply doesn't care for the confines of the real world and, at worst, like an always angry man in search of an outrage.

After 9/11, the challenge of violent, extremist Islam fit their bill, and they went to desperate lengths to fashion an epic struggle with Cold War dimensions. The word "Islamofascism" was invented and rapidly deployed to support President Bush's post-9/11 "global war on terror" doctrine. In the words of one writer, "Islamofascism refers to use of the faith of Islam as a cover for totalitarian ideology."[144] The drive to make any Islamic enemy into Hitler continued in 2008 when President Bush likened then-Senator Barack Obama's proposal to open up diplomatic negotiations with the Iranian government to the British appeasement of the Nazi government before World War II. "As Nazi tanks crossed into Poland in 1939," Bush said in a speech before Israel's Knesset, "an American senator declared: 'Lord, if only I could have talked to Hitler, all of this might have been avoided.' We have an obligation to call this what it is—the false comfort of appeasement, which has been repeatedly discredited by history."[145]

These claims were, generally, part of a political and ideological agenda, rather than a national security strategy supported by objective evidence and rational consideration. Though a serious and dangerous threat that must be attacked and eliminated wherever and however possible, as a strategic concern it's essential to understand that radical Islam does not and cannot pose an existential threat to the United States remotely on par with the Soviet Union's geopolitical policy of bellicose expansion in Europe and the southern hemisphere or Nazi Germany's plan for world domination. The conceptual errors underlying the doctrine were even more evident as a National Intelligence Estimate in July 2007 showed that Al-Qaeda—after five years of the neocons' "global war on terror" approach—was still strong globally.[146] The grasping and unsound theory underlying the "global war on terror" doctrine gradually was repudiated even by the president's closest advisers, as officials ranging from Secretary of Defense Donald Rumsfeld to General David Petraeus recommended removing the term from the military lexicon entirely.[147] Despite the neocons' greatest attempts, they could not reshape the world itself to fit their metaphysical theories. Facts—stubborn things—got in the way, just as the people—also stubborn things—proved to be democracy's greatest obstacle in the neocons' new Iraq.

In the best-selling novel *The Kite Runner*, Afghani children run across the neighborhoods and hills of Kabul with kites, trying to cut the string of a competitor's kite. When they succeed, the kite flies off.[148] For the neocons, democracy was like a kite that has been cut, fluttering far away into the sky because it was never tied to any driving reality or any grounding concern. Strauss's philosophy was rooted in the collapse of Weimar Germany. Irving Kristol's ideas about democracy were formed in response to Stalinism. Jeane Kirkpatrick's foreign policy depended on the Cold War and the active, looming threat of the Soviet Union. For better or for worse, any conception of democracy formed in reaction to actual political events—even Strauss's—was still tethered to the world itself. But in a post–Cold War era, in which the United States seemed not to have any serious challenger and democracy seemed generally unopposed as destiny, the neocons ended up having little concern with the fundamental, grounding elements of democracy. Democracy's native challenges—its intrinsic instability, its need for constitutional commitment by the people, and the organic and primitive threat of the demagogue—were easy to forget. Their ambitions eerily echoed Plato's dream-state project in the *Republic*. Cut loose from the people, the neocons' idea of democracy easily flew off, drifting so far away it became a figment, an abstraction, and, finally, one with the ether.

THE END OF COMPLICITY

GIVEN THE EXTRAORDINARY STORY OF THE NEOCONS' FAILURE TO ABSORB the lessons of democracy's struggle with the demagogue, one might reasonably expect a parade of apologias from leading neocons. The facts are so overwhelming and the failure so stark that they almost demand that Paul Wolfowitz, Bill Kristol, Richard Perle, Charles Krauthammer, Doug Feith, and others step forward, of their own accord, and explain the disconnect between their plan and what happened.

Needless to say, the group confessional hasn't occurred. There have been grudging concessions of practical difficulties from a few quarters, to be sure. Three months after the end of the war, in 2003, Wolfowitz conceded, "Some important assumptions turned out to underestimate the problem."[149] In 2008, Feith wrote a book admitting problems with Iraq but, typically, blaming everyone else for them.[150] Also in that same year, Scott McClellan, President Bush's press secretary for several years during the Iraq War, published a book called *What Happened,* expressing great regret for his part in facilitating a stubborn and recalcitrant foreign policy and disclosing that democracy was indeed the primary motivation underlying the Iraq War.[151] Otherwise, the silence of the war's architects regarding their own intellectual culpability for its considerable failures has been deafening, with one significant exception. In 2006, Francis Fukuyama, long a dominant player deep within the neoconservative infrastructure, issued an extraordinary *mea culpa.*

In 1992, Fukuyama authored a famous essay titled "The End of History," in which he argued that Western-style free-market democracy had become so dominant that we had reached the German philosopher Hegel's conceptual "end of history," when great ideological conflicts cease to generate true political conflict. Many interpreted the essay to argue that the West, finally, had won—that American democracy had become so dominant that we could expect no great ideological struggles between nations over our common political future, ever. Critics saw Fukuyama's thesis as fatuously triumphalist and ahistorical. His defenders, however, thought he offered a patriotic and persuasive vision of a democratic future. In either case, the takeaways from his argument seemed firmly neoconservative: liberals skeptical of American power and American example were wrong and needed to reconsider, his argument went. America held the key to the world's future. And democracy was foreordained.

In 2006, after the failures in Iraq had been laid bare for three years, Fukuyama published a book that broke dramatically with the self-confidence and determinism of "The End of History." The new book, titled *America at the Crossroads: Democracy, Power, and the Neoconservative Legacy*, contained an eloquent and heartfelt exegesis of the neocons' errors. The book began in disenchantment and regret: "The subject of this book is American foreign policy since the Al-Qaida attacks of September 11, 2001. This is a personal subject for me. Having long regarded myself as a neoconservative, I thought I shared a common worldview with many other neoconservatives—including friends and acquaintances who served in the administration of George W. Bush."[152] Fukuyama recited his own neoconservative resume. He worked for Wolfowitz twice in the government and was recruited by Wolfowitz to the Johns Hopkins School of Advanced International Studies while Wolfowitz was the dean there. He worked for Albert Wohlstetter, Wolfowitz's mentor and a leading neoconservative and student of Strauss. Fukuyama was also an analyst at the Rand Corporation, where many neocons also worked; a student of Allan Bloom's; and a classmate of Bill Kristol's in graduate school at Harvard. He later published frequently in the neoconservative journals *The National Interest, The Public Interest,* and *Commentary.*[153]

Fukuyama was, in his words, originally "fairly hawkish on Iraq," but in the year preceding the invasion, after participating in a study on long-term strategy against terrorism, he "finally decided the war didn't make any sense."[154] He abruptly parted ways with the neocons. In February 2004, about a year after the American invasion of Iraq, he attended an annual dinner sponsored by the American Enterprise Institute. Krauthammer delivered a speech that declared the war a "virtually unqualified success."[155] In a crowning irony, the dinner was held in honor of Irving Kristol, the same neoconservative who declared, "It is the fundamental fallacy of American foreign policy to believe, in face of the evidence, that all peoples, everywhere, are immediately 'entitled' to a liberal constitutional government—and a thoroughly democratic one at that."[156]

According to Fukuyama, Krauthammer could have made these claims only by actively ignoring their bankruptcy. At that moment, in a direct assault on Paul Bremer and the Americans in Iraq, Moqtada al-Sadr was vocally threatening to rebel against any Iraqi constitution that did not enshrine Islamic law.[157] His Mahdi army would back up these threats two months later in an offensive against American troops. Sitting in the audience, Fukuyama was confounded by the sea of praise for Krauthammer's cheerleading. "I could not understand why everyone around me was applauding," he wrote with chagrin, "given that the United States had found no weapons of mass destruction in Iraq, was bogged down in a vicious insurgency, and had almost totally isolated itself from the rest of the world by following the kind of unipolar strategy advocated by Krauthammer."[158] That moment marked Fukuyama's departure from the neocon ranks.

As Fukuyama came to realize, the neocons' central intellectual flaw was to believe democracy was a "default condition to which societies would revert once liberated from dictators."[159] Fukuyama argued that even though there may be a universal yearning for freedom and a "broad, centuries-long trend toward the spread of liberal democracy," democracies require institutions to become successful.[160] "And if there is one thing that the study of democratic transitions and political development teaches," he wrote, "it is that institutions are very difficult to establish."[161] But the neocons weren't focused on the tools that America could use to build institutions. They were, instead, riveted by military power. Fukuyama noted that of all the tools to promote democracy, William Kristol and Robert Kagan considered only three in an influential book about Iraq titled *Present Danger:* the ability to project military power, military allies, and ballistic missile defense. "There is not even a nod toward policy instruments that are critical in helping to bring about political transitions, such as the State Department, the U.S. Agency for International Development, or multilateral institutions like the IMF or World Bank."[162]

Fukuyama's ultimate judgment of the neocons was particularly damning: that the unipolar doctrine was constructed largely for rhetorical benefit. He wrote, "The Kristol-Kagan agenda was driven by a belief that this kind of activist foreign policy was in the best interests of the United States. But it was also driven by a less obvious political calculation."[163] The less obvious calculation was an attempt to make our politics aspire to "national greatness," following the *New York Times* columnist David Brooks's argument that Republicans should make the swaggering, dominant administration of Theodore Roosevelt a model for themselves.[164] Fukuyama explained:

> National greatness inevitably manifests itself through foreign policy, since foreign policy is always a public matter and involves issues of life and death. In addition, Kristol noted on several occasions that the Republican Party always did better when foreign policy issues were at stake than when the focus was on domestic policy or the economy. They thus designed a foreign policy around a very abstract view of domestic politics—that America needed a national project to get its mind off issues like the stock market boom and Monica Lewinsky—rather than deriving the foreign policy from the nature of the outside world.[165]

The primary responsibility of foreign policy is to promote America's national security interests in a way that's consistent with our values. But these neocons—who had moved so far from the original neoconservatives—were pursuing instead a different value: a political and rhetorical narrative.

Fukuyama's book did not go unanswered. In a vicious riposte to Fukuyama in *The Washington Post*, Krauthammer dismissed the alternative Fukuyama proposed "for the challenges of September 11" with typically bracing invective. All Fukuyama supported—including the work of institutions such as the State Department and U.S. A.I.D. and new forms of foreign aid—was "a mush of bureaucratic make-work in the face of a raging fire."[166]

It must have been painful to be dismissed so harshly by former friends—and on the pages of *The Washington Post*, at that. The neocons would brook no dissent, and Fukuyama knew the storm he was about to face. There was a palpable sense of loss when he wrote, "I have concluded that neoconservatism, as both a political symbol and a body of thought, has evolved into something I can no longer support."[167] Plato used the metaphor of the winged horses drawing the chariot of the soul for a reason. It's difficult to cut loose from that rush of wind, that sense of ascension to the heavens. Perhaps this explains why more neocons have not made the same move. They are unwilling not only to have their hearts broken, but also to have their universes shattered.

But the rest of us can move ahead. The fact is that America can transcend the bad ideas, the intellectual shambles, and the new demagogues in Iraq and elsewhere. We can reclaim the future of democracy through the constitutionalism we know.

———————————◆———————————

SEDUCTION AND RESOLUTION

WE HAVE JUST EXPLORED THE STORY OF ONE RESPONSE TO HITLER, which began in a kind of elite authoritarian democracy and ended in a metaphysical quest for democratic dominion. But there were other, far more salutary, attempts to bridge the fissures Hitler opened in the democratic project. A German émigré named Hannah Arendt, the sixth and penultimate character in our story of the attempt to save democracy from the demagogue, is the heroine of this book. Just as de Tocqueville responded to the Reign of Terror by turning to the American people as the answer, Arendt answered the turmoil in her native country by developing the boldest, most spiritual, and most powerful idea we have of constitutionalism. Out of the fires of Nazism, Arendt wrought a new idea of constitutionalism that provided a final way out of democracy's demagogue problem and, today, a beacon for those searching for a way to use America's power in a new world.

We first address an event that had a powerful impact on her life and on the formation of her ideas: the seduction of a mentor Arendt trusted and a man she loved by a demagogue. The seizure of Martin Heidegger's great mind by Adolf Hitler was an event that Arendt grappled with throughout her life. It was an episode at once personal and political, and helped spawn a new way of thinking about—and trying to save—democracy.

———————————————

Martin Heidegger was one of the twentieth century's great philosophers, authoring *Being and Time*, a symphonic tome on the relation between *dasein*, or "being," the often-hidden nature of the universe, and our perception of and experience with this mysterious reality. For a time in the early 1930s, Heidegger abandoned his commitment to philosophical objectivity as well as his Jewish friends to side with Hitler. Heidegger spent the rest of his life trying to rationalize and defend his actions.

Heidegger was appointed rector of the university in Freiburg, Germany, in the summer of 1933, after Adolf Hitler was appointed chancellor and the Nazis took over the German government.[168] Heidegger almost immediately joined the Nazi Party. Soon after, he gave his first "rectorial address," which would become one of the most infamous speeches in the history of philosophy. Heidegger summoned the Hegelian idea of Germanic destiny in a bracing call to action by the students assembled before him. "All leading," he told them, "must concede its following its own strength. All following, however, bears resistance in itself. This essential opposition of leading and following must not be blurred let alone eliminated."[169]

In his speech, Heidegger enjoined the students to adopt three kinds of "bonds" to their nation: first, to the "national community" (in German, *Volksgemeinschaft*), which meant they had to provide labor to Germany; second, to the "honor and the destiny of the nation," which meant they had to serve in the military; and, third, to the "spiritual mission of the German people," which meant they had to become— and here Heidegger almost seemed to invoke Plato's *Republic*—a "spiritual people" who would demand "of itself and for itself that its leaders and guardians possess the strictest clarity of the highest, broadest, and richest knowledge."[170]

Heidegger also explained the importance of political theory to his choice of German nationalism and Nazism over all else, which is important because it shows not only how powerful ideas can be *against* the demagogue, but also how much they can *help* the demagogue. Some scholars, he explained to the students, believed the Greek word *theoria* (which, as discussed earlier, meant literally "to see") signified to the Greeks "pure contemplation, which only remains bound to the matter in question and all that it is and demands." Heidegger attacked this notion. Theory was not valuable, he said, "for its own sake." Instead, theory should be pursued "in the passion to remain close to and under the pressure of what is." In other words, a philosopher could—and *should*—subordinate ideas to political ends.

Heidegger ended his speech with a chilling apothegm from Plato's *Republic.* "But we will only fully understand the magnificence and greatness of this new departure," he told the students, "when we carry within us that profound and far-reaching thoughtfulness that gave ancient Greek wisdom the saying: *'All that is great stands in the storm.'* "[171]

To fashion himself as a pillar of greatness amid a hurricane, Heidegger had already capitulated to Hitler in both his heart and his mind well before the speech. Karl Jaspers, a great philosopher and student of Heidegger, was married to a Jewish woman named Gertrud. Heidegger had been a close friend of the Jaspers family and had stayed at their house many times. Yet, as he gravitated toward the demagogue, Heidegger cut them off. In one famous episode, he left the house without saying goodbye properly to Jaspers' wife. In a letter to Arendt years later, Jaspers said his visit was "exceptionally discourteous" and that "I have never forgotten his ungallant behavior toward Gertrud in that situation."[172] Jaspers recalled Heidegger's behavior almost twenty years later in a letter to Heidegger himself: "You will forgive me when I tell you what I had sometimes thought: that you seemed to behave with regard to the national-socialist events like a boy who dreams, does not know what he is doing . . . and soon stands helpless facing a heap of rubble and lets himself be driven deeper and deeper."[173]

For Heidegger as for Plato, concentrating the minds of teachers, students, and political actors on the dream of a perfect society could solve the problem of the demagogue. For Hitler and followers like Heidegger, imagining Germany as "all that is great" bearing up in "the storm" could solve their political problems. By striking a chord with people hungry for greatness, no matter the consequence, the demagogue triggered democracy's collapse into tyranny. Jaspers asked Heidegger once, "How can a man as coarse as Hitler govern Germany?" Heidegger responded, referring to Hitler's powerful gestures before the masses, "Culture is of no importance. Just look at his marvelous hands."[174] Philosophy—high-minded culture—could play a role no longer in saving democracy; indeed, it only got in the way.

In 1924, an eighteen-year-old student sat down in a classroom at the university in Marburg, Germany. She looked toward the front of the room and regarded the reserved, graceless young man pacing in front. A friend and fellow student later described the young woman as "shy and turned inward, with striking, beautiful facial features and lonely eyes." She "immediately stood out," he wrote, "as 'unusual' and 'singular.' "[175] The man she was watching was Heidegger—then thirty-five years old and the father of two in a loveless marriage to a jealous, anti-Semitic wife.[176] He was a "figure out of a romance—gifted to the point of genius, poetic, aloof from both professional thinkers and adulatory students, severely handsome, simply dressed in peasant clothes, an avid skier who enjoyed giving skiing lessons."[177] He was also just beginning to write *Being and Time*.

Martin noticed Hannah. In the coming weeks, as she asked questions and they discussed philosophy in class, he was taken in by the perspicacity and elegance of her intellect. He learned that she had read Kant in high school and had memorized Greek poetry as a hobby.[178] Two months after meeting Arendt, Heidegger wrote her a note asking her to meet with him in his office.[179] Biographers seeking to trace one of the century's most stunning collisions of minds have speculated on exactly what happened next, but the relationship seems at the very least to have moved fast. Three weeks later, Heidegger sent her a note that "indicate[d] . . . the beginning of physical intimacy."[180] The severe philosopher who spent most of his time writing about how to grapple with the metaphysical conundrums of existence was living in the moment—he began writing Arendt poems where he "promised to love her forever."[181]

Heidegger's seduction stemmed at least in part from the metaphysical bent of his philosophy, and of his mind, that was established early in his career—his own "Platonic turn." Arendt took a class from Heidegger in the winter semester of 1924 titled "Interpretation of the Platonic Dialogue *Sophist*." From his lectures, she discerned the Platonism that would ultimately drive his political choices.[182] Heidegger viewed history, and politics, as a struggle to grasp the underlying metaphysical nature of problems. One scholar writes, "[A]ccording to Heidegger, the work of the lives of Socrates, Plato and Aristotle was a 'struggle against sophistry and rhetoric.' This struggle is the conquest of a mode of existence dedicated to the ultimate possibility of uncovering, namely the uncovering of Being itself."[183] The "uncovering of Being itself" divided pursuers of "the truth" into those who understand and are invested in that search and those who are not. Heidegger's rectorial address, one scholar writes, was essentially "a sort of remake of Plato's *Republic*."[184] Ironically, Nazism, the ultimate generator of the cycle of regimes, could sweep up even a Platonic authoritarian like Heidegger, when Plato himself was in fact so desperately trying to solve this threat to democracy.

The Platonic turn can render human beings mechanical instruments of metaphysical will. Anyone who has seen a concentration camp knows their stark horror. I visited the remains of the concentration camp in Dachau in 1997. It was a warm summer day, and tourists streamed in and out of the museum there—entering with uncertain, expectant faces, leaving tear-streaked and stricken. People wandered in and out of the broad grassy expanse through the iron gate with, ARBEIT MACHT FREI ("work will make you free") wrought into the metal. They stumbled into the corridors of tight wooden beds, stacked on top of one another. They walked like ghosts through the oven rooms; in one oven, a visitor had placed a single rose.

I found it hard to breathe. The experience was soul-defeating. It took one's breath away, but in a flattening, suffocating way, like a weight on your chest.

This personal experience with the lasting horror of a Nazi project was also a metaphor for Arendt's celebrated explanation of totalitarianism's particularly devastating quality: that it succeeded precisely by grinding out spontaneity, humanness, and liberty. If people give over their freedom to a demagogue with all the tools of a modern geopolitical titan at his disposal, they empower not only tyranny but totalitarianism. It is, literally, suffocating.

Arendt saw concentration camps as the extreme logical extension of the demagogue's authoritarian assault on constitutionalism, which, brought to its political extreme, enabled the Nazis' totalitarianism. She wrote, "The next decisive step in the preparation of living corpses is the murder of the moral person in man. This is done in the main by making martyrdom for the first time in history, impossible. . . ."[185] The moral person—the person capable of making individual choices on principle and therefore defining herself by those choices—becomes a victim. Totalitarianism then puts the soul itself to death: "Once the moral person has been killed, the one thing that still prevents men from being made into living corpses is the differentiation of the individual, his unique identity."[186] Conversely, the differentiation of the individual is what can *prevent* totalitarianism.

This was a more elaborate and powerful exposition of the same simple answer the Greeks and de Tocqueville found for the defeat of the demagogue—a culture of individual self-reliance, the gift and radical responsibility of the individual burden of political choice, and the cultivation of a constitutional conscience in the hearts and minds of citizens. In reflecting on Heidegger's failure to stand his ground against Hitler, Arendt came to provide the sense of constitutionalism's governing spirit: an almost martial sense of discipline and sacrifice by this soldier in democracy's civil war of the soul. The constitution, to Arendt, was not so much a document as an act that every responsible citizen re-lives every day of his or her life. The "true objective" of the constitution, she wrote, was "not to limit power but to create more power, actually to establish and duly constitute a new power center. . . ."[187] But this power center wasn't actually a "center" at all. Instead, it was a flexible, resilient web connecting people to each other, dispersing authority through a million political filaments.

The final solution Arendt described for the demagogue was a constant state of constitutionalism. This was not a calm state of lawfulness. It was, rather, a vibrant state of continuous revolution—properly understood. She argued that the French Revolution perverted the proper understanding of "revolution." To her, revolution was not the "struggle for liberation" but was, instead, "the foundation of freedom"—a deeply personal commitment with dramatic political consequences. In other words, revolution was not an act of overthrowing something—it was instead ideas and human history literally revolving. It was the constant circulation of ideas, like moral oxygen in a stuffy, oppressive political universe. The ancients saw revolution as a celestial idea that, literally, meant "rotation": "the regular, lawfully revolving motion of the stars."[188] In practical government, this revolution provided a regular, refreshing, natural movement—the change of season to season, the movement of the days. The underlying dynamic, she thought, was not newness but instead restoration. A history based on revolution was always restoring what was lost, returning to its roots. For the same reason, a constitutionalism based in revolution would always restore freedom—the "recovery of the rights and liberties of limited government."[189]

The trinity of restoration, revolution, and constitutionalism was one reason, Arendt thought, that revolutionaries like the Founding Fathers often returned to "terms of ancient liberties."[190] Thus the importance of Athens, once again, in America.

As their affair progressed, the young Arendt received Heidegger as well as her classmates in her attic room near the university. A friend said the young woman had "an intensity, an inner direction, an instinct for quality, a groping for essence, a probing for depth" that together created "a magic about her."[191] She charmed Heidegger by summoning a mouse who lived in the walls out of a hole to eat food she would give it. The mouse, she told a friend, was "as alone" (in German, *so allein*) as she was.[192]

After a year, Arendt left the university to study with two other philosophers—Edmund Husserl and Karl Jaspers. Heidegger did not leave his wife. But Arendt and Heidegger still saw each other off and on for two more years, concluding around 1927.[193] Arendt moved to Berlin in 1929 and began writing by her own lights, in part to escape Heidegger's suffocating, possessive intellectual presence. She soon married another former student of Heidegger, completing her move to philosophical independence.[194]

At the same time, Nazism was beginning to sweep across the country. By 1931, when Hitler was starting to consolidate the Nazi Party,

Arendt was reading Marx, Lenin, and Trotsky and attending public rallies.[195] In 1933, with Hitler's ascension to chancellor and the initiation of public beatings of Jews, Arendt realized that Germans were exchanging the freedom that the democratic Weimar Constitution had granted them for tyranny. Horrified, Arendt exiled herself to Paris. Heidegger, meanwhile, descended into Nazism.

In her search to rescue democracy, Arendt provided two clear and radically different ideas of the word "constitution." The first was the type of written document we all know. The second, far more important, notion was the political life all committed democratic citizens themselves lead. As Thomas Paine said, "A constitution is not the act of a government, but of a people constituting a government."[196] Arendt cited President John Adams with approval: "a constitution is a standard, a pillar, and a bond when it is understood, approved and beloved. But without this intelligence and attachment, it might as well be a kite or balloon, flying in the air."[197]

This second, vital meaning intensified one's self-regard and sense of responsibility. The foundation of the internal life of the constitution is so obvious it is easy to ignore or forget: our own ability to create something new, which Arendt deemed "natality." Natality, to Arendt, was literally each individual's ability to cause something—a word, an idea, an action—to be born. We often forget this extraordinary gift, but it defines the basic idea of what it is to be human. Natality is necessary for freedom, and it begins inside of us—in our hearts and in our minds. "Freedom as an inner capacity of man," Arendt wrote, "is identical with the capacity to begin, just as freedom as a political reality is identical with a space of movement between men."[198] What was so violent about Nazism was that it destroyed individuality—which, to Arendt, was the same as "to destroy spontaneity"—"man's power to begin something new out of his own resources, something that cannot be explained on the basis of reactions to environment and events."[199] Totalitarian demagogues naturally fight natality to the death. "Those who aspire to total domination," Arendt explained, "must liquidate all spontaneity, such as the mere existence of individuality will always engender, and track it down in its most private forms, regardless of how unpolitical and harmless these may seem."[200]

Natality defies the demagogue. No matter how innocent or even apolitical, *any* spontaneity threatens tyranny. When natality, freedom, and spontaneity perish, they leave in their wake an automated, directionless life. Enabled by people like Heidegger, Hitler was able to manufacture inevitability, which made Arendt furious. Arendt provided a haunting metaphor that should stick with any reader and remind her of the horrors of Nazi Germany: "Nothing then remains but ghastly marionettes with human faces, which all behave like the dog in Pavlov's experiments, which all react with perfect reliability even when going to their own death, and which do nothing but react."[201] Nothing captures the inverse of constitutionalism more vividly than this haunting image of inhuman puppets with human faces, yanked to and fro by a demagogue, falling limp without his animating, savage hands.

We should be clear about the relationship among demagogues, authoritarianism, and totalitarianism, which are not the same. Rather, they are marker points along an increasingly extreme scale of tyranny, each enabling a progression to the next stage. Totalitarianism is much worse than authoritarianism. In Arendt's thesis, totalitarianism specifically resulted from the impulse of the Nazi and Stalinist regimes for world domination. That suffocating, all-encompassing ambition in turn resulted in the specifically destructive quality of those regimes. To be sure, many demagogues have never achieved authoritarianism, much less totalitarianism. Josef Stalin did not begin as a demagogue, in that he rose to power not through a connection with the people but rather through internal party machinery. But in Germany, Hitler's demagoguery opened the door to totalitarianism, amid the generous opportunities afforded by the Weimar Constitution.

Arendt's chief hypothesis was that the long slide from demagogue to authoritarianism to totalitarianism was enabled by individuals' loss of their own sense of self-reliance and responsibility for society. The totalitarian model would "rationalize the essentially futile feelings of self-importance and hysterical security that it offered to the isolated individuals of an atomized society."[202] As the twentieth century got under way, people were becoming "atomized, undefinable, unstable and futile."[203] Exploiting the weaknesses of the modern world, totalitarianism rendered individual deliberation pointless. "The propaganda effect of infallibility, the striking success of posing as a mere interpreting agent of predictable forces," Arendt wrote, "has encouraged in totalitarian dictators the habit of announcing their political intentions in the form of prophecy."[204]

The individuality of the totalitarian citizen veered in exactly the wrong direction. Instead of going inward, energizing one's conscience—and sense of integrity, wholeness, and self-respect—this species of individuality instead exploded outward, in a chaos of directionless, angry energy. So Heidegger marched toward the void of German nationalism. So waves of ordinary Germans rose and shouted, *"Heil Hitler!"* These people of the modern machine—all metal edges and furious angles—lacked any organic connection with each other. Loneliness was the enemy.[205] And, in the modern age, loneliness mutated quickly into a lack of trust. "What makes loneliness so unbearable is the loss of one's own self which can be realized in solitude, but confirmed in its identity only by the trusting and trustworthy company of my equals," Arendt concluded, "In this situation, man loses trust in himself as the partner of his thoughts and that elementary confidence in the world which is necessary to make experiences at all."[206]

The loss of natality entailed, naturally, the sacrifice of responsibility. It would be challenging for most Americans to identify with the following passage in which Arendt described the ordinary German's complicity in the Nazi regime: "[N]obody," she writes, "ever experiences a situation in which he has to be responsible for his own actions or can explain the reason for them."[207] Arendt's fury at Heidegger's reluctance to own up to his small but significant role in helping the cycle of regimes turn once again lingered in every one of these lines.

In 1933, Arendt sent her former lover a letter in which she asked whether it was true that he had excluded Jews from his seminars, rejected Jewish colleagues socially, and generally acted like an anti-Semite. Heidegger "vehemently and sarcastically" denied the allegation, listing the favors he had done for Jews at the university.[208] He even brought Arendt into it—saying that he was as much of an anti-Semite in 1933 as he was in Marburg, an allusion to his affair with Arendt herself.[209] Later, Arendt called Heidegger a "potential murderer."[210] Some have speculated that Heidegger's letter sealed Arendt's decision to flee her homeland for France in August of 1933.[211]

Arendt's life in a world now dominated by the demagogue Hitler became even more personally traumatic. When Germany invaded France in 1940, France interned all "enemy aliens"—people of German nationality—even though most of them were already enemies of the Nazis. Arendt was imprisoned in a camp in Gurs, where she helped to organize the inmates.[212] She was eventually released, and moved to the United States in 1941.[213] But Arendt never gave up on Heidegger.

One comes away from reading Arendt with a newfound appreciation for outsiders and even eccentrics in political life—indeed, anyone who displays, or exaggerates, the basic individual creative faculty, which demagogues seek out and suffocate and which we desperately need to nurture today. Arendt wrote, "If [the regime] is still concerned with 'dangerous thoughts,' they are hardly ones which the suspected persons know to be dangerous. . . ." Our capacity to create newness in the world means political systems must respond to us, rather than vice versa: "[T]he regimentation of all intellectual and artistic life demands a constant re-establishment and revision of standards which naturally is accompanied by repeated eliminations of intellectuals whose 'dangerous thoughts' usually consist in certain ideas that were still entirely orthodox the day before."[214]

In other words, we should cradle our individuality, including our "dangerous thoughts," like a lit match on a windy day. Precisely because they are ours, and ours alone, they can strike a fire. We have a political obligation to use our most powerful asset—our humanity—to nip demagogues in the bud. If the cycle of regimes does launch, however, and a demagogue starts becoming a tyrant, the obligation becomes one of active defiance; risking prison or death, truly realized people need to fight for their freedom. But such rebellion is not revolt for its own sake. Rather, when people stand up to an oppressive government or a demagogue, they join the great revolution of humanity, shouldering it back around to the freedom that began it all.

Recall that Polybius likened the "lawless ferocity" of democracy, "inevitably transformed," to a grub devouring timber, an enemy destroying their hosts "without any external injury." If we don't truly believe in the possibility of progress and self-improvement among ordinary people, it becomes difficult to commit to *true* democracy. Just as we saw in Polybius's or Plato's dark view of the human condition and human potential, metaphysical conceptions of democracy can perversely and counterintuitively contain poisonous seeds of authoritarianism, of a politics that refuses to change—through infallible assertions of destiny and through cynical pessimism about the people's own ability to achieve their freedom. On the contrary, Arendt's natality entailed optimism about the potential of innovation, evolution, and resiliency, rooted in human beings and their actions rather than in calcified philosophical ideas. As two Arendt scholars have observed, "The politics of action, as opposed to ruling through the making of institutions, produces a bold vision of how ideational as well as institutional structures might be challenged and changed."[215] Her ideas, once implemented, can help produce the change that intrinsically defies the demagogue.

In the beautiful and haunting conclusion of *The Origins of Totalitarianism*, Arendt described her decision, as an adopted daughter of America fleeing the dual heartbreaks of the collapse of her country and her lover, to put faith in the intrinsic power of each individual person to master democracy: "Beginning, before it becomes a historical event, is the supreme capacity of man; politically, it is identical with freedom. *Initium ut esset homo creatus est*—'that a beginning be made man was created' said Augustine."[216] God created man *in order for* beginnings always to be made. And then, after this rich, intricate Latin phrase, Arendt concluded her great masterwork with a final epochal sentence, one that should ring true to every American who has ever unwittingly waged his or her own war against the demagogue: "This beginning is guaranteed by each new birth; it is indeed every man."[217]

All of this, for Arendt, culminated in her immense admiration for the constitutionalism of Americans. "A brief glance at the various destinies of constitutional governments outside the Anglo-American countries and spheres of influence," she wrote, "should be enough to enable us to grasp the enormous difference in power and authority between a constitution imposed by a government upon the people and the constitution by which a people constitutes its own government."[218] All of the action in this sentence about America takes place in the simple but profound difference between the indefinite and definite articles—"a" constitution and "the" constitution. "A" constitution is the fixed, inorganic artifact machined by a government; "the" constitution is, instead, the culture generated by the American people living in commitment to constitutional values. Arendt observed that the Founding Fathers were preoccupied not solely with the negative enterprise of battling tyranny, but also with the more complex one of creating something new. "Then they declared their independence from this government, and after they had forsworn their allegiance to the crown," Arendt wrote, "the main question for them certainly was not how to limit power but how to establish it, not how to limit government but how to found a new one."[219] As she argued in her conclusion to *The Origins of Totalitarianism*, our ability to "begin" is our ability to be constitutional, to set in motion a historical logic whereby states must bend to the people rather than the other way around—the founding belief of the young American nation.

America's embrace of constitutionalism went back to the very beginning. In 1620, 102 Separatists—hounded in their home country by the Anglican Church—boarded a ship in England for America.[220] On board the ship, rocked by waves, buffeted by winds, they still managed to craft an agreement that many credit with being a first draft for the American Constitution. The "Mayflower Compact," as it would come to be known, described how the men "solemnly & mutually in the presence of God, and one of another, covenant & combine our selves together into a civil body politick, for our better ordering & preservation & furtherance of the ends aforesaid; and by virtue hereof to enacte, constitute, and frame such just & equal laws, ordinances, Acts, constitutions, & office."[221]

Forty-one of the colonists signed the Compact on November 11, 1620, after disembarking from the Mayflower in what is now Provincetown—the fist of the crooked arm of Cape Cod.[222] In Arendt's view, the Compact was powerful because it demonstrated to the men who signed it, and generations of Americans who followed them,

that "newly discovered means of promise and covenant" could create responsible, constitutional power.[223] Previously, power was created
through princely inheritance or tyrannical domination. The colonists
sailing on the Mayflower devised a third way: to covenant, to create
under the eye of God a new "civil body politick." The act of making
promises to one another created a new kind of politics and a new constitutional conscience. Experience, "rather than theory or learning,"
taught these early Americans a final lesson: "the real meaning of the
Roman *potestas in populo,* that power resides in the people."[224]

With Heidegger's capitulation to Hitler in mind, Arendt was fascinated by the worship of the Constitution in America and how steadily
it eroded any demagogue's grip on the country. She wrote: "The great
measure of success the American founders could book for themselves,
the simple fact that the revolution here succeeded where all others were
to fail, namely, in founding a new body politic stable enough to survive the onslaught of centuries to come, one is tempted to think, was
decided the very moment the Constitution began to be 'worshiped,'
even though it had hardly begun to operate."[225] The worship of the
Constitution set in motion a great historical wheel. America's body
politic absorbed the lessons and dicta into the way we thought and felt
about political matters. We *became* the Constitution.

Though she was greatly impressed by America's constitutional
accomplishments, Arendt subjected Americans to the same searching critique as their counterparts in other nations, and often found us
wanting. She was alarmed by many aspects of American life: the racism, the anti-communism in the Republican Party and McCarthyism,
the failure of the American left sufficiently to denounce totalitarianism, and the conformity of American society.[226] Arendt thus joined
the same culture of self-critique that led Americans to revolt against
F.D.R.'s court-packing plan and became, like the early Americans she
so admired, an active bearer of our constitutional conscience.[227]

After World War II, Arendt renewed her relationship with Heidegger
through voluminous trans-Atlantic letters.[228] In the late 1940s she
described him as a "typical European philistine who had been attracted
to 'the mob' but had found no place ultimately in the party of the mob,

which had no interest in creative individuals like him."[229] This was the unsteady beginning of her attempt to rehabilitate Heidegger. Beginning in the 1950s, Arendt began seeing Heidegger during trips to Germany. The incredibly baroque relationship—Heidegger stayed with his wife, who over the years came to a grudging acceptance of his intense Platonic relationship with his former lover—took increasing twists and turns, as Arendt tried to work out for herself, over the decades, the implications of Heidegger's complicity in Hitler's rise. It took Arendt until the 1960s truly to forgive Heidegger, on the twin bases of his argument that he really could not have seriously influenced the Nazis and his complete renunciation of politics for a life of the mind.[230]

Heidegger's conscience, desolate and alone as it was, lived on. In the 1940s, after the fall of the Nazis, Heidegger began to recognize his seduction by Hitler but still refused to take responsibility in any satisfying way. Heidegger had dedicated the 1927 edition of *Being and Time* to his teacher, Edmund Hüsserl, who was Jewish, but had removed the dedication from the 1941 reissue.[231] Hüsserl was also barred from the Freiburg library, for which some scholars blame Heidegger, though Heidegger denied it. Heidegger told Arendt in a letter, however, that when Hüsserl died he became "sick, in bed."[232] He attributed his illness to "painful shame over what was meantime . . . done to the Jews and that one was helpless when confronted with it."[233] In the letter, however, Heidegger "included himself among the countless millions the Nazis had destroyed."[234] True, he did not recant, apologize, or specifically condemn the atrocities, which Jaspers opined later was because Heidegger was "incapable of grasping the depth of his failure as a human being."[235] But there's no doubt Heidegger was haunted by his sins. In 1946, as denazification proceeded throughout Germany and Heidegger was put increasingly on the defensive, he took refuge in a sanatorium and met with his archbishop. The archbishop said that Heidegger "conducted himself in a genuinely edifying manner." When the archbishop "told him the whole truth," the philosopher "accepted it, in tears."[236]

There are eerie parallels between the Platonic turn that drove Heidegger's thought and the confusions in our neocon foreign policy.

Arendt hated Heidegger's philosophy for its "Self-centeredness, attraction for nothingness, irresponsibility, deceptive genius, despair, Romanticism."[237] These are all qualities in generous supply in the neocons' foreign policy. But most dangerous to Arendt was the allure of abstraction, of theory. The fixation on deep thinking about the abstract required metaphysical reasoning not where it belonged—in philosophy—but instead in politics. Arendt wrote, "[F]requently leaders not only have abstract projects, they also experience their projects abstractly—that is, invisibly, impalpably, in a manner that is abstract to the senses."[238] Metaphysical reasoning led to the dehumanization of actual people, a problem Arendt strikingly saw as a problem of vision, of a flawed *theoria:* "Relatedly, many of those who sustain the policy by administering it, or by carrying it out every day, may literally see what they do, but the division of labor separates some people from all visibility and parcels out visibility to others who do not literally see."[239]

The consequences of policymakers' failure to "literally see" were dire for anyone unlucky enough to become a pawn on their chessboard. Arendt observed, "It is as if the epitome of evil on a large scale is raining bombs from a great height. No one engaged in a policy of evil, on any level, can see or feel the whole policy."[240] The metaphor of an ideological plane raining bombs down on minute targets shows exactly what a foreign policy of democracy promotion must avoid. As Shakespeare wrote in *Romeo and Juliet:* "These violent delights have violent ends,/ And in their triumph die; like fire and powder,/ Which, as they kiss, consume."[241] Politics belongs to the earth, to people, sentiments, and reasoning. When politics gropes instead for metaphysical targets, its "violent delights" can eclipse, and even extinguish, actual people.

The neocons' worst error was to convert both democracy and American "greatness" into metaphysical goals that could not be validated by empirical evidence or even by experience. You only knew them if you *knew them,* just as only the Straussians understood the lost "nobility" of the ancients. The greatest danger of all was the lure of the abstract reasoning originally fashioned by Georg Wilhelm Friedrich Hegel, the great nineteenth century German philosopher. Hegel wrote in his *Lectures on the Philosophy of World History:* "For world history moves on a higher plane than that to which morality properly belongs." This means that "whatever is required and accomplished by the ultimate end of the spirit . . . and whatever providence does, transcends the obligations, liability, and responsibility which attach to individuality." Ordinary men could not plead ordinary morals and law against such heaven-bound greatness: "The litany of private virtues . . . must not be raised against them." They were, after all, operating in the realm of "world history," which Hegel wrote "might well disregard completely the sphere to which morality . . . belongs . . . by ignoring individuals altogether."[242]

The contemporary political theorist George Kateb has written, with perceptible horror, of Hegel's reasoning in this passage: "It is hard to imagine a greater license for evil than these words."[243] Although they certainly would not agree, the great irony is that American neocons converted democracy, the most hopeful of human endeavors, into something bearing a certain resemblance to a Hegelian pursuit. For them, democracy—by definition, the rule of the people—became instead a goal in service of "world history" that ended up "disregarding completely the sphere" of ordinary people and "ignoring individuals altogether."

Soon after World War II ended, Arendt wrote a letter to Karl Jaspers diagnosing Heidegger's problem. Heidegger, she wrote, lacked character—"in the sense that he literally has none and certainly not a particularly bad one." She continued: "At the same time, he lives in depths and with a passionlessness that one can't easily forget. The distortion is intolerable."[244] But she still couldn't relinquish him to his sins. In 1952, Arendt returned to Europe and visited Freiburg in Germany. At her hotel, she used the stationery to draft a handwritten letter to Heidegger that she left unsigned—and he immediately came to the hotel.[245] Heidegger launched into a recitation, in Arendt's words, of "a sort of tragedy in which, presumably, I had participated in the first two acts."[246] The next day, he returned and told Arendt that his wife now knew that Arendt had been "the passion of his life" and the inspiration for his work.[247] He visited Arendt again, bringing manuscripts and letters.[248] But while she still desired to save Heidegger, she refused to allow him to seduce her. She quickly returned to her husband.

Throughout Arendt's career as a philosopher and public intellectual, Heidegger dismissed her—wrongly—as a minor philosopher. But Arendt clearly dominated the erstwhile Nazi's life, and vice versa. One of Arendt's most perceptive commentators, Julia Kristeva, speculates that the problem of how to forgive Heidegger controlled Arendt's concept of forgiveness, which itself lay behind her idea of "judgment"—the ultimate requirement for a civilized people to drive tyranny out of the government and out of their own hearts. Kristeva argues that Arendt believed Heidegger deserved forgiveness because this "revelation of love" would help "awaken a respect for a thought unique among all others."[249] In other words, rehabilitating a single flawed individual—even after he had yielded to and was trampled by a demagogue—rendered the project of constitutional democracy worthwhile.

PART IV

DEFYING THE DEMAGOGUE

THE PRECEDING SECTIONS HAVE EXAMINED WHERE DEMOCRACY HAS been. We now move to the question of where we should go—how we can salvage the goal of freedom from the neocons' misadventures. We need to work to help empower the peoples of the world with constitutional values that cultivate a sense of both the gift and the burden of freedom and that encourage them always to "chasten authority" in their own countries. But this will demand a substantial shift in our foreign policy.

In the wake of the neocons' foreign policy and a world of unstable, implosive democracies looming ahead, the challenge is how to weave Arendt's repudiation of the demagogue into a political theory that can guide our foreign policy. America should pursue freedom in the world while also staying true to our values. We can begin by changing our focus from *democracy* to *constitutionalism*. Democracy is a noble, formal structure for a government and an inspiring set of practical expectations for laws and for people. But, taken by itself, democracy is something like a body without a soul. What powers a successful constitutional democracy is a constitutional conscience among the people. Our foreign policy should therefore seek to cultivate constitutionalism among the peoples of the world, as a matter of our national security—rather than just impose democratic structures and institutions upon them.

◆

CONSTITUTIONALISM

FOR DECADES, POLITICAL SCIENTISTS HAVE DEBATED THE PROPER ROLE of variables like economics and political institutions in a successful constitutional democracy. Since James Madison, however, some have argued that democracies succeed instead because of elements like the checks and balances in America's Constitution. Samuel Huntington, for instance, lists no fewer than twenty-seven variables that may explain democratic success, including a country's experiences as a feudal aristocracy or a British colony, or its possession of a market economy.[1]

Although such variables are unquestionably significant, a great number of countries—whether in Latin America, Russia, the Middle East, Iraq itself, or Weimar Germany—have abandoned them entirely in favor of demagogues. These "illiberal democracies" reveal the importance of the citizens' commitment to constitutionalism. As one scholar of ancient Greece puts it: "No set of laws, no institutions, no complex bureaucracy, no intricate mechanisms of checks and balances is sufficient to preserve a democracy and maintain its health if the democratic spirit takes leave of the hearts of the people. Institutions help, making a democracy possible, but they are lifeless without the democratic genius."[2] Like Americans, the Greeks grasped that the "democratic genius" resides in the people, who provide the ultimate barrier to a demagogue's misuse of power.

The idea of constitutionalism builds instead on a different school of political science—one focused on political *culture*. Beginning in the early 1960s, political scientists began moving from views of democracy that took into account only formal structures to an approach that looked at the habits and attitudes of the general public. Over time, many recognized that the most important aspect of political culture for democratic success was a "long-term commitment to democratic institutions among the public."[3] The most important variables in a political culture of democracy, in the words of one study, are "deeply-rooted orientations of tolerance, trust, and a participatory outlook."[4] People must trust that their institutions reflect and are bound to their preferences; for a democracy to be effective, citizens need to do their part to keep leaders accountable.

The concept of constitutionalism explains how the constitutional conscience of Athens and America can inform a political theory to guide any country at any time. Considering the deep importance of the idea of constitutionalism both to America's own development and to the prospects for democracy throughout the world, the scholarship on constitutionalism is in a diffuse state—perhaps explaining why we see relatively little consistent use of the term. Some see constitutionalism as an exclusively legal matter, having to do with decisions by the Supreme Court on cases impacting constitutional rules.[5] Others view constitutionalism instead as a philosophical construct about the abstract relationship between freely choosing individuals and the state that would constrain them.[6]

But there has been less attention to the most robust and useful idea of constitutionalism, which Alexis de Tocqueville described most powerfully: a living culture of political values among ordinary people that (1) promotes the individual's private sense of self-worth and responsibility for democracy's success and (2) publicly operates as a countervailing political force on those who would gather power and break rules in doing so.[7] The sum of constitutionalism is that it controls those who seek an undue amount of authority.[8] The contemporary political theorist George Kateb has written that constitutionalism works by "chastening authority."[9] Mark Brzezinski explains that constitutionalism "is a state of mind, an expectation, a norm in which politics must be conducted in accordance with standing rules or conventions, written or unwritten, that cannot easily be changed; it is a principle whereby all power is limited, and whereby forces of power can act and decide only within strict limits defined by the national constitution."[10] The two valences of constitutionalism—the internal and the external—allow the people collectively to militate against demagogues and constantly perpetuate a just, equal, and fair political order. In the words of one political scientist, a "positive requirement of a working democracy is an intelligent distrust of its leadership, a skepticism stubborn but not blind, of all demands for the enlargement of power, and an emphasis upon critical method in every phase of social life."[11]

The limiting of authoritarian tendencies reinforces the spirit of self-reliance so powerfully invoked by Arendt. In an evocative passage, Kateb describes constitutionalism as generating "several commendable moral phenomena that, together, conduce to the emergence of a certain kind of *culture*. These phenomena," he explains, "include: independence, in a twofold sense of a wish to be autonomous (to lead one's own life, to make one's own soul) and of a disposition to say no, to resist inclusion in collective mindlessness or wrongdoing. . . ." Ultimately, the "twofold sense" of self-ownership, on the one hand, and resisting "collective mindlessness," on the other hand, generates a "sense of moral indeterminacy, a sense that though there are absolute limits, a voluptuous uncertainty as to how to judge and what to think about what, even, to want, both is a sign of life and is life itself."[12] The "voluptuous uncertainty" has joys of its own, capturing the sense of possibility in Arendt's idea of natality. In other words, constitutionalism helps one live life itself.

In the end, constitutionalism is about ordinary people doing ordinary things in their ordinary lives to an extraordinary end. As Voltaire said in *Candide*, "Cultivate your garden." Constitutionalism is not a glamorous affair; it is, instead, weeding and tending. As Arendt argued, a constitution can be both a written document and a constant act of a people constituting their government. In the case of the Greek constitution, the Greeks used the richer term *politeia*, and Leo Strauss, to his credit, got the definition exactly right: "The classics called the best society the best *politeia*. By this expression they indicated, first of all, that, in order to be good, society must be civil or political society, a society in which there exists government of men and not merely administration of things." But constitutionalism isn't about *laws*, precisely—it's about the spirit that underlies those laws. As Strauss put it, "The *politeia* is more fundamental than any laws; it is the source of all laws."[13] Constitutionalism is the culture that fights concentrated authority; it is a constant warning, in the people's hearts and minds, to those who would be strongmen.[14]

THE ERRORS OF THE PAST

IN THINKING ABOUT HOW TO GET DEMOCRACY RIGHT IN THE FUTURE, we need to draw a crucial distinction between democracy *installation* and democracy *promotion*.[15] The former can occur through regime change and was a key feature in "nation-building," as was the case with America's recent efforts in Afghanistan and Iraq. The latter describes our ongoing efforts with many countries in the world through American agencies like the National Democratic Institute, the Millennium Challenge Corporation, and their partner agencies in many developed nations, as well as private organizations like George Soros's Open Society Institute. Democracy promotion has a checkered history, but at least lacks the lavish, self-defeating errors of democracy installation in countries such as in Iraq.

In the summer of 2008, I traveled to Berlin to serve as a panelist at an event at a German *stiftüng*. *Stiftüngen* are foundations allied with each of Germany's four political parties created after World War II to help rebuild Germany's democratic institutions. The panel was on the topic of American foreign policy in the presidential election. After the panel concluded, I went to dinner with several of the panel's organizers, where the conversation turned to a discussion of the post–World War II laws, still in place in Germany, that prohibit anyone from denying the Holocaust. One man at the dinner raised the question of whether the laws were still necessary, suggesting that the opinions should be allowed so they could be soundly defeated in the marketplace of ideas—a proposition familiar from John Stuart Mill's *On Liberty*, a foundational text for American freedom of speech theory.

A young woman at the dinner reacted vehemently. "No, absolutely not," she said, putting down her glass. "With our history, I just don't think we can trust that." Sixty-three years after Hitler's suicide and the fall of Nazi Germany, it was striking how strongly a Berliner like this young woman was committed to fighting her own culture's historical tendency to authoritarianism and violence. Like many other Germans, she saw holding the line against Nazism as so important that they should be willing to sacrifice the freedom of speech for it.

Notably, the conversation occurred under the auspices of a *stiftüng*. By the late 1970s, these organizations, essentially the in-house think tanks of Germany's four political parties, were playing a prominent role in democratic transitions taking place on the Iberian Peninsula.[16] The perceived success of their work helped lay the groundwork for the U.S. Congress to institutionalize democracy promotion. In 1980, the American Political Foundation was established in Washington, directed by a former Republican National Committee chairman and a current Democratic National Committee chairman.[17] Two years later, President Ronald Reagan proposed an initiative "to foster the infrastructure of democracy—the system of a free press, unions, political parties, universities—which allows a people to choose their own way, to develop their own culture, to reconcile their own differences through peaceful means."[18] Ultimately, the National Endowment for Democracy was created.[19]

In 2004, President George W. Bush created the Millennium Challenge Corporation (MCC), a bold new step in democracy promotion. In contrast to previous efforts that funneled money into programs or took direct actions, the new program set up an incentive system. If nations achieved a set of criteria, or "indicators," demonstrating they were developing strong governance and accountability systems, they would be eligible for increased levels of American aid. For all of the vituperation that the Bush administration rightly deserves for the belligerence of its foreign policy and its policies in places like Iraq and Afghanistan, the MCC was a substantial step in the right direction. It was, unfortunately, eclipsed in popular understanding and world reputation by the administration's mistakes in Iraq. Even though the MCC should be better funded and its indicators expanded to better address constitutionalism, the effort reveals the power of an American democracy policy focused on people and their governments, rather than dreams of grandeur and the adrenaline of American might.

Democracy *installation* is another story entirely. According to one study, over the last century the United States has deployed its military to impose democratic rule in foreign lands on nineteen occasions: Cuba in 1906 and 1917, Nicaragua in 1909 (twice), Mexico in 1914, Honduras in 1924, Haiti in 1915, the Dominican Republic in 1916 and 1965, Italy in 1944, West Germany in 1944, Japan in 1945, South Vietnam in 1965, Cambodia in 1970, Grenada in 1983, Panama in 1989, Haiti in 1994, Afghanistan in 2001, and Iraq in 2003. Of the *regimes* we replaced with force, democracy was sustained within ten years of our action in only six countries: Germany, Japan, Italy, Panama, Grenada, and Nicaragua.[20] In Cuba, the Dominican Republic, and Haiti, among others, repeated direct American military interventions, including lengthy occupations, resulted only in new dictatorships.

Noah Feldman, a law professor who consulted on the constitutional process in Iraq, recalls flying to Iraq in May 2003 in a military transport plane. On the plane, Feldman was reading a book about the Iraqi Shi'a and familiarizing himself with Iraq's colloquial dialects. His colleagues on the flight were also reading intently, but they had dramatically different material in hand. "Without exception," Feldman writes, "they were reading new books on the American occupation and reconstruction of Germany and Japan."[21] As Feldman observed, Germany and Japan were foremost in the minds of the planners of Iraq. During the first weeks of the occupation, Paul Bremer instructed his staff on the causes underlying successful democracies. "Let's keep in mind the relevant lessons of Germany and Japan," he said. "Democracies don't work unless the political structure rests on a solid civil society . . . political parties, a free press, an independent judiciary, open accountability for public funds. These are society's 'shock absorbers.' They protect the individual from the state's raw power."[22]

Bremer's words showed he understood the importance of a "solid civil society." Yet, perversely, this appropriate goal would fall victim to the overwrought, neocon-influenced drive to make the Iraq project into an epic great-power battle, analogous to our world-historical victories over totalitarianism in World War II. Bremer's flip reference to "the relevant lessons of Germany and Japan" revealed how grossly misconceived and executed the Iraq adventure was. These policymakers simply didn't seem to appreciate that Germany and Japan differed radically from Iraq, especially when it came to post-war policy and democracy promotion. In Germany, several factors completely differentiated the approach and the result from Iraq. In post-war Germany, a totalitarian regime had failed in a belligerent foreign policy, leading to a collapse of the Nazi ideology and a resulting vacuum ready to be filled—as it turned out, in West Germany by American democracy and in East Germany by Soviet Communism. The West, the United States and its allies, principally the United Kingdom and France, reeducated the German citizenry through a comprehensive denazification educational regime aimed at millions of children and adults. The laws were also altered to criminalize Nazism itself. In both cases, the resources of the state were employed to shift the citizenry's priorities toward constitutionalism and away from the belligerent nationalism and virulent anti-Semitism that had marked the Nazi era. As we discussed at my dinner in Berlin, some of these prohibitions stand today, including German laws that prohibit Holocaust denial. Together, these measures continue to militate over the slippage of German *mores*.

America also initiated purely positive efforts in Germany—not to prohibit the bad, but to build the good. The United States launched the Marshall Plan throughout Europe, including Germany, plowing billions of dollars into the re-creation of institutions, employment, and the basic building blocks of society, practically as well as culturally undermining hatreds that otherwise could have taken root again. Through the Marshall Plan, the United States proved itself deeply sensitive to and sensible about the people's role in the ultimate success of constitutionalism. Finally, the United States undertook actions that gave us tremendous moral authority, undermining any Germans who would reflexively undertake the demagogue's proven technique of creating and attacking a hated foreign enemy. Andrei Cherny's recent book *The Candy Bombers* illuminates how the controversial Berlin Airlift, during which American bombers provided sustenance to millions of Berliners starving behind Soviet barricades, helped earn America a lasting reputation for good works in Germany and a natural friendship with generations of post-Nazi Germans.[23]

In all of these instances, Germany couldn't have been more different from Iraq, where for too many years a fitful American presence and an inattentive post-war regime had predictably allowed society to adopt harsh anti-Americanism, letting violent militias and insurgent groups gain a toe-hold in a fractious and barely surviving civil society and pushing millions of ordinary citizens into a demagogue's embrace.

Japan, too, was a distinct case. During World War II, millions of the country's citizens readily supported an extremely belligerent foreign policy toward the United States, China, and Korea. Despite the formal existence of the Meiji Constitution that General Douglas MacArthur relied upon in post-war Japan, constitutionalism had played only a small role in Emperor Hirohito's imperial Japan. A culture of military nationalism had prevailed instead among the citizens, who embraced policies that culminated not only in Pearl Harbor but also in the celebration of *kamikaze* fighters, who subsumed even their own identities to individual military suicide bombings in service of the nationalistic cause. The situation after the war led to tectonic shifts in the underlying citizen culture that had previously supported the imperial culture. Millions of the country's citizens had suffered the devastating psychological and practical effects of two nuclear bombs, including the deaths of hundreds of thousands of fathers, mothers, sons, daughters, neighbors, and political and civic leaders. As with Nazism, the ruling regime had been not only defeated but humiliated, losing any moral or practical authority whatsoever. The vacuum was filled by an occupying power's complete domination.

And, as in Germany, the United States was deeply attentive to the role of the citizenry in whether a democratic post-war Japan could survive. Under the reign of MacArthur, the steel grip of American policy came in a velvet glove. Local customs were incorporated in the new constitution, and MacArthur took care to craft a benevolent image. The United States was in for the long haul. Utter domination was combined with a constructive and long-term constitutionalism.

Again, the contrast with Iraq could not be greater. In the early years, our troops never achieved the monopoly on violence that was the prerequisite to citizen control. Instead of sustained commitment, ordinary Iraqis saw the confused and lean staffing of a hesitant occupier. Instead of a hard-earned security environment, ordinary Iraqis witnessed an engaged internal insurgency comprising multiple warring groups—and, of course, Moqtada al-Sadr leading the poor Shi'a masses.

Setting aside Germany and Japan and leaving Afghanistan and Iraq as open cases for now, when democracy was installed by force it lasted for a reasonable period of time in only a very few cases. As noted, these include Nicaragua in 1909, Italy in 1944, Grenada in 1983, and Panama in 1989. In our earlier discussion of Bill Kristol's promotion of forcible democracy installation, we saw how each of his cited successes was a nation especially amenable to the creation of democracy. In Italy, the demagogue and dictator Benito Mussolini's movement utterly collapsed, the people savagely turned on him, and the country was a substantial recipient of Marshall Plan funds and programs. Grenada is a tiny island whose political society was relatively easy to recreate. Panama, another very small country, was dominated by tens of thousands of American troops and a long-standing relationship with America through the Panama Canal. When American troops withdrew from Nicaragua in 1934 after an intermittent twenty-four year occupation, the country pitched into turmoil, first under the Somoza family's decades-long brutal dictatorship, then as it was overthrown by the Sandinistas and later challenged by the Contras. Its history makes clear that democracy installation isn't a matter simply of military will or commitment. An occupation of substantial length didn't make much of a difference in Haiti, either, where American troops were continuously engaged for nineteen years.[24]

Part of the problem in both democracy promotion and installation has been a disconnect between our rhetoric and our actions. The history of democracy promotion is filled with braggadocio and backfires, offenses that crossed party lines. Thomas Carothers observes that the Clinton administration, like the senior Bush's administration before it, was "addicted to sweeping statements about promoting democracy abroad that simply do not correspond to policy reality."[25] The result was extremely high expectations about U.S. policy, which can result in "self-inflicted wounds of considerable severity."[26] These excesses were evident from Woodrow Wilson's rhetoric and policies in the early part of the twentieth century to George W. Bush's missionary theme.

Another error has been to identify democracy too closely with formal institutions, rather than underlying values and processes.[27] "Supporting democracy too often resembles the application of a preprinted checklist in which the institutional forms of U.S.-style democracy are financed and praised," Carothers writes, "while the more complex and more important underlying realities of political life are ignored."[28] If we focused more on people than institutions, we could understand better when democracy is veering off course. We've made similar errors in equating democracy with particular rulers. Constitutional democracy should be defined by the trees, not the forest. If we associate democracy exclusively with a particular leader—something Carothers terms the "Great Leader" approach to democracy—then we risk actually undermining democracy, creating a brittle and top-heavy structure that can crumple when the top layer of society or an individual leader is displaced.[29] While we obviously must work with institutions and rulers, we should see them as a means to an end, not the end itself. The ultimate goal of a foreign policy of constitutionalism should be to focus on people rather than leaders and cultivate constitutional values among them; they, in turn, will pressure their institutions and leaders to adopt more equal power arrangements and more stable politics.

Finally, American attempts to address issues raised by democracy's paradox occasionally have supported the opposite of democracy. Throughout the twentieth century, American policymakers launched a series of covert operations that aimed to subvert, replace, or assassinate democratic leaders who were seen as a threat to the United States and her allies. The efforts included covert American involvement in the toppling of the democratic prime minister Mohammed Mossadeq in Iran, the overthrow of prime minister Patrice Lumumba in the Republic of Congo in 1960, the attempt to overthrow the demagogue Fidel Castro in the Bay of Pigs invasion in 1961, the overthrow of the democratic leader Salvador Allende in Chile in 1973, and illegally funding and supporting the war of the Contras against the socialist Sandinista government in Nicaragua during the 1980s.

In most cases, these efforts violated international law and even American law. They deeply contradicted the moral principle underlying America's foreign policy. Finally, they often backfired, serving to empower anti-American forces. Our actions in Latin America helped create generations of deep suspicion and hostility. The strength of anti-Americanism in Iran today is partly attributable to the tendency of Iranian leaders to characterize many public policies as a continuation of the vengeful 1979 White Revolution, when radical Muslims overthrew the autocratic Shah of Iran, who had been installed by the United States and the United Kingdom after they deposed Mossadeq in 1953.

These efforts almost always ignored the people and their constitutional culture. There was little attention given to ensuring that the nations would become, over the long haul, stable constitutional countries friendly to America and open to the world. Instead, America sided with dictators such as the Shah of Iran and Augusto Pinochet in Chile, reaping not peace and security, but resistance or worse.

MOVING FORWARD

THE ERRORS OF THE PAST EXERCISES IN DEMOCRACY MAKE CLEAR THE urgent need for a coherent strategy that will comprehensively turn away from failed ideas and resolve democracy's demagogue problem rather than regenerate it. In short, we need a political theory to guide the proper pursuit of democracy through our foreign policy.

The idea of constitutionalism resolves the platitude we often hear about democracy promotion—that a society must have either a history of democracy or inherited democratic institutions for democracy to take hold.[30] A culture is different from a history or from institutions. Like steel, culture is malleable, but only under tremendous force. Germany and Japan both became democracies fairly rapidly, but their cultures were forced to change very rapidly and under great duress by an overwhelming occupying power. In Iraq, however, the neocons wrongly assumed the Iraqis would use their freedom to embrace their constitution while under military occupation; instead, many turned their freedom over to al-Sadr. We failed to concentrate enough on cultivating constitutionalism among the ordinary people of Iraq—the housekeepers and engineers, the poets and architects, the surveyors and the police officers.

All this means that we should be working directly with people around the world to cultivate their constitutional values and to defuse demagogues. America must reach out to the peoples of the world and avoid actions that walk directly into the demagogues' trap by suggesting that we are belligerent and arrogant unilateralists who *want* mutually hostile relations. We also need to tend our garden carefully here at home, a necessity Larry Diamond, the democracy expert who witnessed the manifold failures of democracy installation in the first years in Iraq, crisply describes under the injunction, "Physician, heal thyself."[31] We cannot cultivate constitutionalism abroad if we take it for granted—or, worse, if we neglect it—here in the United States. In general, we have a highly engaged, reflective, and progressive relationship with our constitutional values. There are times, however, when we make terrible mistakes. The inattention to some civil rights and related issues during the course of the recent administration—for instance, the hasty passage of the Patriot Act; the current highly qualified status of *habeas corpus;* the shaky regulatory environment for voting; and the fact that socioeconomic status routinely impedes quality elections in certain communities—undermines our constitutional culture. We are strong, but we are not perfect, and we simply must remain vigilant at home as well as abroad.

A foreign policy of constitutionalism will present a new way of looking at the world, of relating to other peoples, and of understanding how constitutional democracy flourishes. We are looking to inculcate in ordinary citizen's a spirited dedication to the laws that transcends the laws. Democracy includes not only institutions and ideals but also a citizen's expectations of herself. Above all, constitutional democracy is a product of the people and their own values. George Kateb writes about Emerson's famous sentence in his essay "Politics," that "Good men must not obey the laws too well" (where Emerson was discussing the challenge of citizenship in a corrupt state): "Private moral feeling, when the individual stops and takes time to think in the forum of his individual mind, is likely to be better than the moral feeling embodied in laws that are made by a process of publicity, exaggeration, competition, and compromise."[32] Our evaluation of successful democracy should begin and end with the people's own "private moral feelings" *about* their democracy.

Such constitutionalism intrinsically defies the demagogue. "Citizens must build links across ethnic and regional divides to challenge elitist hierarchies and rule by strongmen," Larry Diamond writes. All hands must be on deck for this enterprise, including "dense, vigorous civil societies, with independent organizations, mass media, and think tanks, as well as other networks that can foster civic norms, pursue the public interest, raise citizen consciousness, break the bonds of clientelism, scrutinize government conduct, and lobby for good-government reforms."[33] Through these practices, a citizenry alert to authoritarian excesses will intrinsically inhibit ambitious political figures from attempting to become demagogues.

This is a highly practical goal, to be sure, but we must begin our pursuit of it with theory. As we saw in the Introduction, the ancient Greeks saw theory as a matter of *vision*. At this time in our history, we most urgently need conceptual goals that will help describe the state of the world our foreign policy hopes to achieve. They should include:

- Conceiving of other countries as composed of individuals, grouped into peoples, who each have hopes, dreams, and responsibilities for the direction of their nations.
- Communicating directly with the peoples of the world and understanding that a rapport with them undermines demagogues and redounds to our national security interest.

- Equipping people across the world with deep, enduring constitutional values through sweeping new educational and informational campaigns.
- In every country, placing the highest priority on an educated people's own judgment of their own abilities and importance, as against the state and centralized authorities.
- Creating the sense that the most value for a democracy comes from a boundless, limitless sense of individual possibility.
- Cultivating among citizens of the world, and society at large, the sense of revolution as a constant restoration of their natural right to freedom.
- Generating the recognition that each citizen can always create something new—a word, an idea, an action—for which she is responsible, and that the government must respect for that reason.
- Cultivating a common understanding among the peoples of the world that anyone who would use the people's approval to create powers that transcend the people themselves does democracy the greatest harm and must be stopped.

These conceptual goals are like facets of a prism through which we can view the world, rather than a to-do list of specific policies. However, this doesn't mean policy isn't important. On the contrary, constitutionalism will matter only if it leads to practical steps.

Before we get to these measures, we first need to flag the danger of a quest for a silver bullet. The history of democracy promotion is riddled with policymakers' infatuations with particular ideas that will make democracy take hold immediately.[34] These fads have included elections, civil society, rule of law, decentralization, and anticorruption. (In recent years, for instance, nongovernmental organizations [NGOs] were seen as *the* key to democracy.) Democracy promotion organizations proceeded, willy-nilly, to build and fund thousands of these groups and programs in developing nations around the world—sometimes without regard for whether they actually created the constitutional culture that was really needed. All such approaches suffer from the same flaw—the idea that "democratization is amenable to magic bullets."[35] We've seen the consequences, whether in Plato or Strauss, of the quest for a perfect "solution" to the demagogue problem—a solution that itself takes on ideal, almost metaphysical, qualities. If we convert our desire to make democracy work into a spiritual, even religious, quest, we will neglect the very ordinariness of a successful constitutionalism. And the demagogue who understands the advantage the ordinary has over the extraordinary will always be able to find the seams in democracy and rip it apart.

With this cautionary note firmly in mind, we move to the final question of this book—how to increase constitutionalism around the world through our foreign policy. We should take action in the following ways.

Civic education

The best-selling book *Three Cups of Tea* dramatically recounts the efforts of a Westerner to help rebuild Pakistan's educational system through local schools.[36] Countries like Pakistan desperately need assistance to build up their public education system; otherwise, thousands of young children will receive their only education through *madrassas,* many of which are operated by extremist clerics. With little or no training in basic constitutional values, children will more likely be educated in the values of authoritarianism and anti-Americanism. We should increase educational programs through a sweeping effort to train students across the world in constitutional values and inculcate these values at an ethical level. This education should include training in separation of powers, equal rights, judicial review, and the preeminence of the law (rather than authority).

Market economics

We should support programs that equip people with the self-possession and independence to hold the line against demagogues. The scholar Michael Mandelbaum credits "market activities" with triggering the cultural changes that can cause democracy to suddenly appear in

countries like a "rabbit being pulled out of a hat."[37] Participating
in a free market cultivates values in citizens that apply equally well
to constitutionalism. Acting as a consumer cultivates the "exercise,
and the expectation of exercising, sovereignty," as citizens think of
themselves as individuals in control of their own choices.[38] Market
practices also help citizens take on the habits and values of trust
and compromise, because you must trust someone to buy and sell
from that person, and you must often haggle and compromise—
accepting the other as an equal partner in the process.[39] Programs
that help to set up and monitor local stock markets, train citizens
in the basic elements of a free market, and expand microfinance
programs to increase small business will help lay the foundation for
constitutionalism.

Sharing the vision

America should commit to spreading the vision of constitutionalism,
both the internal value of a self-respecting citizenry and the external
value of chastening authority. Our leaders, whether at the highest
levels, including the president, or at levels including officials of the
State Department, USAID, or other international agencies, should
make a distinct effort to share our foundational ideals of the active
pursuit of political freedom, the free exchange of ideas between citizens, and the tolerance of dissent in their interactions with the people
of the world.[40] Two prominent examples of such direct connection
with the citizenries of other countries are the appearance of John
F. Kennedy in Berlin in 1963, where he proclaimed, "All free men,
wherever they may live, are citizens of Berlin, and, therefore, as a free
man, I take pride in the words '*Ich bin ein Berliner!*'" and Ronald
Reagan's 1987 speech, also in Germany at the Berlin Wall, where he
implored, "Mr. Gorbachev, tear down this wall!" These actions will
reveal the ideas that generate constitutionalism. In practice, they will
also share with the world the confidence of the constitutional experiment and how citizens take part in it, without fear of reprisal, and
with the self-reliance of a citizen who fully shoulders the burden of a
constitutional society.

Election training

People need training in actual elections because elections can be intimidating to new voters and, as in any new activity, information and practice can make a great difference. Ordinary citizens need basic education in how to participate in elections—reviewing campaign arguments and materials; using blind ballots; understanding, evenly evaluating, and filtering the electioneering that takes place around the election; and taking responsibility for the gift and burden of the franchise by participating in public deliberations and by voting. The administrators of the election process itself need support and training, as well—in conducting impartial elections, helping less-skilled citizens make their choices, preventing pressure tactics, and generally cultivating public confidence in the elections. Thomas Carothers observes that, in the area of election monitoring, too many democracy promoters focus simply on the election itself. But related activities deserve attention as well, such as the passage of election laws, registration of parties and candidates, creation of voter lists, the media coverage of the process, the campaign finance system, and the system for dealing with voter complaints.[41] Again, all of this should be viewed through the lens of the ordinary person's experience of democracy, with an eye toward strengthening and deepening the constitutional values currently in practice.

Respect

The people in other countries need to know and believe that the United States is affording them the respect of free-choosing individuals who are electing a constitutional system over the incitements of leaders who prioritize other goals, such as nationalism. The same values that Arendt emphasized in constitutionalism—trust, responsibility, self-ownership—must connect, at the "macro" level, to the "micro" level of the individuals in the societies we want to become democratic. When we condescend to or seek to control the thought of other societies, these actions often backfire. Conversely, we can expand constitutional democracy by sharing our own tolerance and the broader message that constitutional democracy succeeds when the citizens embrace and respect debate, rather than reject it. Diamond, for instance, argues that the United States' Voice of America international broadcast agency ought to include opposing viewpoints. "Nothing the United States can broadcast so powerfully conveys the democratic idea as its own willingness to air and tolerate criticism of its policies."[42]

Direct engagement with the people

The United States needs to broadly engage directly with the peoples of the world, enlisting them in the constitutional enterprise and helping them to bypass, where possible, prudent, and desirable, the elites and structures that otherwise would block them from sharing these values. This direction will allow constitutionally engaged citizens to question and pressure established governments, whether in the Middle East, Africa, Asia, or Latin America. But there are softer paths, as well. One example is increasing foreign student exchanges with countries with democratic difficulties. We should increase the number of students from countries like Venezuela, Iran, Lebanon, and Iraq studying in the United States, specifically so they will understand constitutionalism and return home able to share those values with their fellows and their children and grandchildren.

Tailor constitutionalism to underlying cultural values

Constitutionalism is an artifact of culture and belief. We therefore need to begin where the people *are* and accept that constitutionalism will naturally differ from place to place. Historically, political scientists have determined that norms for civil liberties can vary dramatically from country to country and that the "role played by democracy is mediated by how that concept is understood in the political culture of the country."[43] From America's perspective, as long as a nation's constitutionalism produces a common wariness about strong men, a desire for broad and deep rights, a chastening of authority, and pride in the ownership by each citizen of their democracy, it will be a powerful step in the right historical direction. As

Diamond writes, "There must be unifying principles and overarching objectives, but every country is distinctive, and strategies to assist democratic development must be specific to the time and place."[44] Douglas MacArthur's decision to retain the emperor in the Japanese constitution would be anathema in the United States, but was the right decision. Similarly, in Iraq or other Muslim countries, *sharia* law—or parts of it—might well make the most sense for their legal system.

A world of individuals

The deeper underlying value of a diverse constitutionalism is a recognition—and embrace—of the pluralism of the world. One scholar writes, "Arendt's appeal to a universal feature of humanity arguably makes her a cosmopolitan, but that feature is plurality, rather than the more common ideas of universal human rights, universal human reason or a universal humanity as the basis of utilitarian calculation."[45] This strongly contrasts with the approaches of Samuel Huntington and some neocons today, who envision other nations and cultures as fixed.[46] In other words, we need to stop reductively lumping people together, conceptually or practically as, say, "Sunni," "Arab," "Middle Eastern," or "African." A post-neocon, pro-constitutionalism foreign policy will view other nations and groups not primarily as calcified categories that operate in an unchanging, preset manner, but more fundamentally as groups of individuals, each of whom possesses the same characteristics (natality, uniqueness, rights) that we do. The political systems and cultures in which these people operate can certainly impinge upon their individual freedoms. But they are all, first, individuals, and we need to begin from that premise.

Increased civilian capacity on humanitarian and democracy missions

The American military has done an impressive job adapting to the civil components of missions in Iraq, Afghanistan, and elsewhere, including helping with educational, legal, and even transportation issues.

The Pentagon has created small and nimble Provincial Reconstruction Teams (PRTs) to enable the military to better tailor their actions to civilians' needs in Iraq and Afghanistan. The PRTs have allowed our troops to better relate to the peoples of countries where we are engaged. President Bush also recently implemented a program called the Civilian Reserve Corps, which at full strength is supposed to have more than 3,000 civilian professionals who can deploy to assist on missions where their expertise is required. Finally, the Department of Defense also recently created a new command center in Djibouti, called AFRICOM, with the express intent of working on civil and humanitarian missions.

We should take these efforts to the next level by creating a substantial new corps of civilian professionals who can help cultivate constitutionalism around the world. We should dramatically expand and institutionalize the Civilian Reserve Corps to resemble a democracy-promoting equivalent of the Peace Corps; it would thus become a well-known, well-funded, and substantial program consisting of the equivalent of two to three brigades. These doctors, lawyers, financial experts, civil engineers, teachers, and other expert professionals (under the direction of the State Department and in coordination with the Department of Defense) would deploy to weak and failing states. They would promote democracy and address humanitarian issues by working directly with civilian populations. They would be the advance guard of a United States that's newly committed to cultivating a constitutional culture among the peoples of the world.

Finally, we should take the simple but profound step of denying demagogues what they seek the most—an easily hated enemy to agitate the masses against. Any garden-variety demagogue can exploit another nation's belligerence, and it takes only arrogance or stupidity—or both—to play into their hands. It's no surprise that during the years of the Bush administration, when the neocons in power were pursuing an "imperium" idea, anti-American demagogues such as Chávez, Nasrallah, Ahmadinejad, and Sadr flourished. The greatest irony of all is that democracy, at the hands of the neocons, ended up damaging prospects for spreading constitutionalism by fomenting demagogues in countries newly rebellious against the United States.

Anne-Marie Slaughter, the dean of Princeton's Woodrow Wilson School of Public and International Affairs, makes this point in her important book *The Idea that Is America*. She observes that polls have shown that majorities in Turkey, Morocco, Jordan, and Pakistan believed the "war on terror," including Iraq, really was about "world domination." And majorities in these countries have also concluded that the Iraq War has decreased their confidence that the United States wants to promote liberty and democracy globally. Slaughter tells an illuminating story about a conversation with a Palestinian cab driver in Denmark:

> He was at pains to explain that he had no quarrel with the American people. But he asked how on earth America could say it was fighting for democracy in Iraq when it had completely ignored even the limited measure of global democracy established through the United Nations in choosing to go to war against the wishes of the Security Council. If the world didn't want war, he asked, including almost all of the closest U.S. allies, how could we go ahead? Surely, he thought, it was because we had other motives—oil, money, and power.[47]

As we've seen, from Cleon to Hitler, demagogues often need an external force to agitate. The neocon foreign policy seeded suspicion and enmity among the peoples of the world, not just their leaders and their institutions. These masses then became easy targets for the demagogues who simply wanted power.

If we choose to bury other nations in bluster and bullying, demagogues will sprout like mushrooms in manure. The point is particularly acute in light of the central role of democracy in the wars in Iraq and Afghanistan. We must decouple democracy and military interventionism.[48] When democracy becomes a pawn in regime change, the cause of freedom can erode rather than expand. Democracy's confluence with regime change also leads to gross contradictions that infuriate the world, such as when America advances tactical relationships with non-democratic regimes such as Saudi Arabia and Egypt with the one hand, while attempting to force democracy with the other.

It's a deceptively obvious point. If we want the world's nations—and the people who live in them—to desire democracy, these people must themselves not resent, fulminate against, and attack history's greatest democracy. The peoples of the world are citizens of a democratic planet, in the same sense that Americans are citizens of our constitutional democracy. Whether in Athens or America, the dedication of ordinary people to constitutional principles can resolve democracy's primitive threat from the demagogue. Similarly, if we want the citizens of the world to adopt and support constitutionalism, we have to offer them a light to follow on an often dark path instead of a whip to drive them forward. This means American power, both in theory and in application, must become an authority that works *with* the peoples of the world, rather than threatening and demanding things from them.

Properly pursued, this orientation could lead to adjustments of all of the instruments of the American government that perform before and interact with the peoples of the world, ranging from the president and his counselors to the State Department and the Pentagon to agencies including USAID and the National Endowment for Democracy. Thousands of Americans work in these government agencies and regularly represent the United States to the world's citizens. In many cases, they do a splendid job of fostering constitutionalism. Yet the unfortunate reality is that the exceptions can swallow the rules. The Bush administration deserves compliments for the creation of the Millennium Challenge Corporation and for the AFRICOM base in Djibouti, for instance; yet these accomplishments were largely eclipsed by the mistakes of the Iraq War. The lesson is that constitutionalism and a rebuilding of America's reputation among the peoples of the world will require vigilance. All hands are needed; every relevant government agency and individual, from the president to each civil servant, should help steer America in a new direction.

————————————◆————————————

THEORY AND PRACTICE

A NEW, PROGRESSIVE DEMOCRACY AGENDA MAY SOUND AMBITIOUS, BUT the United States shouldn't have to reinvent the wheel to promote constitutionalism. At a small level, often through pilot programs, governmental organizations such as the National Democratic Institute (NDI) have been acting in this area for years. But to make a real difference, these programs need to be made a priority, expanded, monitored, and held to high standards. The efforts so far have been promising. Since 1997, for instance, NDI has run a program in Haiti called the Civic Forum, which aims to provide Haitians with the knowledge and confidence to effect change at the grassroots level. With relatively low funding, nearly 200 Initiative Committees were formed throughout Haiti to promote civic education on democratic norms and values and to act upon those values through initiatives at the community level. Thousands of impoverished citizens have taken part in these groups, realizing that the "best way to bring initial relief to their communities and get themselves out of their dilemma is through citizen participation and community action."[49]

In certain cities in Kosovo, NDI has run a program for several years with the aim of instructing citizen groups in organizing and advocacy, the overarching goal being to help them force an "appropriate balance of power between citizens, their public officials and institutions." NDI aimed to give citizens the tools needed to scrutinize government and influence decisions, and found, over three years of the program, a marked increase in organized citizen participation and in the improvement of the performance of city assemblies.[50]

In Lebanon, NDI worked on the pervasive apathy among the country's marginalized groups, especially youth. NDI started a pilot program training youth in seven villages to run for and serve on city councils. The project included training sessions on strategic thinking, community organizing, fund raising, coalition building, Lebanese municipal code, advocacy campaigns, and the assessment of results. Participants also took part in activities to promote team building.[51]

Programs like these are not earthshaking, but neither are they the "mop-up work" Charles Krauthammer derided in his exchange with Francis Fukuyama. Remember that the individual components of the Marshall Plan—building hospitals, roads, schools, and financial institutions—also weren't revolutionary. The difference is in the scope and emphasis, not the kind of activity. The National Endowment for Democracy (NED), the umbrella organization for NDI and its sister organization, the International Republican Institute (IRI), is a nonprofit organization funded by grants from Congress. It's relatively inexpensive, with a budget of $74 million in 2006. We could expand this budget dramatically without significantly impacting our overall expenditures on foreign affairs and national security, while achieving an exponential impact on constitutionalism in the world.

But we don't just need to expand existing programs. In keeping with the underlying conceptual basis of constitutionalism, America ought to strengthen democracy beginning from *where the people are.* Whether ethnic or civic, nations are, above all, local. The essence of constitutionalism is the experience of a lawful society in one particular place. Constitutionalism, like nations, requires a profound sense of identity rooted in place, history, and, more importantly, culture.

A study of democracy promotion efforts conducted in 2000 by the Carnegie Institute of Peace concluded that they need to be carefully tailored to "specific sectors and contexts." If they are not, they can have little impact or can "even backfire, provoking unintended harassment of both locals and Western groups."[52] The study focused on actions by democracy organizations in post-Soviet countries in four areas: political parties and elections, independent media, public advocacy groups, and ethnic conflict.[53] The researchers uncovered interesting stories. In Russia, for instance, NDI and IRI helped train citizens in modern Western political campaigning and election technology, such as how to make political ads (including negative ones), how to conduct direct mail campaigns, and how to use polls in developing one's "message."[54] The researchers found that campaigning practices with a local cultural correlate were more likely to take hold. When trying to teach the Western practice of monitoring elections, for instance, they found that the Russian Communist Party far more readily adopted the practice than the various liberal parties, in large part because the Communist Party had substantial experience in monitoring citizens under the Soviet regime, and the liberal parties were too uncomfortable with the idea to do it very well.[55]

Another sector was advocacy groups focused on women's rights, the environment, and civic education, including organizations such as the Soros Foundation, the Ford Foundation, the German Marshall Fund, and the MacArthur Foundation.[56] Again, the researchers found that local culture was a critical variable. In Poland, for instance, American feminism-influenced advocacy for women had a difficult time taking hold. An example was a series of seminars by a Western organization on how to establish women-run banks in Warsaw and Lodz, cities with large populations of female workers. The models on which the seminars were based were drawn from countries substantially different from Poland, and the students protested that they were unhelpful. The administrators, however, refused to alter the models, so no banks were ever constructed.[57] In the civic education area, another example occurred in Romania. American donors imported an American pedagogical model focused on substantial teacher–student interaction, which conflicted with traditional Romanian ideas of teacher-centered lectures. Local teachers who were supposed to give the civic education lectures resisted participating at all.[58] Ultimately, the organization was forced to create a new vocabulary, a new field of study, and a new training program, revealing the promise of adaptation.[59]

In the end, a democracy promotion policy focused on constitutionalism will need to begin with the people and their culture. The neocons got it exactly wrong, viewing democracy as destiny and America as above such "mop-up work." The truth is that just as democracy is not deterministic, America shouldn't be above anything having to do with the growth of actual freedom and the ultimate resolution of the cycle of regimes. In fact, this is exactly where we should start.

---◆---

FROM HUBRIS TO STRENGTH

FINALLY, WE MUST THINK ABOUT OUR IDEA OF AMERICA HERSELF IN relation to democracy in the world. The answer to the question of how to absorb the lessons of Iraq and redirect our foreign policy to constitutionalism must begin with our vision of the United States. We have already seen how much damage hubris can cause, in the form of the idea of a quasi-imperial superpower. But there is another vision we can borrow for America, one that sees the nation not as an arrogant crusader but instead as a wise and reflective leader, seared by our own experiences and reflective about the burden of our unique moral and political capabilities. We again need to travel back in time for the richest picture of this America, as drawn by our seventh and final character: the poet Walt Whitman.

In 1855, Ralph Waldo Emerson, the essayist and famous Yankee dean of American letters, boarded a train in Cambridge, Massachusetts, where he was enshrined at Harvard. Over a decade earlier, Emerson had published "Self-Reliance," an essay that quickly became something like American scripture on the topic of our constitutional conscience. Despite his preeminence, Emerson knew his limitations. He was a gifted intellectual who could explain to the public complex philosophical arguments about America's uniqueness and the promise of freedom. He could craft arguments and articulate positions on par with the world's great public intellectuals. But he knew his machine of democracy also needed a soul.

Emerson stepped onto the train, took a seat, and watched through the windows as the station slowly receded—and wondered what he had gotten himself into. He was traveling to New York to meet Walt Whitman, a young man he had seen only in the frontispiece of a first volume of poetry called *Leaves of Grass*. In the engraving, Whitman seemed at once insouciant and tough, with a broad-brimmed hat hovering above an enigmatic stare and a brazenly open flannel shirt. The equally rough-hewn volume of poetry had been savaged by the Brahmins in Emerson's hometown. The Boston *Intelligencer* called it "this heterogeneous mass of bombast, egotism, vulgarity, and nonsense."[60]

Emerson, however, had discovered something so special in the book that he had written Whitman, out of the blue, a letter so ecstatic its prose was downright giddy:

> Dear Sir,
>
> I am not blind to the worth of the wonderful gift of *Leaves of Grass.* I find it the most extraordinary piece of wit and wisdom that America has yet contributed. I am very happy in reading it, as great power makes us happy. . . . I did not know until I last night saw the book advertised in a newspaper that I could trust the name as real and available for a post-office. I wish to see my benefactor, and have felt much like striking my tasks and visiting New York to pay you my respects.[61]
>
> R. W. Emerson

Emerson had gotten caught up in *Leaves of Grass,* yes, and deservedly so. The collection of poems read like the literary equivalent of a burst of lightning—a shockingly new, self-aware, brash, intensely personal, and deeply political work. The poems spanned a tremendous range of ideas, from Whitman's desires for freedom and complete self-expression and self-realization, to his argument that America had a unique capability in the world. It was, as Emerson had written Whitman, the most extraordinary piece of wisdom that America had yet contributed.

Despite his excitement, Emerson had mixed feelings about the meeting. Whitman seemed to have a disturbing penchant for boundary-crossing self-promotion. Emerson wrote his letter to Whitman on July 21; on October 10, Whitman had the letter published in the New York *Tribune* without Emerson's permission or knowledge.[62] Emerson was perplexed, irritated by what he called a "strange, rude thing."[63]

———

It's difficult to imagine a more bizarre person becoming the authoritative chronicler of America's dream of democracy—particularly one who contradicted so dramatically the other tenders of the flame, bewigged and priggish as they seemed to be. As he grew older and more famous, Whitman's image would become something of a caricature. Thoreau wrote about him as having a "remarkably strong though coarse nature, of a sweet disposition and much prized by his friends. . . . He is very broad, but not fine."[64] Whitman was large, slow-moving, and unkempt, with a big beard and mustache and what another poet described as a "cloud of Jovian hair."[65] He weighed two hundred pounds and had big feet, big hands, and a broad, open face. He liked rough, common food—buckwheat cakes, beef steak, oysters, and strong coffee. Left to his own devices, he would drink directly from a water pitcher or a bottle of sherry or rum.[66] Career-wise, he was a mess—an erstwhile journalist who toiled for years in the cavernous marble halls of Washington bureaucracies while retooling and retooling again the growing manuscript that would become American scripture—and who suffered the trauma of being fired from the Department of the Interior after the secretary of the Interior discovered a copy of the sexually explicit *Leaves of Grass* in his desk drawer.

He was *yang* to Emerson's *yin*—an unabashed egotist and sensualist, whose appetites provided him with the raw material for some of his most vivid and celebrated injunctions to celebrate the whole potential of human experience. Yet underlying Whitman's checkered professional career was a profound conception of America, democracy, and the role of the citizen—at once spiritual, serious, and boundlessly optimistic.

Whitman saw himself as not only a poet, but as a *political* poet. Beginning as a pure exercise in self-publishing in 1855, *Leaves of Grass* went through multiple editions, with Whitman's political ambitions increasing with each edition. In the edition published in 1857, Whitman saw his mission as expressly political: to address the president, the Congress, the Supreme Court, and the nation on issues "as some great emergency might demand" and to "keep up living interest in public questions."[67] Whitman's democracy captivated Emerson because it fused a soaring political theory with a haunting meditation on America's spiritual beauty. Taken together, Whitman's ideas were a call for his readers to embrace a self-sustaining constitutionalism. In reading his words—in grasping his ideas—you were meant to come away bearing part of America's democracy burden, but with joy. In a poem called "Thoughts," Whitman wrote: "Of these years I sing,/ How they pass and have pass'd, through convuls'd pains as through parturitions;/ How America illustrates birth, muscular youth, the promise, the sure fulfillment, the Absolute Success, despite of people—Illustrates evil as well as good. . . ."

This was a constitutionalism of the future, a vertiginous vision of a great nation's potential. Whitman dismissed those who wouldn't take part for failing to join the march of democracy: "How many hold despairingly yet to the models departed, caste, myths, obedience, compulsion, and to infidelity . . . / How the great cities appear—how the Democratic masses, turbulent, willful, as I love them,/ How the whirl, the contest, the wrestle of evil with good, the sounding and resounding, keep on and on,/ How society waits unform'd, and is for awhile between things ended and things begun. . . ." These reprobates, wedded to the past, risked falling off the path. They would never join America's march under the banner of freedom. Whitman described the "birth" and "muscular youth" of America's "Absolute Success" and how we are the "continent of glories" and of the "triumph of freedom." This constitutionalism was at once deeply rooted and flourishing, tended by the caring hands of millions.

In Whitman's vision, democracy was destiny, but not reached via a magical path. Every individual shared responsibility for laying the brick and toiling in the sun. In his famous anthem, "By Blue Ontario's Shore," he wrote, between enigmatic parentheses: "(Democracy—the destin'd conqueror—yet treacherous lip-smiles everywhere,/ And Death and infidelity at every step.)" The constitutional conscience was our "great Idea." Like a lantern, it would give us the light we needed to build the path: "For the great Idea, the idea of perfect and free individuals,/ For that idea the bard walks in advance, leader of leaders,/ The attitude of him cheers up slaves and horrifies foreign despots."[68]

Whitman described the stirring part of constitutionalism that involves the very soul and being of every individual. This is the stark opposite of the raw destiny the neocons imagined, which barely requires individual effort at all. To Whitman, democracy was participatory art, not state-driven science. The most significant element of Whitman's democracy was the element of obligation. Each citizen had to pay for the gift of freedom. We had to earn the right to be a member of democracy. Democracy could succeed only through the people—ordinary people, not cultivated, learned leaders. "I must insist on the masses," Whitman once said. "I never have any doubts of the future when I look at the common man."[69] But the common man couldn't just *accept* such praise. He had to earn it by constantly living the democratic creed: "Underneath all, individuals!/ I swear nothing is good to me now that ignores individuals,/ The American compact is altogether with individuals,/ The only government is that which makes minute of individuals,/ The whole theory of the universe is directed unerringly to one single individual—namely, to You."[70]

What Whitman gave us, most powerfully, was a different sense of America's destiny. Like the neocons to come, Whitman believed America was exceptional, with a special responsibility for building democracy in the world. But where the neocons' America would be a hungry, arrogant, and hubristic bully, Whitman's America was instead a giant, at once fierce, humble, and grave, deeply cognizant of being bound up with the rest of humanity, and aware of the special burdens of being the world's greatest—and then still young—democracy. The "You" in the poem above was Whitman himself, each individual reader, and any man or woman in the street. It was everyone together, bound up in the common mission of a great nation—the world's greatest. "[A]merica is the continent of the glories, and of the triumph of freedom, and of the Democracies, and of the fruits of society, and of all that is begun . . ."[71] Whitman wrote. America was "all that is begun." Our constitutionalism, a gift to the world, would become the world's, but only if we loved it as much as we loved ourselves.

———

The two men met in Brooklyn. We can imagine Whitman clasping his rough hand over the pale Yankee's prim fingers, and Emerson eyeing the poet with a mixture of wonder and suspicion. Perhaps Whitman roared with laughter at the older man's nervousness. Whitman was like his poetry: garrulous, generous, and self-important. During this first meeting, the pair spent an hour talking in Whitman's small wooden house. They then went, at Whitman's urging, to eat dinner at Fireman's Hall, a raucous social club frequented by common folk,[72] with Emerson, according to a later account of Whitman's, doing most of the talking. Later, Emerson recorded the day with a single entry in his diary: "Brooklyn."[73]

During their meeting, Emerson couldn't contain himself. He needed to communicate to Whitman how much he admired the poet's ability to convey in words of hot feeling, rather than cool analysis, America's extraordinary accomplishment. Whitman, after all, could write words like this, in his short poem "America": "Centre of equal daughters, equal sons,/ All, all alike endear'd, grown, ungrown, young or old,/ Strong, ample, fair, enduring, capable, rich,/ Perennial with the Earth, with Freedom, Law and Love,/ A grand, sane, towering, seated Mother,/ Chair'd in the adamant of Time."[74]

Whitman's unique combination of humility and nationalism can perhaps be explained through the America of his time. Just as the neocons responded to the power vacuum of the post–Cold War era with a swaggering foreign policy, Whitman developed his political ideas in response to the trauma of the Civil War. Whitman himself dedicated years to serving the troops directly. He worked as a nurse in the wartime hospitals in Washington, while also working part-time as a copyist in the Army Paymaster's Office. He visited the hospitals twice a day, six or seven days a week—first in the afternoon and then for three or four hours at night, amazed that injured soldiers were sometimes housed in buildings that had hosted parties for Abraham Lincoln's Inaugural Ball in 1861. "To-night, beautiful women, perfumes, the violins' sweetness, the polka and the waltz," Whitman wrote, "then the amputation, the blue face, the groan, the glassy eye of the dying, the clotted rag, the odor of wounds and blood."[75] He frequently sat up all night with injured soldiers.

For Whitman, the achievement of America's dignity would forever be linked with its cost. During these years, his brother George's safety constantly weighed on his mind. George had joined a New York regiment in September of 1861 and spent four years fighting in a number of important battles. In late 1864, George was imprisoned by Confederate forces, prompting Walt to write one of his "angriest letters ever," in one biographer's words, about the secretary of war's decision that a prisoner exchange was not in the Union's interest.[76] George almost died in prison, but he was finally freed in a prisoners' exchange the next February, to Whitman's eternal relief.[77]

Whitman was emotionally and personally involved, and he can't be accused of any sort of weak-kneed, dovish qualities during the war. On the contrary, he was a passionate advocate of the Union's cause, crediting the war with reversing a decadent, downward direction for the nation. "There were years in my life—years there in New York—when I wondered if all were not going bad with America—the tendency downward," he wrote, "but the war saved me: what I saw in the war set me up for all time—the days in the hospitals."[78] He saw the war itself as a painful but necessary birth for a magnificent new nation, one that wouldn't be defined by perfection but rather by reconciliation of its own conflicts. "What is any Nation, after all—and what is a human being—but a struggle between conflicting, paradoxical, opposing elements," Whitman wrote, "and they themselves and their most violent contests, important parts of that One Identity, and of its development?"[79] By his reference to "One Identity," Whitman was linking America's internal struggle, and its birth through conflict, to the human condition itself and to our brothers and sisters in other nations across the world. He didn't think we should turn inward after the Civil War; in 1865, he told a friend the Civil War had rendered America "a gigantic embryo or skeleton of Personality, fit for the West, for native models."[80]

The figure of Abraham Lincoln looms large in Whitman's writing about America. If anyone best captured the elevated, powerful, grave, and ultimately philosophical character of American might and American democracy that Whitman envisioned, it was the president who prevailed over America's bloodiest conflict. Whitman saw the president frequently in the streets of Washington, writing in the summer of 1863 that "I see the president almost every day. We have got so that we exchange bows and very cordial ones."[81] Contrary to images of America as a sea of Platonic perfection, Whitman's beloved president was deeply flawed, but lovable for those flaws. His face, Whitman wrote, was "so awful ugly it becomes beautiful, with its strange mouth, its deep cut, criss-cross lines, and doughnut complexion."[82] And he was plebeian, looking "about as ordinary in attire, &c., as the commonest man."[83] But this friend of the common people was no demagogue. He instead staked his conflicted and controversial presidency on a singular claim about America herself, binding his own character and identity to the fate of a unified nation. "UNIONISM, in its truest and amplest sense," Whitman wrote, "form'd the hard-pan of his character."[84]

After Lincoln was assassinated, Whitman's eulogistic poems "O Captain! My Captain!" and "When Lilacs Last in the Dooryard Bloom'd" went on to become his most famous and most identifiably American poems. In these poems, the fusion of death and life, of reverence and ambition, and most importantly of the sacrifice at the heart of the American experiment, set Whitman's ideas apart from more naïve, reckless, and hubristic conceptions of American greatness, all wrapped up in the storied image of the great Lincoln.

After his meeting, Emerson boarded the return train, stirred and unsettled by his encounter with the wild-haired poet. He felt strangely infected by Whitman's reckless, jovial spirit, even if he was still irritated by the publication of his letter in the *Tribune*. The poet's lively, generative presence seemed to capture something of the fire of American democracy.

The two would go on to have a long mentor–mentee relationship, with Emerson advising Whitman to exclude some of the explicit poems from new editions of *Leaves of Grass*.[85] But it did not always go well between them. Just as he rebelled in all else, Whitman would also rebel against the occasionally suffocating influence of his mentor. Years after his meeting with Emerson, Whitman criticized to a friend the "bloodless intellectuality" of Emerson's writing. Of their first meeting, when Emerson talked so much, he said: "If I were to unbosom to you in the matter I should say that I never cared so very much for Emerson's writings, prose or poems, but from his first personal visit and two hours with me . . . I had a strange attachment and love for *him* and his contact, talk, company, magnetism."[86]

Whitman's restless, independent spirit perhaps helps explain how a poet's ideas, like those of a great political theorist, have actually mattered in politics. In a book published in 1944, for instance, when Nazi Germany seemed poised for world conquest, a well-known critic of communism named Samuel Sillen claimed Whitman as a fighter for freedom across the world. "This volume has a definite purpose," Sillen wrote. "It aims to present Walt Whitman as a living force in the war against fascist barbarism as well as in the peace which America and the other United Nations seek to achieve through unconditional victory."[87] He went further: "Our richest poetic interpreter of democracy, Whitman speaks directly to those who are battling today at the gates of a new era in which it will be possible, for the first time in history, to fulfill his vision of world liberty and fraternity."[88] Although it might seem like an overreach to credit a poet with teaching us about the "imperishable dignity of man" and how to "strengthen the concord of free peoples," this was the power of Whitman's vision of America's true authority.

Whitman, as the final character in our story, joins the six other great thinkers who grappled with the problem of democracy's own worst enemy. In the end, those who understood the true promise of democracy—Aristotle, Jefferson, de Tocqueville, and, most impressively, Arendt—argued that in equipping the people to protect democracy, we would, together, bend the arc of history upward (to paraphrase Martin Luther King, Jr., and, today, Barack Obama). With constitutionalism, they felt we could escape the dark spiral of our worst collective instincts and move toward the luminous horizon of a future where humanity can always transcend itself.

Nowhere was the ground more fertile for these new ideas than America. As Whitman explained so well, America is an optimistic nation. We believe in the frontier. At our best, however, we are grounded by our common recognition of the most basic tragedies of the human condition: the unintended consequences of unfounded ambition, the suffering and death when hubristic plans go awry, the hearts broken by a patriotism of word but not of deed. For America and Americans, democracy, held and nurtured by the people, *is* the answer—not only for ourselves, but for history. As we strive to meet the demands of the extraordinary gift of political freedom, we cannot—we must not—ever rest.

Conclusion

America the Exceptional

AMERICANS HAVE ALWAYS BEEN INTERESTED IN THE NOTION THAT America has exceptional capabilities, as have observers in other countries. The nineteenth-century German chancellor Otto von Bismarck famously (and bemusedly) observed, "God has a special providence for fools, drunks and the United States of America."[1] The idea of American exceptionalism draws in part from the American people's deep reservoirs of moral idealism and civic responsibility, but it's also rooted in hard facts about America herself. America is geographically privileged, has the most successful representative democracy in the world, and in domestic political affairs has long held a distaste for the rule of force common to European democracy and colonialism, embracing instead the rule of law.[2] American exceptionalism, as the human rights expert Michael Ignatieff has explained, manifests itself in four distinct ways: the realist, based on America's unique power relative to other nations; the cultural, stemming from "an American sense of Providential destiny"; the institutional, rooted in America's "specific institutional organization"; and the political, related to the distinctive conservative and individual character of America's political culture.[3]

The scholar Walter Russell Mead has gone further to identify four distinct strands of exceptionalist thought, each tied to an authoritative American political figure. Wilsonians are moral missionaries, committed to using American might and creating international institutions to make the world safe for democracy. Hamiltonians support international engagement, but through markets and economic measures. Jacksonians pursue a strong military that can apply overwhelming force against enemies. Finally, Jeffersonians, primarily concerned with liberty at home, avoid military and large-scale projects.[4] As different as they are, all of these groups are united by a common theme: a deep and abiding faith in America's unique capability and responsibility to do good in the world through democracy.

The Wilsonian missionary tradition was powerfully realized in the presidency of George W. Bush and the quasi-imperialism of the neocons, with a perverse bent. They twisted exceptionalism to suggest that

America is an "exception" to the world, rather than an "exceptional"—meaning excellent—nation. The disregard for the world that led to the Iraq War was consistent with the approach that led the administration to dismiss or withdraw from international agreements such as the Kyoto Protocol on climate change and the International Criminal Court; to withdraw from diplomatic engagement in challenging areas such as Russia, the Middle East, and China; and to scoff at multilateral institutions such as the United Nations. As Harold Koh, the dean of Yale Law School, has written, "The greatest tragedy is when America's 'bad exceptionalism,' its support for double standards, undermines its ability to engage in 'good exceptionalism,' or exceptional human-rights leadership."[5] This brand of exceptionalism undermined America's potential, rather than strengthened it.

Good people can differ on exceptionalism. Some find the idea that Americans at once bear a unique burden to solve the world's problems and an exceptional gift for that task obnoxiously self-important. They believe the weight would be better distributed around the nations of the world. Others find the idea of exceptionalism simply does not square with the facts of our history as they see them. In some respects, they are certainly right. We have made horrible choices as a nation, to be sure. For every advance in constitutional rights, there were Indian wars, Jim Crow, lynchings, the oppression of women, Massive Resistance, Japanese internment, and, today, Guantanamo and Abu Ghraib. These injuries may never be undone and must never be forgotten.

But the fact cannot be ignored that America *is* an exceptional nation. There is simply no other way to understand our history, our values, and our ambitions. From the Founding Fathers to the Monroe Doctrine, the War of 1812 to the Spanish–American War, the Civil War to Woodrow Wilson's quest for a League of Nations, Theodore Roosevelt's presidency to F.D.R.'s Four Freedoms, the Nuremberg trials to the American-influenced Universal Declaration of Human Rights, Harry Truman's Marshall Plan to J.F.K's Peace Corps, Jimmy Carter's emphasis on human rights to Ronald Reagan's call to end communism, Bill Clinton's assumption of the leadership of a globalized world to George W. Bush's call for a world of universal freedom—America has pursued an exceptional mission in the world. And we have put our money where our mouth is, with the world's largest economy and a military that is larger than those of the rest of the world combined. No serious political leaders—themselves responsive and accountable to the American people—ever really seek to undo these fundamental underpinnings of the still-unfolding American experiment. In short, American exceptionalism is a function of the American people themselves. It is deeply and uniquely American, originating in our essential national character—our generosity, our hopefulness, our ambition, and our sense of frontier and endless possibility.

But you wouldn't have known this in recent years. In a time when America most needed to present the world with our best character—generosity, confidence, and reflection—the world instead saw the worst—arrogance, ignorance, and hubris. This "vulgar exceptionalism" stemmed from a fundamental intellectual mistake: that the road to democracy could circumvent ordinary people. The people who directed our foreign policy during the last several years wanted arrogance for its own sake. Just as constitutionalism uses the best in the people to deny the demagogue the raw material he needs, in the coming years we will need to use the best in America to deny any policymakers the raw material they need for the hubris they seek.

Building a political theory of constitutionalism into our foreign policy vis-à-vis democracy will reverse this vulgar exceptionalism and turn us toward a different, more hopeful direction—an idea I suggested should be called "exemplarism" in the inaugural issue of *Democracy: A Journal of Ideas.*[6] This foreign policy concept would seek to draw the world to us through inspiring and resolute moral conduct.[7] Borrowing from Whitman's invocation of Lincoln, we should present a face to the world that is at once wise, strong, ambitious, and charismatic, but also gravely aware of the human costs of adventure as well as our own very real limitations. Past examples of exemplarism range from Truman's Marshall Plan to J.F.K.'s Peace Corps to Bill Clinton's Kosovo invasion. In each of these instances, the United States put something of value on the line for the sake of foreign policy decisions that at once created a safer world for America and our allies and reinforced the deserved reputation of America as a moral leader. And in each, we were rewarded for our actions with admiration and loyalty throughout the community of nations.

———————

An exemplarist foreign policy of democracy promotion through constitutionalism would view the peoples of the world as members of a great partnership with us. In helping guide them toward the constitutional values that we know work well from our own experience, we should understand that we are in a direct relationship with them, both through the policy of our government as well as through the basic humanity we all share. When we look at other nations that we hope will seek freedom, we should therefore also see millions of people like us—working, thinking, talking, acting, with governments responding to them (or not), as they demand it. These people in this global mirror will look back at us with eyes as intelligent, as discerning, and as open as ours. Like us, they will try to resolve the basic paradox of the human condition that generates demagogues: that democracy, left to its own devices, can produce not constitutionalism but tyranny. And like us, they will choose freedom, if they have the education, the understanding, and the constitutional values they need.

But they will turn on freedom—and on us—if they are not enabled to defend themselves and a demagogue arises to take advantage. Democracy, as de Tocqueville predicted, is almost certainly the path most of the world will follow most of the time. But that does not mean democracy will always succeed. If history teaches us anything, it's that the demagogue always lies in wait. Given a momentary opportunity, he will take hold and invade the body politic. The demagogue will never let go and will never disappear. Only vigilance among the people will keep him at bay and expand the reign of liberty. America can help save democracy in its eternal struggle with the demagogue. We can help slow, if not stop altogether, the cycle of regimes. And we can add to the victories of humanity's better angels over our own worst demons. Our unique position in the community of nations, and our extraordinary history, demands, once again, that we strike out on the path to true freedom.

NOTES

INTRODUCTION: FREEDOM AT THE BRINK

1. Gen. Rick Sanchez (ret.), "Muqtada al-Sadr," Time.com, http://www.time.com/time/specials/2007/article/0,28804,1733748_1733757_1735554,00.html
2. Ibid.
3. Samuel Huntington, *The Third Wave* (Tulsa: University of Oklahoma Press, 1991), 16–26.
4. Chávez: "Bush 'Devil'; U.S. 'On the Way Down,'" September 26, 2006, CNN. com, http://www.cnn.com/2006/WORLD/americas/09/20/chavez.un/index. html (accessed on July 10, 2008).
5. Nicholas Noe, *Voice of Hezbollah: The Statements of Sayyed Hassan Nasrallah 1* (London: Verso, 2007).
6. Arch Puddington, "Freedom in Retreat: Is the Tide Turning?," Freedom House, http://www.freedomhouse.org/uploads/fiw08launch/FIW08Overview.pdf (accessed on May 18, 2008).
7. Thomas Carothers, *Funding Virtue: Civil Society Aid and Democracy Promotion* (Washington, DC: Carnegie Endowment for International Peace, 2000).
8. George Athens Billias, ed., *American Constitutionalism Abroad* (Westport, CT: Greenwood Press, 1990).
9. Michael Mandelbaum, *Democracy's Good Name: The Rise and Risks of the World's Most Popular Form of Government* (Jackson, TN: Public Affairs, 2007).
10. George Kateb, *The Inner Ocean: Individualism and Democratic Culture* (Ithaca, NY: Cornell University Press, 1992), 43.
11. Robert Dahl, *A Preface to Democratic Theory* (Chicago: University of Chicago Press, 2006), 143.
12. Survey by Associated Press and Ipsos-Public Affairs, (February 11–13, 2005) [USIPSOSR.022305.R2]. This was not an isolated result. Throughout the second half of the twentieth century, one organization had conducted polls asking participants how important the goal of "helping to bring a democratic form of government to other nations" should be for America's foreign policy. The number saying it was "very important" had always hovered around 33 percent. But in 2006, that number dropped in half to 17 percent. Christopher Whitney, ed., "The United States and the Rise of China and India: Results of a 2006 Multination Survey of Public Opinion," The Chicago Council on Foreign Affairs, http://www. asiasociety.org/publications/GlobalViews06.pdf, 17 (accessed on July 11, 2008). In June 2006, the German Marshall Fund asked Americans whether "it should be the role of the United States to help establish democracy in other countries." Only 45 percent said yes, a drop of six points from the previous year. Survey by the German Marshall Fund of the U.S. and the Compagnia di San Paolo, Italy, with additional support from the Luso-American Foundation, Portugal, Fundacion BBVA, Spain, and the Tipping Point Foundation, Bulgaria, and TNS Opinion and Social Institutes, June 6–24, 2006 [USTNS.06TRANS.R23].
13. Survey by the Third Way and Penn, Schoen, and Berland Associates, January 30–February 4, 2007, http://www.thirdway.org/data/product/file/76/americas_role-poll.pdf (accessed on July 11, 2008). Granted, this was a false choice, given

that advancing democracy is most often complementary with protecting our security, but the fact that people embraced the false choice is itself instructive about changing attitudes about democracy. In another poll conducted in 2005, only 38 percent agreed with the statement that, "As a rule, U.S. foreign policy should encourage countries to be democratic." Fifty-four percent believed this instead: "As a rule, U.S. foreign policy should pursue U.S. interests, which sometimes means promoting democracy and sometimes means supporting non-democratic governments." "US Role in the World" PIPA-Chicago Council, 2005, http://www.americans-world.org/digest/overview/us_role/democracy.cfm (accessed on July 11, 2008).

14. "American Attitudes: America and the World," WorldPublicOpinion.org, http://www.americans-world.org/digest/overview/us_role/democracy.cfm (accessed on July 11, 2008).

15. PIPA-Chicago Council September 2005. In the 2007 Third Way poll, 40 percent thought "People all over the world share the desire to live in freedom and govern themselves democratically," while a strong majority, 55 percent, agreed that "People in some countries want freedom and democracy more than people in other countries." Survey by Third Way and Penn, Schoen, and Berland Associates, January 30–February 4, 2007, http://www.thirdway.org/data/product/file/76/americas_role-poll.pdf (accessed on July 11, 2008).

16. Fareed Zakaria, *The Post-American World* (New York: W.W. Norton, 2008).

17. Parag Khanna, *The Second World* (New York: Random House, 2008).

18. Immanuel Kant, *A Project for Perpetual Peace: A Philosophical Essay* (London: Stephen Couchman, 1796).

PART I: THE CYCLE OF REGIMES

1. Benjamin Jowett, trans., The Politics of Aristotle (Mineola, NY: Dover Publications, 2001), 154.

2. Jeffrey Tulis, *The Rhetorical Presidency* (Princeton, NJ: Princeton University Press, 1987), 27.

3. Alexander Hamilton, "Number 1," *The Federalist Papers* (New York: Penguin, 1961), 35.

4. Ibid., 527.

5. Adrienne Koch, *Jefferson and Madison* (New York: Oxford University Press, 1964), 18.

6. Ibid., 19.

7. Max Farrand, ed., *The Records of the Federal Convention of 1787,* vol. II (New Haven, CT: Yale University Press, 1911), 114.

8. Ibid., 582.

9. Ibid., 57.

10. Larry Diamond, *Consolidating Democracy* (Baltimore, MD: Johns Hopkins University Press, 1999).

11. Ibid., 10.

12. Fareed Zakaria, "The Rise of Illiberal Democracy," *Foreign Affairs,* November 1997.

13. John Milton. "Eikonoklastes," in *The Prose Works of John Milton,* vol. I (London: George Bell and Sons, 1881, originally published in 1649), 348.

14. See Reinhard H. Luthin, *American Demagogues: Twentieth Century* (Gloucester, UK: Peter Smith, 1959) and David H. Bennett, *Demagogues in the Depression: American Radicals and the Union Party, 1932–1936* (New Brunswick, NJ: Rutgers University Press, 1969).

15. James Fenimore Cooper, *The American Democrat* (New York: Knopf, 1956), 97.

16. James Ceaser, Presidential Selection: Theory and Development (Princeton, NJ: Princeton University Press, 1979), 12.
17. Aristotle, Benjamin Jowett, trans., *The Politics of Aristotle* (Mineola, NY: Dover Publications, 2001), 1212.
18. Plato, "Republic" in Benjamin Jowett, trans. *The Dialogues of Plato* (Gloucestershire, UK: Clarendon Press, 1908), 274.
19. F. W. Walbank, *Polybius: Classical Lectures* (Berkeley, CA: University of California Press, 1990), 7–8.
20. Polybius, *Histories,* vol. 9, http://www.yorku.ca/inpar/polybius_six.pdf (accessed on April 27, 2008), 355.
21. Ibid.
22. Ibid.
23. Ibid.
24. Arthur O. Lovejoy, *The Great Chain of Being: A Study of the History of an Idea* (Cambridge, MA: Harvard College, 1936).
25. Polybius, *Histories,* vol. 9, 355.
26. Thucydides, *History of the Peloponnesian War* (New York: Viking Penguin, 1987), 214–15.
27. J. K. Davies, *Democracy and Classical Greece* (Cambridge, MA: Harvard University Press, 1963), 100.
28. James Loeb, *Aristophanes and the Political Parties at Athens,* trans. Maurice Croiset (London, UK: Macmillan and Co., 1909), 22.
29. Plutarch, *The Rise and Fall of Athens: Nine Greek Lives* (New York: Penguin Classics, 1960), 167.
30. Ibid., 169.
31. Thucydides, *History of the Peloponnesian War,* 164.
32. Plutarch, *Rise and Fall of Athens,* 169.
33. Ibid., 172.
34. Thucydides, *History of the Peloponnesian War,* 163–64.
35. Ibid., 145 (emphasis added).
36. Benjamin Jowett, trans., *Thucydides* (Gloucestershire, UK: Clarendon Press, 1881), 129.
37. Ibid.
38. Hubert Ashton Holden, *Plutarch's Life of Pericles* (Highstown, NJ: Macmillan, 1894), 60.
39. Jowett, *Thucydides,* 129.
40. Hubert Ashton Holden, *Plutarch's Life of Pericles* (Highstown, NJ: Macmillan, 1894), 61–62.
41. Ibid., 164.
42. Aristophanes, *The Acharnians,* in *Aristophanes: The Eleven Comedies.* (New York: Liveright Publishing Corporation, 1943), 105.
43. Lowell Edmunds, *Cleon, Knights, and Aristophanes' Politics.* (Lanham, MD: University Press of America, 1987), 7.
44. Aristophanes, *The Knights* in *Aristophanes: The Eleven Comedies* (New York: Liveright Publishing, 1943), 65.
45. Ibid., 65.
46. Ibid., 48.
47. Ibid., 24.
48. Eli Sagan, *The Honey and the Hemlock: Democracy and Paranoia in Ancient Athens and Modern America* (Princeton, NJ: Princeton University Press, 1994), 128.
49. Plato, *Republic,* trans. G.M.A. Grube (Indianapolis, IN: Hackett, 1992), viii.
50. Ibid., viii–ix.
51. Ibid., ix.
52. Ibid., 216.
53. Ibid., 233.

54. Ibid., 232.
55. Ibid.
56. Ibid., 233.
57. Ibid.
58. Ibid., 234.
59. Ibid.
60. Ibid., 236.
61. Ibid.
62. Ibid.
63. Ibid.
64. Karl Popper, *The Open Society and Its Enemies* (London, UK: Routledge, 1945).
65. Plato, *Republic,* trans. G. M. A. Grube (Indianapolis, IN: Hackett, 1992), 95.
66. Ibid., 91.
67. Ibid., 148.
68. Plato, *The Republic of Plato,* trans. Benjamin Jowett, *The Dialogues of Plato* (Gloucestershire, UK: Clarendon Press, 1908), 250.
69. Ibid., 252.
70. Ibid.
71. Ibid.
72. Ibid., 260.
73. Ibid., 252–53.
74. Aristotle, Richard McKeon, ed., *The Basic Works of Aristotle* (New York: Random House, 2001), xiv.
75. Irving Kristol, "Confessions of a True, Self-Confessed—Perhaps the Only— 'Neoconservative,' " in *Reflections of a Neoconservative: Looking Back, Looking Ahead* (New York: Basic Books, 1983), 76.
76. Aristotle, *The Politics of Aristotle,* trans. Benjamin Jowett (Oxford: Oxford University Press, 1941), 1190.
77. Ibid.
78. Ibid., 1206.
79. Ibid., 1207.
80. Ibid.
81. Ibid., 1212.
82. Ibid., 1212–13.
83. Ibid., 1213.
84. Adolf Hitler, *Mein Kampf* (Boston: Houghton Mifflin Company, 1943), 338.
85. Josiah Ober, *Mass and Elite in Democratic Athens* (Princeton, NJ: Princeton University Press, 1989), 169.
86. Ibid., 95.
87. Ibid.
88. "The Birth of Democracy: An Exhibition Celebrating the 2500th Anniversary of Democracy," catalogue (National Archives, Washington, D.C., 1993), 95.
89. Sagan, *Honey and the Hemlock,* 91.
90. Ibid.
91. Ibid.
92. Ibid., 92.
93. Ober, *Mass and Elite,* 301.
94. Ibid., 323.
95. Ibid., 322.
96. Ibid.
97. "The Birth of Democracy: An Exhibition," 35.
98. I. F. Stone, *The Trial of Socrates* (Boston: Little, Brown and Company, 1988). See also "I. F. Stone Breaks the Socrates Story," *The New York Times Magazine,* April 8, 1979.
99. Sagan, *Honey and the Hemlock,* 128.

PART II: DEMAGOGUERY IN AMERICA

1. James Madison, Alexander Hamilton, and John Jay, The Federalist Papers (New York: Penguin Books, 1987), 345.
2. David Leonhardt and Marjorie Connelly, "81 Percent in Poll Say Nation Is Headed on Wrong Track," New York Times, April 4, 2008.
3. "Historical Bush Approval," http://www.hist.umn.edu/~ruggles/Approval.htm (accessed on July 11, 2008).
4. David P. Szatmary, Shays' Rebellion: The Making of an Agrarian Insurrection (Amherst, MA: University of Massachusetts Press, 1980), 49.
5. Marion L. Starkey, A Little Rebellion (New York: Alfred A. Knopf, 1955), 33.
6. George Richards Minot, The History of the Insurrection in Massachusetts in the Year Seventeen Hundred and Eighty-Six and the Rebellion Thereon (Freeport, NY: Books for Libraries Press, 1970), 151.
7. Szatmary, Shays' Rebellion, 59.
8. "John Jay to General Washington, June 27, 1786," in Gaillard Hunt and James Brown Scott, eds., The Debates in the Federal Convention of 1787 which Framed the Constitution of the United States of America, vol. 2. (New York: Prometheus Books, 1987), 587.
9. Letter from General Knox to General Washington, October 23, 1786, in Ibid., 586.
10. Letter from General Washington to John Jay, August 1, 1786, in Ibid., 587.
11. Szatmary, Shays' Rebellion, 73.
12. Szatmary, Shays' Rebellion, 74.
13. Bruce Ackerman, We The People: Volume I: Foundations (Cambridge, MA: Harvard University Press, 1991).
14. Thomas Jefferson, Merrill D. Peterson, ed., The Portable Thomas Jefferson (New York: Penguin Books, 1977), 417.
15. Jefferson's initial view on Shays' Rebellion, Ibid., 414; later view in letter to William Smith in Adrienne Koch and William Peden, eds., The Life and Selected Writings of Thomas Jefferson (New York: The Modern Library, 1944), 436.
16. David N. Mayer, The Constitutional Thought of Thomas Jefferson (Charlottesville, VA: University of Virginia Press, 1994), 3–4.
17. Adrienne Koch, Jefferson & Madison: The Great Collaboration (New York: Oxford University Press, 1964), 3–15.
18. Peterson, Thomas Jefferson, 417.
19. Ibid., 431.
20. Ibid., 430.
21. Mayer, Constitutional Thought, 318.
22. Ibid.
23. Thomas Paine, Thomas Philip, ed., Thomas Paine: Rights of Man, Common Sense, and Other Political Writings (New York: Oxford University Press, 1995), 122.
24. Peterson, Thomas Jefferson, 432.
25. E. M. Halliday, Understanding Thomas Jefferson (New York: HarperCollins, 2001), 129.
26. Ibid., 221.
27. Thomas Jefferson, "Report to the Commissioners for the University of Virginia," in Merrill D. Peterson, ed., The Portable Thomas Jefferson (New York: Penguin Books, 1977), 334.
28. Thomas Jefferson, "Letter to Destutt deTracy, December 26, 1820," University of Virginia, Jefferson Quotations, http://www.monticello.org/reports/quotes/uva.html (accessed on June 28, 2008).
29. Wilbourn E. Benton, ed., 1787: Drafting the U.S. Constitution, Volume I (College Station, TX: Texas A&M University Press, 1986), 89.

30. Farrand, Max, ed., *The Records of the Federal Convention of 178*, vol. 1 (New Haven, CT: Yale University Press, 1911), 299.
31. Ibid., 299–300.
32. James Madison, *Notes of Debates in the Federal Convention of 1787* (New York: W.W. Norton, 1987), 73.
33. Benton, *1787,* 456.
34. Ibid., 802.
35. Mayer, *Constitutional Thought,* 205.
36. Ibid.
37. Clare Priest, "Colonial Courts and Secured Credit: Early American Commercial Litigation and Shays' Rebellion," *The Yale Law Journal* 108:8 (June 1999), 2414–15, 2418.
38. Ibid., 2447–50.
39. Jonathan Smith, "The Depression of 1785 and Daniel Shays' Rebellion," *The William and Mary Quarterly* 5:1 (January 1948), 87.
40. Leonard Richards, *Shays's Rebellion: The American Revolution's Final Battle* (Philadelphia: University of Pennsylvania Press, 2002), 144.
41. Szatmary, *Shays' Rebellion,* 99.
42. Alexis de Tocqueville, *Democracy in America* (Chicago: University of Chicago Press, 2000), 326.
43. Halliday, *Understanding Thomas Jefferson,* 54.
44. Joseph Ellis, *American Sphinx: The Character of Thomas Jefferson* (New York: Thomas A. Knopf, 1996).
45. Annette Gordon-Reed, *Thomas Jefferson and Sally Hemings: An American Controversy* (Charlottesville, VA: University of Virginia Press, 1997), 108–09.
46. Bob Herbert, "The Blight That Is Still With Us," *The New York Times*, January 22, 2008.
47. "Death of the Wild Man," *Time Magazine,* http://www.time.com/time/magazine/article/0,9171,934786,00.html (accessed on June 28, 2008).
48. Reinhard H. Luthin, *American Demagogues: Twentieth Century* (Gloucester, UK: Peter Smith, 1959), 54.
49. Ibid., 63.
50. Michael Klarman, *From Jim Crow to Civil Rights: The Supreme Court and the Struggle for Racial Equality* (New York: Oxford University Press, 2006), 407.
51. Andrew Burstein, *The Passions of Andrew Jackson* (New York: Knopf, 2003), 5.
52. Ibid., 34–61.
53. Sean Wilentz, *Andrew Jackson* (New York: Times Books, 2005), 47.
54. Francis J. Grund, "General Jackson Understands the People of the United States," in Miller, ed., *The Nature of Jacksonian America* (New York: John Wiley & Sons, 1972), 120.
55. Arthur M. Schlesinger, Jr., "An Impressive Mandate and the Meaning of Jacksonianism," in Charles Sellers, ed., *Andrew Jackson: A Profile* (New York: Hill & Wang, 1971), 119.
56. Ibid., 121.
57. Michael Chevalier, "Symptoms of Revolution," in Douglas T. Miller, ed., *The Nature of Jacksonian America* (New York: John Wiley & Sons, 1972), 89–90.
58. Wilentz, *Andrew Jackson,* 55.
59. Mayer, *Constitutional Thought,* 107.
60. Oliver Wendell Holmes, *The Common Law* (New York: Little, Brown and Company, 1963), 36.
61. Thomas P. Abernethy, "Tennessee Nabob," in Charles Sellers, ed., *Andrew Jackson: A Profile* (New York: Hill & Wang, 1971), 40.
62. Ibid.
63. Burstein, *The Passions,* 27.

64. Abernethy, "Tennessee Nabob," 45.
65. Wilentz, *Andrew Jackson,* 76–78.
66. Ibid., 97.
67. Gerard N. Magliocca, *Andrew Jackson and the Constitution: The Rise and Fall of Generational Regimes* (Lawrence, KS: University Press of Kansas, 2007), 12.
68. John Spencer Bassett, "A Remarkable Man," in Charles Sellers, ed., *Andrew Jackson: A Profile* (New York: Hill & Wang, 1971), 102.
69. Joseph Epstein, *Alexis de Tocqueville: Democracy's Guide* (New York: Harper Collins, 2006), 10.
70. Susan Banfield, *The Rights of Man, The Reign of Terror: The Story of the French Revolution* (New York: J.B. Lippincott, 1989), 159.
71. Simon Schama, *Citizens: A Chronicle of the French Revolution* (New York: Viking Penguin, 1989), xv.
72. Epstein, *Alexis de Tocqueville,* 10.
73. Ibid., 11.
74. Harvey Mansfield and Delba Winthrop, Introduction, Alexis de Tocqueville, *Democracy in America* (Chicago: University of Chicago Press, 2000), xix.
75. de Tocqueville, *Democracy in America,* 6.
76. Ibid., 7.
77. Ibid., 10.
78. Ibid., 7.
79. Ibid.
80. Ibid.
81. Ibid., 12.
82. Ibid., 295.
83. Ibid., 275.
84. Ibid.
85. Ibid., 228.
86. Ibid., 229.
87. Ibid.
88. Ibid.
89. Ibid., 297.
90. Ibid., 298.
91. David Ross Locke, *The Demagogue: A Political Novel* (Boston: Lee and Shepard Publishers, 1891), 389.
92. Ibid., 19.
93. Ibid., 151.
94. Ibid.
95. Ibid., 153.
96. Ibid., 159.
97. William J. Locke, *The Demagogue and Lady Phayre* (London: John Lane, The Bodley Head, 1911), 39.
98. Ibid., 128.
99. Ibid., 43.
100. *The Compact Edition of the Oxford English Dictionary* (New York: Oxford University Press, 1971), 172.
101. Ibid.
102. Ibid., 51.
103. Arthur M. Schlesinger, Jr., *The Politics of Upheaval* (Boston: Houghton Mifflin Company, 1960), 20.
104. Ibid., 24.
105. "'Demagogues:' Johnson Lambastes Senator and Priest; Long Counters with Utopia; Coughlin Parries With Spirit of '76,'" *News-week.* March 16, 1935, 6.
106. T. Harry Williams, *Huey Long* (New York: Alfred A. Knopf, 1970), 89.

107. Ibid., 200.
108. Luthin, 236.
109. Williams, *Huey Long,* 37.
110. See Alan Michie and Frank Ryhlick, *Dixie Demagogue* (New York: The Vanguard Press, 1940).
111. Alan Brinkley, *Voices of Protest: Huey Long, Father Coughlin, and the Great Depression* (New York: Vintage Books, 1983), 31.
112. Ibid., 42.
113. Ibid., 36.
114. Huey Long, *My First Days in the White House* (Harrisburg, PA: Telegraph Press, 1935), 4.
115. Ibid., 110.
116. Williams, *Huey Long,* 37.
117. Ibid., 341–43.
118. Ibid., 657–58.
119. Ibid., 78.
120. Arthur M. Schlesinger, Jr., "Messiah of the Rednecks," in *The Age of Upheaval,* (New York: Houghton Mifflin, 1960), 58.
121. Ibid., 82.
122. Ibid.
123. Ibid.
124. Ibid.
125. Ibid., 80.
126. Ibid., 82.
127. Hermann B. Deutsch, "Paradox in Pajamas," *The Saturday Evening Post,* October 5, 1935, 14.
128. Ibid.
129. The novelist Robert Penn Warren uses a similar description to introduce his novel about Huey Long, *All the King's Men.* In the scene, Willie Stark alternately soothes and attacks his driver, Sugar-Boy, on a hectic trip on a country road. Robert Penn Warren, *All the King's Men* (New York: Harcourt Brace & Jovanovich, 1946).
130. Ibid., 15.
131. Russell Owen, "Huey Long Gives His View of Dictators: He Says That They Have No Place in America and Denies That He Himself Is One," *The New York Times Magazine,* February 10, 1935, 3.
132. T. Harry Williams, *Huey P. Long: An Inaugural Lecture Delivered before the University of Oxford on 26 January 1967,* (Oxford, UK: The Clarendon Press, 1967), 6.
133. Henry C. Dethloff, *Huey Long: Southern Demagogue or American Democrat?* (New York: Heath, 1967), ix, xiii.
134. Hodding Carter, "Bogeyman," in "How Come Huey Long," *New Republic,* February 13, 1935, 11.
135. Kenneth S. Davis, *FDR: The New Deal Years, 1933–1937* (New York: Random House, 1986), 494.
136. Arthur Krock, "In Washington: Ways Are Sought to Counteract Huey Long's Program," *New York Times,* January 10, 1935, 18.
137. Francis Brown, "The Political Pot Boils Ahead of Time," *New York Times,* April 7, 1935, 3.
138. Williams, *Huey Long,* 844.
139. Ibid.
140. Ibid., 845.
141. Felix Belair, Jr., "Radical Party Wedge Goes with Huey Long," *New York Times,* September 15, 1935, E3.
142. Carter, "Bogeyman," 14.

143. David Bennett, *Demagogues in the Depression* (New Brunswick, NJ: Rutgers University Press, 1969), 309.

144. Ibid., 263.

145. Rita James Simon, "Introduction," in Rita James Simon, ed., *As We Saw the Thirties: Essays on Social and Political Movements of a Decade* (Champaign, IL: University of Illinois Press, 1967), 46.

146. Gerald L. K. Smith, "The Huey Long Movement," in Rita James Simon, ed., *As We Saw the Thirties: Essays on Social and Political Movements of a Decade* (Champaign, IL: University of Illinois Press, 1969), 61.

147. T. Harry Williams, "Gentleman from Louisiana: Demagogue or Democrat?," in Henry C. Dethloff, ed., *Huey Long: Southern Demagogue or American Democrat?* (Boston: Heath, 1967), 73.

148. Arthur M. Schlesinger, Jr., "Messiah of the Rednecks," 92.

149. Ibid.

150. Williams, *Huey Long*, 844.

151. Ibid., 862.

152. Ibid., 865.

153. Ibid., 872.

154. Ibid.

155. Ibid., 869.

156. Sinclair Lewis, *It Can't Happen Here* (New York: Signet, 1970), 28.

157. Philip Roth, *The Plot Against America* (New York: Houghton Mifflin, 2004).

158. Marian C. McKenna, *Franklin Roosevelt and the Great Constitutional War: The Court-Packing Crisis of 1937* (New York: Fordham University Press, 2002), 73.

159. Ibid., 301–02.

160. Ibid., 303.

161. Ibid., 240–41.

162. Ibid., 344–47.

163. Ibid., 348.

164. Ibid., 352.

165. Ibid., 521.

166. Ibid., 555.

167. Prima Facie Guide: *The Rise and Fall of Senator Joseph R. McCarthy* (Wilmington, DE: Scholarly Resources Inc., 1982), 7.

168. Robert Griffith, *The Politics of Fear: Joseph R. McCarthy and the Senate* (Amherst, MA: University of Massachusetts Press, 1987), 29.

169. Tom Wicker, *Shooting Star: The Brief Arc of Joe McCarthy* (New York: Harcourt, 2006), 165.

170. Ibid., 162.

171. Ibid., 165.

172. William Manchester, *American Caesar: Douglas MacArthur 1880–1964* (Boston: Little, Brown and Company, 1978), 119.

173. Ibid., 152.

174. Ibid., 590.

175. Ibid.

176. Ibid., 648.

177. Ibid.

178. Ibid., 658.

179. Ibid., 661.

180. Ibid., 662.

181. Ibid., 663.

182. Ibid.

183. Ibid.

184. Ibid., 685.

185. Ibid., 671.

186. Ibid., 471.
187. Ibid., 454.
188. Ibid., 461–62.
189. Ibid., 500.
190. Ibid.
191. Ibid., 501.

PART III: THE MODERN STRUGGLE

1. Ben Wattenberg, "First Universal Nation: Leading Indicators and Ideas," in *Surge of America in the 1990s* (New York: Simon & Schuster, 1992), 196.
2. George Packer, "Dreaming of Democracy," *New York Times Magazine*, March 2, 2003.
3. Ibid.
4. David Isenberg, "Imperial Overreach: Washington's Dubious Strategy to Overthrow Saddam Hussein," *Policy Analysis* 360 (November 17, 1999), 1.
5. Ibid., 8.
6. Ibid., 13.
7. Yash Ghai, "Constitution-Making in a New Iraq," in Yahia Said, Mark Lattimer and Yash Ghai, eds, *Building Democracy* (London: Minority Rights Group International, 2003), 30.
8. Ibid.
9. Ibid.
10. John F. Burns, "Transition in Iraq: The Departing Administrator," *New York Times*. June 29, 2004, 9.
11. Larry Diamond, *Squandered Victory: The American Occupation and the Bungled Effort to Bring Democracy to Iraq* (New York: Times Books, 2005), 72.
12. Ibid., 82.
13. Jonathan Morrow, "Iraq's Constitutional Process II: An Opportunity Lost," Special Report 155, US Institute of Peace (November 2005).
14. Ibid., 86.
15. Ibid., 183.
16. Ibid., 185.
17. Ibid., 191.
18. Ibid., 198.
19. Thomas O. Melia and Brian M. Katulis, "Iraqis Discuss Their Country's Future: Post-War Perspectives from the Iraqi Street," July 28, 2003 (National Democratic Institute for International Affairs), 18.
20. Ibid.
21. Ibid., 17.
22. Ibid.
23. Thomas Melia and Brian Katulis, "To Win Over Iraqis," *The Washington Post*, August 10, 2003, B7.
24. Diamond, *Squandered Victory*, 83.
25. Eric D. Weitz, *Weimar Germany* (Princeton, NJ: Princeton University Press, 2007), 32.
26. Ibid.
27. Ibid., 33.
28. Ibid., 1.
29. William Shirer, *The Rise and Fall of the Third Reich: A History of Nazi Germany* (New York: Exeter Books, 1987), 23.
30. Ibid.
31. Adolf Hitler, *Mein Kampf* (Boston: Houghton Mifflin Company, 1943), 373.

32. Shirer, *Rise and Fall,* 44.
33. Ibid., 45.
34. Ibid.
35. Ibid.
36. Ibid., 48.
37. Ibid., 56.
38. Hitler, *Mein Kampf,* 580.
39. Daniel Goldhagen, *Hitler's Willing Executioners* (New York: Alfred A. Knopf, 1996), 395.
40. Ibid., 32.
41. Lawrence Rees and Tilman Remme, dirs., *The Nazis: A Warning from History* (1998).
42. Weitz, *Weimar Germany,* 33.
43. Plato, "Phaedrus," in Benjamin Jowett, trans., *The Dialogues of Plato* (Gloucestershire, UK: Clarendon Press, 1908), 252.
44. Catherine and Michael Zuckert, *The Truth about Leo Strauss* (Chicago: University of Chicago Press, 2006), 27.
45. Ibid.
46. Nicholas Xenos, "Leo Strauss and the Rhetoric of the War on Terror" in *Logos: A Journal of Modern Society and Culture* 3.2 (Spring 2004), http://www.logosjournal.com/issue_3.2/xenos.htm (accessed on June 23, 2008).
47. Ibid.
48. Zuckert, *Truth about Leo Strauss,* 27–28.
49. George Anastaplo, "Leo Strauss at the University of Chicago" in Kenneth Deutsch and John Murley, eds., *Leo Strauss, The Straussians, and the American Regime* (Lanham, MD: Rowman & Littlefield, 1999), 3.
50. Zuckert, *Truth about Leo Strauss,* 27–28.
51. Shadia Drury, *Leo Strauss and the American Right* (New York: St. Martin's Press, 1997), 5.
52. Zuckert, *Truth about Leo Strauss,* 54.
53. Leo Strauss, *Natural Right and History* (Chicago: University of Chicago Press, 1952), 42.
54. Hilail Gildin, "Introduction," in *An Introduction to Political Philosophy: Ten Essays by Leo Strauss* (Detroit, MI: Wayne State University Press, 1975), xix.
55. Leo Strauss, *On Tyranny* (London: The Free Press of Glencoe, 1963), 21–22.
56. Anne Norton, *Leo Strauss and the Politics of American Empire* (New Haven, CT: Yale University Press, 2005), 96.
57. See, for example, this representative passage from his seminal *Natural Right and History,* where Strauss took a conservative position on the importance of natural law versus changing value systems that evolve with time: "The philosophic quest for the first things," he wrote, "presupposes not merely that there are first things but that the first things are always and that things which are always or are imperishable are more truly beings than the things which are not always" (Leo Strauss, *Natural Right and History,* 89). Strauss's peculiar use of the adjective "always" rather than "forever," his lack of commas, the expansive breadth of this sentence's metaphysical reach ("first things are always"), and the poetic meter he employs, all combined in a charismatic intensity. This quality mounted as Strauss built both the rhetorical and logical case for natural law: "Beings that are always are of higher dignity than beings that are not always," he asserted, "because only the former can be the ultimate cause of the latter, of the being of the latter or because what is not always finds its place within the order constituted by what is always" (*Natural Right and History,* 89). The answer? Strauss leveled a final condemnation with a suffocating certainty: "Beings that are not always, are less truly beings than beings that are always, because to be perishable

means to be in between being and not-being" (*Natural Right and History*, 90). The benighted life of being "less truly" a being awaited anyone who refused to participate in Strauss's project. Everything that was "not always" was relegated to a half-status, presumably undeserving of moral commendation, the sanction of law, or any public policy not founded on an absolute, unshifting, "natural" morality. This was the universe Strauss creates and invokes—an intoxicating blend of certainty, incantation, and yearning for a grander, nobler time of absolutes and crystallized truths.

58. Leo Strauss, *Persecution and the Art of Writing* (New York: The Free Press, 1952).

59. Francis Fukuyama, *America at the Crossroads: Democracy, Power and the Neoconservative Legacy* (New Haven, CT: Yale University Press, 2006), 21.

60. Here is how one devotee of the neoconservatives describes the progression: "John Doe writes an article on welfare reform and single mothers for *The Public Interest*. William Raspberry of the *Washington Post* devotes a column to it, and a *Wall Street Journal* editorial questions Raspberry's interpretation two days later. George Will is intrigued by the article, devotes a *Newsweek* column to it, and invites Doe to appear on *This Week with David Brinkley*, where Doe is questioned by Will, Brinkley, and Sam Donaldson before a national audience. *The New York Times* condenses the article into an op-ed, and runs the next Sunday. Pretty soon, Doe receives speaking engagements from around the nation, and is able to explain his insight to thousands of people directly. Public officials from both parties call him for advice, and Doe is invited to testify before Congress. If the timing is right, Doe may receive a phone call from the president of the United States offering a high appointment. After all this, maybe only 10,000 people have read Doe's article—but his main idea is conveyed in one form or another to millions of others." Michael Gerson, *The Neoconservative Vision* (Lanham, MD: Madison Books, 1996), 5–6.

61. Anne Norton, *Leo Strauss*, 14–16.

62. Derek Chollet and James Goldgeier, *America between the Wars: From 11/9 to 9/11: The Misunderstood Years between the Fall of the Berlin Wall and the Start of the War on Terror* (New York: Public Affairs, 2008), 219.

63. Paul Wolfowitz, interview with Sam Tannenhaus, *Vanity Fair*, May 9, 2003, http://www.defenselink.mil/transcripts/transcript.aspx?transcriptid=2594 (accessed on July 11, 2008).

64. Saul Bellow, *Ravelstein* (New York: Viking, 2000), 59.

65. Leo Strauss, *Natural Right and History* (Chicago: University of Chicago Press, 1965), 141.

66. Ibid.

67. See, e.g., William Pfaff, "The Long Reach of Leo Strauss," *Policy Review*, Spring 1987; Shadia Drury, *Leo Strauss and the American Right* (New York: St. Martin's Press, 1997).

68. Strauss, *Natural Right and History*, 141.

69. Aristotle, Jowett, trans., *Politics*, 1190.

70. Strauss, *Natural Right and History*, 287.

71. Ibid., 286.

72. Ibid., 287.

73. See, e.g., Jim George, "Leo Strauss, Neoconservatism and US Foreign Policy: Esoteric Nihilism and the Bush Doctrine" in *International Politics* 42:2 (June 2005): 174–202; Nicholas Xenos, "Leo Strauss and the Rhetoric of the War on Terror" in *Logos*, 3:2 (Spring 2004): 12–14, http://www.logosjournal.com/issue_3.2/xenos.pdf; and James Atlas, "A Classicist's Legacy: New Empire Builders" in *New York Times* (accessed on May 4, 2003).

74. Leo Strauss, "Plato," in *An Introduction to Political Philosophy: Ten Essays by Leo Strauss* (Detroit, MI: Wayne State University Press, 1975), 210.

75. Leo Strauss, "Liberal Education and Responsibility," in *An Introduction to Political Philosophy: Ten Essays by Leo Strauss* (Detroit, MI: Wayne State University Press, 1975), 341.
76. Ibid., 341.
77. Ibid.
78. Carl Schmitt, *The Concept of the Political* (New Brunswick, NJ: Rutgers University Press, 1976).
79. Strauss, *Natural Right and History*, 103.
80. Ibid., 311.
81. Ibid., 305.
82. Ibid.
83. Irving Kristol, "'Moral Dilemmas' in Foreign Policy," in *Reflections of a Neoconservative: Looking Back, Looking Ahead* (New York: Basic Books, 1983), 263.
84. Lawrence F. Kaplan and William Kristol, *The War over Iraq: Saddam's Tyranny and America's Mission* (San Francisco: Encounter Books, 2003), 98.
85. Maureen Dowd, *Bushworld: Enter at Your Own Risk* (New York: Putnam, 2004).
86. Irving Kristol, "Memoirs of a Trotskyist," in *Reflections of a Neoconservative*, 5–6.
87. Ibid.
88. Ibid.
89. Ibid., 9–10.
90. Ibid., 7.
91. Ibid.
92. Irving Kristol, "Introduction," in *Reflections of a Neoconservative*, xii.
93. Irving Kristol, "'Moral Dilemmas' in Foreign Policy," in *Reflections of a Neoconservative*, 263.
94. Ibid.
95. Ibid., 262.
96. Ibid., 12.
97. Ibid., 13.
98. Ibid.
99. David Harvey, *The New Imperialism* (New York: Oxford University Press, 2005), 191–92.
100. Kaplan and Kristol, *War over Iraq*, ix.
101. Ibid.
102. Ibid., 98.
103. Ibid.
104. Ibid.
105. Ibid., 99.
106. Ibid.
107. Ibid., 105.
108. Ibid.
109. Pew Research Center, *Pew Global Attitudes Project: Global Unease with Major World Powers*, June 27, 2007, http://pewglobal.org/reports/pdf/256.pdf, 3, 25.
110. James Mann, *Rise of the Vulcans* (New York: Viking, 2004), 352–53.
111. George W. Bush, "Second Inaugural Address," http://www.whitehouse.gov/inaugural/index.html
112. Jacob Weisberg, "Fishing for a Way to Change the World," *Newsweek*, January 28, 2008.
113. "President Bush Discusses Freedom in Iraq and Middle East," November 6, 2003, http://www.whitehouse.gov/news/releases/2003/11/20031106-2.html (accessed on July 11, 2008).
114. Ibid.

260 • NOTES •

115. Weisberg, "Fishing for a Way."
116. Natan Sharansky, *The Case for Democracy: The Power of Freedom to Overcome Tyranny and Terror* (New York: Public Affairs, 2004), xxv.
117. Ibid., 244.
118. Ibid., 75.
119. For an excellent general treatment of the neoconservative movement, with a particular focus on many of the less popularly known formative figures, including Max Schachtman, Lionel Trilling, Gertrude Himmelfarb, Albert Wohlstetter, and Paul Berman, as well as the legacy of Scoop Jackson, see Jacob Heilbrunn, *They Knew They Were Right: The Rise of the Neocons* (New York: Doubleday, 2008).
120. Jeane J. Kirkpatrick, "Dictatorships and Double Standards," *Commentary* 68, No. 5 (November 1979), cited in Gary Dorrien, *The Neoconservative Mind: Politics, Culture, and the War of Ideology* (Philadelphia: Temple University Press, 1993), 326.
121. Jeane J. Kirkpatrick, "A Normal Country in a Normal Time," *National Interest* 21 (Fall 1990), cited in Dorrien, *Neoconservative Mind,* 327.
122. Dorrien, *Neoconservative Mind,* 327.
123. Ibid., 339–40.
124. Ibid., 377.
125. Joshua Muravchik, *Exporting Democracy: Fulfilling America's Destiny* (Washington, D.C.: The AEI Press, 1991).
126. Ibid., 227.
127. Mann, *Rise of the Vulcans,* 133.
128. Ibid., 129.
129. Ibid., 136.
130. Ibid., 134.
131. Biography of Charles Krauthammer, http://www.jewishworldreview.com/cols/krauthammer1.asp (accessed 8 July 2008).
132. Ibid.
133. Lionel Barber, "Views of the world: Who is the most influential commentator in China?" *Financial Times,* May 20, 2006.
134. Charles Krauthammer, "The Unipolar Moment," *Foreign Affairs* (Winter 1990/1991): 26.
135. Ibid., 33.
136. Charles Krauthammer, "Universal Dominion: Toward a Unipolar World," *The National Interest,* (Winter 1989/90): 48.
137. Ibid., 49.
138. Ibid.
139. Ibid., 48.
140. Ibid.
141. Ibid., 47.
142. Ibid.
143. Michael Lind, *The American Way of Strategy* (New York: Oxford University Press, 2006), 252.
144. Stephen Schwarz, "What Is Islamofascism?" *The Weekly Standard,* August 17, 2006.
145. Steve Holland, "Democrats Outraged by Bush 'Appeasement' Remark," Reuters, May 15, 2008, http://www.reuters.com/article/topNews/idUSN0839956720080515?feedType=RSS&feedName=topNews (accessed on June 29, 2008).
146. Tom A. Peter, "National Intelligence Estimate: Al Qaeda Stronger and a Threat to U.S. Homeland," *Christian Science Monitor,* July 19, 2007.
147. See, generally, Samantha Power, "Our War on Terror," *New York Times,* Sunday Book Review, July 29, 2007.
148. Khaled Hosseini, *The Kite Runner* (New York: Riverhead Books, 2003).

149. Mann, *Rise of the Vulcans,* 360.
150. Douglas Feith, *War and Decision* (New York: HarperCollins, 2008).
151. Scott McClellan, *What Happened: Inside the Bush White House and Washington's Culture of Deception* (New York: Public Affairs, 2008).
152. Fukuyama, *America at the Crossroads,* ix.
153. Ibid., ix–x.
154. Ibid., x.
155. Ibid., xi.
156. Irving Kristol, "'Moral Dilemmas' in Foreign Policy," in *Reflections of a Neoconservative,* 263.
157. Gettleman, Jeffrey and Filkins, Dexter. "Pending Vote, Some Iraqis See Larger Council." *New York Times.* February 20, 2004.
158. Fukuyama, *America at the Crossroads,* xi.
159. Ibid., 116.
160. Ibid.
161. Ibid., 117.
162. Ibid.
163. Ibid., 42.
164. Ibid.
165. Ibid., 43.
166. Charles Krauthammer, "Fukuyama's Fantasy," *Washington Post,* April 28, 2006, A23.
167. Fukuyama, *America at the Crossroads,* xi.
168. Elzbieta Ettinger, *Hannah Arendt Martin Heidegger* (New Haven, CT: Yale University Press, 1995), 4.
169. Martin Heidegger, "The Assertion of the German University," http://www.eco.utexas.edu/~hmcleave/350kPEEHeideggerSelf-Assertion.pdf (accessed on May 14, 2008).
170. Ibid.
171. Ibid.
172. Ettinger, *Hannah Arendt,* 118.
173. Ibid., 50.
174. Ibid.
175. Hanna Fenichel Pitkin, *The Attack of the Blob: Hannah Arendt's Concept of the Social* (Chicago: University of Chicago Press, 1998), 39.
176. Ibid, 39, 34.
177. Elisabeth Young-Bruehl, *Hannah Arendt: For Love of the World* (New Haven, CT: Yale University Press, 1982), 49.
178. Pitkin, *Attack of the Blob,* 39.
179. Ibid., 40.
180. Ibid.
181. Ibid.
182. A distinction should be drawn between Heidegger's moral and ontological Platonism. In *Being and Time,* he argued that the Western history of "forgetfulness of Being" began with the ideas of Socrates, Plato, and Aristotle, who had moved away from the pre-Socratic philosophical attempts truly to grasp the reality of being. Martin Heidegger, John Macquarrie and Edward Robinson trans., *Being and Time* (New York: Blackwell Publishing, 1962), 38–40.
183. Jacques Taminiaux, *The Thracian Maid and the Professional Thinker: Arendt and Heidegger* (Albany: State University of New York, 1997), 4.
184. Ibid., 9.
185. Hannah Arendt, *The Origins of Totalitarianism* (New York: Harcourt, Inc., 1976), 451.
186. Arendt, *Origins of Totalitarianism,* 453.
187. Hannah Arendt, *On Revolution* (New York: The Viking Press, 1965), 152.

188. Arendt, *On Revolution*, 35.
189. Ibid., 153.
190. Ibid.
191. Young-Bruehl, *Hannah Arendt*, 61.
192. Ibid.
193. Pitkin, *Attack of the Blob*, 40.
194. Ibid., 43.
195. Ibid., 44.
196. Ibid., 143.
197. Ibid., 145.
198. Arendt, *Origins of Totalitarianism*, 473.
199. Ibid., 455.
200. Ibid., 456.
201. Ibid., 455.
202. Ibid., 357.
203. Ibid., 356.
204. Ibid., 349.
205. Ibid., 476.
206. Ibid., 477.
207. Ibid., 375.
208. Ettinger, *Hannah Arendt*, 35.
209. Ibid., 36.
210. Ibid., 37.
211. Ibid.
212. Pitkin, *Attack of the Blob*, 55.
213. Ibid., 52.
214. Ibid., 429.
215. Anthony F. Lang, Jr. and John Williams, *Hannah Arendt and International Relations: Reading Across the Lines* (New York: Palgrave Macmillan, 2005), 7–8.
216. Arendt, *Origins of Totalitarianism*, 479.
217. Ibid.
218. Arendt, *On Revolution*, 144.
219. Ibid., 146.
220. Henry Dexter and Morton Dexter, *The England and Holland of the Pilgrims* (Wilmington, MA: Houghton, Mifflin, and Company, 1905), 589.
221. James Thatcher, *History of the Town of Plymouth* (Boston: Marsh, Capen and Lyon, 1835), 18.
222. Ibid., 18–19, and Diane Ravitch, *The American Reader* (New York: HarperCollins, 2000), 3.
223. Arendt, *On Revolution*, 175.
224. Ibid., 178.
225. Ibid., 199.
226. Julia Kristeva, *Hannah Arendt* (New York: Columbia University Press, 2001), 113.
227. Occasionally, Arendt let her passions for saving America from democracy's paradox get the better of her. She found something she called the "social" particularly disturbing—the tendency of people to group themselves into homogeneous and unthinking groups that would "keep[] us from our lost freedom." But her pursuit of this hazy target led her into muddy philosophical waters. The contemporary political theorist Hanna Pitkin has written that Arendt's invocation of the "social" was so obsessive, broad, and internally contradictory that it might as well be likened to a "blob" out of a 1950s science fiction movie. Of the "social" in Arendt's work, Pitkin writes, "Even more telling is how often and how powerfully her imagery personified and even demonizes this entity. . . . In *The Human*

Condition, society is variously said to 'absorb,' 'embrace,' and 'devour' people or other entities; to 'emerge,' 'rise,' 'grow,' and 'let loose' growth; to 'enter,' 'intrude' on, and 'conquer' realms or spheres; to 'constitute' and 'control,' 'transform' and 'pervert'; to 'impose' rules on people, 'demand' certain conduct from them, 'exclude' or 'refuse to admit' other conduct or people; and to 'try to cheat' people." Pitkin, *Attack of the Blob*, 2, 3, 4.

228. Elisabeth Young-Bruehl, *Why Arendt Matters* (New Haven, CT: Yale University, 2006), 23.
229. Ibid., 24.
230. Ibid., 24–25.
231. Ibid., 96.
232. Ibid., 64.
233. Ibid.
234. Ibid.
235. Ibid.
236. Ibid., 65.
237. Taminiaux, *Thracian Maid*, 10.
238. Kateb, *Inner Ocean*, 206.
239. Ibid.
240. Ibid.
241. William Shakespeare, "Romeo and Juliet," in *The Works of Shakespeare* (New York: Oxford University Press), 260.
242. Kateb, *Inner Ocean*, 207.
243. Ibid.
244. Young-Bruehl, *Why Arendt Matters*, 195.
245. Young-Bruehl, *For Love of the World*, 246.
246. Ibid.
247. Ibid., 247.
248. Ibid.
249. Kristeva, *Hannah Arendt*, 234.

PART IV: DEFYING THE DEMAGOGUE

1. Huntington, *The Clash of Civilizations* (New York: Touchstone, 1996), 37.
2. Eli Sagan, *The Honey and the Hemlock: Democracy and Paranoia in Ancient Athens and Modern America* (Princeton, NJ: Princeton University Press, 1994), 88.
3. Ronald Inglehart, "The Renaissance of Political Culture," *American Political Science Review* 82:4 (December 1988): 1205.
4. Ronald Inglehart and Christian Welzel, "Political Culture and Democracy: Analyzing Cross-Level Linkages," forthcoming article in *Comparative Politics*, 4.
5. Sandra F. VanBurkleo et al., ed., *Constitutionalism and American Culture: Writing the New Constitutional History* (Topeka, KS: University of Kansas Press, 2002).
6. See, e.g., Jon Elster and Rune Slagstad, eds., *Constitutionalism and Democracy* (Cambridge, MA: Cambridge University Press, 1988).
7. For an overall account of the idea of political culture in explaining why democracies succeed or fail, see Larry Diamond, "Political Culture and Democracy," in Larry Diamond, ed., *Political Culture and Democracy in Developing Countries* (Boulder, CO: Lynne Rienner Publishers, 1993), esp. 12.
8. In the words of another scholar, constitutionalism aims to ensure that "the coercive power of the state is constrained." Scott Gordon, *Controlling the State: Constitutionalism from Ancient Athens to Today* (Cambridge, MA: Harvard University Press, 1999), 5.
9. George Kateb, *The Inner Ocean: Individualism and Democratic Culture* (Ithaca, NY: Cornell University Press, 1992), 43.

10. Mark Brzezinski, *The Struggle for Constitutionalism in Poland* (Oxford: St. Antony's Press, 2000), 11.
11. Sidney Hook, Reason, *Social Myth, and Democracy* (New York: Humanities Press, 1950), cited in Larry Diamond, *The Spirit of Democracy* (New York: Times Books, 2008), 12.
12. George Kateb, *Hannah Arendt: Politics, Conscience, Evil* (Totowa, NJ: Rowman & Allanheld, 1983), 145.
13. Leo Strauss, *Natural Right and History* (Chicago: University of Chicago Press, 1965), 136.
14. A useful book distinguishing legal from political constitutionalism—a constitutionalism that requires the active participation of the citizenry and robust processes to ensure freedom—is Richard Bellamy, *Political Constitutionalism: A Republican Defence of the Constitutionalism of Democracy* (Cambridge, MA: Cambridge University Press, 2007).
15. My thanks to Mike Gubser for emphasizing this distinction.
16. David Lowe, "Idea to Reality: A Brief History of the National Endowment for Democracy" (April 10, 2003), http://www.ned.org/about/about.html (accessed on July 11, 2008).
17. Ibid.
18. Ibid.
19. Ibid.
20. Minxin Pei and Sara Kasper, "The 'Morning After' Regime Change: Should U.S. Force Democracy Again?," *Christian Science Monitor* 95:35 (January 15, 2003), 9.
21. Noah Feldman, *What We Owe Iraq* (Princeton, NJ: Princeton University Press, 2004), 1.
22. L. Paul Bremer, *My Year in Iraq: The Struggle to Build a Future of Hope* (New York: Simon & Schuster, 2006), 19.
23. Andrei Cherny, *The Candy Bombers* (New York: G.P. Putnam's Sons, 2008).
24. Pei and Kasper, "'Morning After' Regime Change."
25. Thomas Carothers, *Critical Mission* (Washington, DC: Carnegie Endowment, 2004), 34.
26. Ibid.
27. Ibid., 35.
28. Ibid.
29. Ibid.
30. See, e.g., Seymour M. Lipset, "Some Social Requisites of Democracy: Economic Development and Political Legitimacy," *The American Political Science Review* 53:1 (March 1959): 69–105, and Robert Dahl, *Polyarchy: Participation and Opposition* (New Haven: Yale University Press, 1971), 208: ". . . a country that has had little or no experience with the institutions of public contestation and political competition and lacks a tradition of toleration toward political opposition is most unlikely to turn into a stable polyarchy in the space of a few years."
31. Larry Diamond, *The Spirit of Democracy,* 345–70.
32. Kateb, *Inner Ocean,* 87.
33. Larry Diamond, "The Democratic Rollback: The Resurgence of the Predatory State," Foreign Affairs, March/April 2008.
34. Thomas Carothers, "Introduction," in Critical Mission: Essays on Democracy Promotion at 5 (Washington, D.C.: Carnegie Endowment for International Peace, 2004).
35. Ibid., 5–6.
36. Greg Mortenson and David Oliver Relin, *Three Cups of Tea: One Man's Mission to Promote Peace . . . One School at a Time* (New York: Viking, 2006).
37. Michael Mandelbaum, *Democracy's Good Name: The Rise and Risks of the World's Most Popular Form of Government* (Jackson, TN: Public Affairs, 2007), 118.

38. Ibid., 113.
39. Ibid., 115–16.
40. Larry Diamond, *Spirit of Democracy,* 330.
41. Thomas Carothers, *Critical Mission,* 88.
42. Larry Diamond, *Spirit of Democracy,* 330.
43. J. L. Sullivan and J. E. Transue, "The Psychological Underpinnings of Democracy: A Selective Review of Research on Political Tolerance, Interpersonal Trust, and Social Capital," *Annual Review of Psychology,* 50 (1999): 636.
44. Larry Diamond, *Spirit of Democracy* (New York: Times Books, 2008), 332.
45. Anthony F. Lang, Jr. and John Williams, *Hannah Arendt and International Relations: Reading Across the Lines* (New York: Palgrave Macmillan, 2005), 11.
46. Ibid., 10.
47. Anne-Marie Slaughter, *The Idea That Is America* (New York: Basic Books, 2007), 70.
48. Thomas Carothers, "Repairing Democracy Promotion," *The Washington Post,* September 14, 2007.
49. "Community Transformation-Haiti," National Democratic Institute, February 2007, 5.
50. "Community of Advocates Monitors Government," National Democratic Institute February 2004, 7.
51. "Lebanese Youth Step Forward," National Democratic Institute, September 2007, 5.
52. Sarah E. Mendelson and John K. Glenn, Carnegie Endowment for International Peace, "Democracy Assistance and NGO Strategies in Post-Communist Societies" (February 2000), https://www.policyarchive.org/bitstream/handle/10207/6464/final.pdf?sequence=1 (accessed on July 11, 2008), 65.
53. Ibid., 13.
54. Ibid., 23.
55. Ibid., 24.
56. Ibid., 40.
57. Ibid., 42–43.
58. Ibid., 52.
59. Ibid.
60. Hugh I'Anson Fausset, *Walt Whitman: Poet of Democracy* (New Haven, CT: Yale University Press, 1942), 101.
61. Ibid., 101–02.
62. Justin Kaplan, *Walt Whitman: A Life* (New York: Bantam Books), 205.
63. Ibid., 211.
64. Fausset, *Walt Whitman,* 109.
65. Samuel Sillen, *Walt Whitman: Poet of American Democracy* (New York: International Publishers, 1944), 42.
66. Kaplan, *Walt Whitman,* 15.
67. Ibid., 223.
68. Walt Whitman, *Songs of Democracy* (Philadelphia: David McKay, Publisher, 1919), 103–104.
69. Sillen, *Walt Whitman,* 41.
70. Whitman, *Songs of Democracy,* 110.
71. Ibid., 71–72.
72. Ibid., 212.
73. Ibid.
74. Ibid., 56.
75. Kaplan, *Walt Whitman,* 273.
76. Jerome Loving, *Walt Whitman: Song of Himself* (Berkeley, CA: University of California Press, 1999), 282.
77. Ibid., 283.

78. David A. Reynolds, *Walt Whitman* (New York: Oxford University Press, 2005), 127.
79. Kaplan, *Walt Whitman,* 300.
80. Ibid.
81. Reynolds, *Walt Whitman,* 129.
82. Ibid.
83. Ibid., 130.
84. Ibid., 129.
85. Fausset, *Walt Whitman,*138.
86. Ibid., 103.
87. Sillen, *Walt Whitman,* 9.
88. Ibid.

CONCLUSION: AMERICA THE EXCEPTIONAL

1. Walter Russell Mead, *Special Providence: American Foreign Policy and How it Changed the World* (New York: Routledge, 2002), vii.
2. Stanley Hoffman, "American Exceptionalism: The New Version," in Michael Ignatieff, ed., *American Exceptionalism and Human Rights* (Princeton, NJ: Princeton University Press, 2005), 225.
3. Ignatieff, *American Exceptionalism,* 11.
4. See, generally, Mead, *Special Providence.*
5. Harold Hongju Koh, "On America's Double Standard: The Good and Bad Faces of Exceptionalism," *The American Prospect,* October 1, 2004.
6. Michael Signer, "A City on a Hill," *Democracy: A Journal of Ideas,* 1 (Summer 2006).
7. The historian H. W. Brands has employed the term "exemplarism" differently, to apply to America's conduct of its affairs domestically as an example we can set for the purposes of foreign policy, in *What America Owes the World: The Struggle for the Soul of Foreign Policy* (Cambridge, MA: Cambridge University Press, 1998). Here, I mean instead to suggest that our foreign policy *itself* can serve as exemplary.

INDEX

CPSIA information can be obtained
at www.ICGtesting.com
Printed in the USA
LVHW111653090919
630448LV00005B/67/P

9 780230 606241